OTHER IIE PUBLICATIONS

English Language and Orientation Programs in the United States. 1969. $1.00.

Graduate Study in the United States. 1967. 40 cents.

International Awards in the Arts: For Graduate and Professional Study. 1969. $3.00.

Open Doors: Report on International Exchange. Statistics and text. Annual. $3.00.

The Two-Year College in the United States. 1967, reprinted in 1969 with a list of new colleges. 30 cents. (Bulk-order discounts are available on all of the above.)

Handbook on International Study: For Foreign Nationals. Available in 1971. $5.00.

Meet the U.S.A.

Meet the U.S.A.

by HENRY STEELE COMMAGER

Including A Practical Guide
For Academic Visitors to
the United States

IIE *Institute of International Education*

foreword

Meet the U.S.A. was first published by IIE in 1945 to provide an introduction to America — its land, its people, its institutions — for foreign students and other academic visitors who were then beginning to come to the U.S. in substantial numbers. Since then the number of such visitors has grown dramatically: there were approximately 7,500 foreign students in our colleges and universities in 1945 and a much smaller number of visiting professors; in 1969 there were 135,000 foreign students and more than 12,600 scholars. Since then, too, 70,000 copies of Meet the U.S.A. have been printed and distributed. Thousands more in foreign language editions have also been distributed.

On three occasions in the past twenty-five years, Meet the U.S.A. has been revised to take note of major developments and to keep its contents current. Now, however, we have thought it time to offer a fresh perspective, which takes into account the powerful forces and dramatic events which have so profoundly affected American life in the last generation. To do so, we have asked a distinguished historian, Henry Steele Commager, to write this entirely new edition of Meet the U.S.A.

To this presentation he has brought his great learning, his gifted pen, and his challenging point of view. He has described and analyzed the major elements of American life: its government, its economic system, its social and cultural patterns, its role in world affairs, and, in so doing, he has drawn a sharp and provocative portrait of the American character. We know that our readers will be informed by his interpretations; we hope that they will also be stimulated to explore American life further through other books (a list of recommended readings is appended) and more important, by personal observation and first-hand experience.

As another appendix to the book, IIE staff has provided an extensive section of practical information which will help prospective foreign students and other academic visitors on such subjects as the U.S. higher education system, the costs of study in the U.S., government regulations concerning foreign visitors, travel and recreation within the U.S., and social customs.

The Institute is grateful to the Old Dominion Foundation (since merged with the Avalon Foundation into the Andrew W. Mellon Foundation), whose generous support has made this publication possible.

Kenneth Holland
President
Institute of International Education

v

contents

illustrations

1. geography

Ever since "our fathers brought forth a new nation," back in 1776, foreign interpreters of the American scene—students, journalists, scholars —have compared the United States with their own nation—England, France, Germany, Norway, Spain, China—and that approach has lingered on into our day; it is the natural, almost the inevitable, approach that each visitor takes as he familiarizes himself with the United States. But it is nevertheless a distorted, even a misleading, view. The United States is, to be sure, a single nation but, like Russia and China, it is a nation of continental dimensions. If we are to understand it aright we must look at it not within the framework of the old world nations from which it arose— as another but somewhat different France or Germany or Ireland—but as we would look at the whole European continent. The United States is continental in size; continental in its immense variety of climate, soil, flora and fauna, and resources; continental in its social, ethnic, and, for that matter, religious ingredients. Much that seems otherwise incomprehensible about the United States becomes clear or at least understandable when we think of it in continental terms.

From the beginning the land took over. Size was the first thing that impressed the discoverers and explorers of the new world, impressed the colonists and settlers and, in time, impressed the Americans themselves. Everything was, or seemed, on a gigantic scale. It was, after all, as far from Maine to Florida as from Sweden to Sicily, and from the Chesapeake Bay to the Golden Gate of San Francisco harbor was farther than from Lisbon to St. Petersburg. Never had European man known such mighty rivers—the St. Lawrence, the Mississippi, the Columbia—nor such vast lakes as Huron, Michigan, Superior. The mountains seemed immense and impassable, as if two sets of Alps should have stretched from the Mediterranean to the Arctic, and early travelers reported wildly that some of them towered fifty miles into the skies. Once the first great range of mountains was conquered, prairie and plain stretched forever towards the limitless horizon, and even in 1801, when the western boundary of the United States was still the Mississippi River, Jefferson could speak of "land enough for our descendants to the thousandth and thousandth generation." Not only was everything somehow larger than life or nature: everything was abundant beyond the dreams of avarice. Fish swarmed in the rivers and bays, and

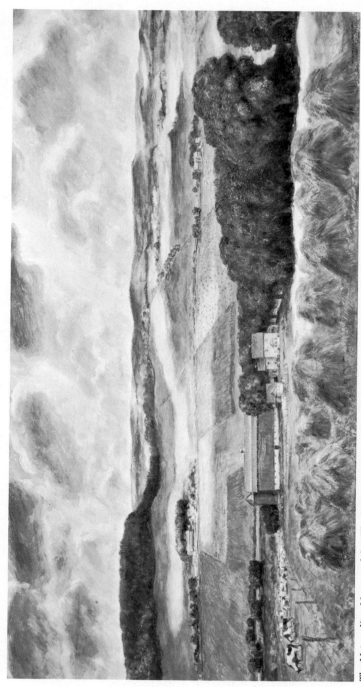

The Metropolitan Museum of Art. The George A. Hearn Fund, 1942.

Wisconsin Landscape. John Steuart Curry. 1938-39. To the first settlers, the fertile Midwestern plains represented endless abundance. They are still the prime source of the U.S.A.'s food.

you had only to dip down your net to duplicate the parable of the fishes; pigeons darkened the skies for a week on their migrations; herds of buffalo thundered across the prairies for days at a time. Virgin forests covered millions of acres; trees grew to gigantic size, as did the fruit that hung from them so plentifully; wild grapes and berries were to be had for the picking; corn grew tall overnight ("the corn is as high as an elephant's eye," the chorus was to sing in the popular folk opera *Oklahoma!*). Even the animals, as Jefferson was careful to point out to European critics, were larger in the new world than in the old—moose whose antlers stretched to ten feet, cattle and pigs twice the size of their European ancestors. Everything was immense, abundant, and easily available.

The Spaniards, who were the first settlers in the southern regions of the new world, found an environment exotic and inhospitable: vast jungles, fetid swamps, towering mountains, strange flora and stranger fauna, clouds of poisonous insects, venomous snakes; many of the conquistadors and priests thought, at first, that all this was part of Satan's kingdom. It took them two centuries to adjust to their new American environment. The French, too, found Canada vast, cold, and forbidding, so unlike the familiar provinces of the mother country that the new settlements simply did not flourish. After almost two centuries the population of French Canada had reached only some sixty thousand.

By great good luck that part of the new world that became the United States was geographically very much like Britain and northern Europe. The climate was much the same—a bit warmer in the summer, a bit colder in the winter. The land was densely wooded with oak and elm and maple and sycamore and fir, with hickory nut and walnut and chestnut—all familiar in the old world. Once cleared the land was open and the soil rich and varied, fit for all the familiar crops and for new produce like the potato and maize and squash and tobacco. In short it did not require any convulsive effort for the English and after them the Germans, the Irish, the Swedes, to make themselves at home along the Eastern seaboard or in the great Ohio-Mississippi valley. They could plant familiar crops, cultivate the soil with familiar tools, raise their pigs and cattle, sheep and poultry, and have turkey and venison pretty much for the shooting. They could build houses of familiar materials—wood or stone or bricks from local clay; they had ample stone for walls and wood for fences to mark off boundary lines and fence in cattle. In short, Europeans could put down roots in familiar soil, apply all their traditional skills, not only be secure, but feel secure.

Conditions were not everywhere, nor always, so favorable. When, about the 1840s, pioneers reached the edge of the Great Plains—western Iowa, Kansas, Nebraska—they found, for the first time, an environment that was unfamiliar and even hostile: arid land, with a rainfall less than half that to which they were accustomed; streams that were too shallow to float boats and that dried up during the summer months; thick matted

3

4

Wood engraving. From *Frank Leslie's Illustrated Newspaper*, May 24, 1879. The lure of gold drew men across the plains and mountains to the Pacific Coast. The caption, from a contemporary illustration, reads: "Prospectors and emigrants crossing the parks among the mountains, 10,000 feet above the sea, en route to Leadville — loss of animals on the road."

Fur Traders Descending the Missouri. George Caleb Bingham (1811-1879).

grass that did not yield to the plow; vast plains without trees with which to build houses and fences; summer heat that raised the temperature above a 100° F. day after day, parching the soil and searing the crops; winter blizzards that drove the temperature below zero for weeks on end, killing off cattle—and people too. No wonder settlement dragged to a halt and then, in one of the great dramas of history, vaulted fifteen hundred miles across plain and mountain and desert to the distant Pacific coast. For fifty years the intervening area was left to the Indian or given over to miners and cattlemen; not until irrigation, the windmill, dry farming, and the introduction of new strains of wheat made it profitable to farm on the Great Plains did the pioneer resume his advance into that great area. The geographical differences between the plains area and the rest of the United States can still be traced not only in statistics of population and of farming, but in the habits and the accents of the people.

No wonder that from the beginning the immensity of the continent

5

and the abundance of resources fired the imagination of the American people, excited their pride, stimulated their cupidity, and gave them imperial notions about themselves and the destiny of their country. No sooner were they settled along the Atlantic seaboard—itself larger than any western European country and amply adequate for their needs—than they were off into the interior, looking for more lands. And not the English alone: the frontiers beckoned everywhere, and to everyone. The handful of French in Quebec explored far into the interior, along the Great Lakes, into the Canadian West, down the network of rivers that led to the Mississippi and the Gulf of Mexico where they created a second new France. The Spaniards, too, were bemused by space; they pushed their frontiers northward into New Mexico and Texas and westward into California. Even the Russians, who had swept across Siberia in the seventeenth and eighteenth centuries, leapfrogged along the Aleutians to Alaska, and pushed a thousand miles down the coast to San Francisco where they met the Spanish pioneers from the South. But where the French and the Spanish and the Russians expanded as fur traders or soldiers or missionaries, the English and Americans expanded as farmers, and therefore took possession of the land, as others did not. The Americans alone could speak of the "conquest" of the West. But "the land was ours before we were the land's" wrote Robert Frost, the greatest of modern American poets, and it took time for the land, that is, the environment, to impose itself on the American character and the American imagination.

The eighteenth century—following the argument of Montesquieu—believed that climate (by which they meant environment) largely determined civilization. That was one way to explain the differences between Frenchmen and Germans, Englishmen and Italians, Chinese and Arabs. If different climates did indeed make different civilizations, then the new United States would have displayed not one but a dozen different civilizations. For the United States was not only larger than all of Europe west of Russia, but had within its spacious boundaries as many climates, soils, resources as the whole of western Europe, and a dozen distinct geographical areas, each one comparable in size and resources to most European nations. Had the principle of particularism triumphed over the principle of unity, as it did in Europe and Latin America, and as it has since in Asia and Africa, there would have been a valid basis for ten or twenty separate nations. But, in defiance of history, these large and populous regions, with their distinctive geographical and economic features, did not become separate states, but regions within a single nation.

6

The explanation of this is simple enough.

Except for the Indians (several millions of them) and scattered groups of French and Spaniards, the territory that is now the United States was empty. There were no fixed populations for Americans to absorb, no deeply rooted cultures to assimilate. The expansion of the American people into their successive wests differed therefore profoundly from the expansion of the British in India or South Africa, for example, or of the French in North Africa or the Japanese in Asia. Americans did not have to come to terms with an existing population; once they had killed off or pushed aside the Indians, they were the only population, and the speech, law, religion, and culture that they carried with them became native to their new societies. Some of their habits and institutions, to be sure, were modified by new environments or by the economy. The South is a monument to this kind of modification, and the South was, in mid-nineteenth century, enough of a separate section to seek independence in order to preserve its own way of life, its own plantation economy, its own "peculiar institution" of slavery. Some regions were modified by the large-scale influx of immigrants—Germans to Missouri, Norwegians and Swedes in Minnesota, Mexicans in the Southwest. But for the most part cultural uniformity imposed its pattern upon regional disparity.

It would be a mistake to give the impression that regionalism is wholly a thing of the past. New England still has a character of its own, and so, too, the Deep South, the Southwest, and the Great Plains. No one could mistake President Kennedy for a Southerner, nor President Johnson for a Yankee; Willa Cather is indubitably a spokesman for the Midwest, and William Faulkner for the Deep South. Climate continues to be important: the sharp seasons of New England; the almost tropical warmth of the Gulf Coast. The blue skies and the balmy breezes of California impose a pattern of outdoor life and architecture as surely as the cruel winters of the Dakotas impose a pattern of indoor life. Ethnic ingredients are still important: the predominance in the South of English, Scots, and Scots-Irish stock and of the Negro; the ethnic variety of the North and the Middle West, the product, in large part, of immigration. History and tradition are still important. New England retains not only some of the physical inheritance of Puritanism, but its intellectual and moral inheritance as well; it has not only white-steepled churches and Georgian houses and town commons, but scores of colleges and universities, dedicated to truth and light. Some words from the school song of the most famous of them, Harvard University, express their commitment:

Let not moss-covered error moor thee at its side,
As the world on truth's current glides by;
Be the herald of light, and the bearer of love,
Till the stock of the Puritans die.

"Fair Harvard"

7

The Middle West, for all its urbanization, retains something of its corn-belt and wheat-belt psychology, as well as something of the spirit of enterprise that we associate with the spectacular rise of cities like Chicago and St. Louis and, more recently, Denver, and something of the diversified social pattern woven by Germans and Scots, Cornishmen and Swedes, Bohemians and Poles. The South, of all sections of the country the most self-conscious about its history and traditions, still thinks of itself as the land of cotton—"old times there are not forgotten," as "Dixie" the war song of the South, tells us. It still cherishes the memory, or the illusion, of a planter aristocracy that was civilized and gracious; it still, on occasions sometimes appropriate but usually inappropriate (football games, for example), waves the Stars and Bars, the banner of the Confederate States of America. Though genuine regional differences are fast evaporating the memory of them lingers on.

Sectional characteristics, we are tempted to say, linger on only in memory and in legend. For it is not only history that has consigned regionalism to the realm of literature and memory, it is economy and technology as well. The United States is the only major nation the whole of whose history is embraced in the era of the industrial revolution. The land was there to be occupied, but had it not been for science and technology it might have taken as long to conquer the American West as it took Rome to spread throughout the Mediterranean and western Europe. It was the steamboat, the canal, the railroad that enabled pioneers to penetrate into the interior and establish permanent settlements there; it was the reaper and harvester and, later on, the windmill and the barbed wire fence that enabled homesteaders to farm the new land; it was iron and steel, oil and gas, that built the new cities. From the beginning the American was prepared, like Huckleberry Finn, to "light out for the territory," and, what is more, he was able to get there and once there to make a go of it. No wonder the process went faster than at any other time in history. As a boy John Quincy Adams was with his father, John Adams (both were to be elected President) when he signed the Treaty of 1783 acknowledging the independence of the new United States; the same John Quincy Adams was in Congress when California came under the American flag in 1848.

Mobility is common enough in the modern world—witness the migration of English to their colonies and commonwealths, of Germans and Italians to the countries of South America, of French to North Africa — but only in the United States was it an almost entirely internal affair. The millions who migrated from Germany, Sweden, Italy, Poland, for the Americas, North and South, were lost to their countries; those who "migrated" in the United States simply moved to some other part of the vast country. The United States, in short, kept its emigrants; European countries—and Asiatic as well—almost always lost them. The United States was the greatest colonizing country of the nineteenth century, but her colonies were all in the national domain and became commonwealths.

8

Nothing contributed more to the encouragement of a sense of nationalism than this process of building new commonwealths. It was one in which all could participate, foreign-born as well as native, women as well as men. It was one that brought together people from different states, sections, regions, brought them together not only geographically but politically and culturally as well, thus substituting understanding for suspicion and cooperation for animosity. It was a process that went on almost entirely under the auspices of the national government, for the new commonwealths were carved out of the national domain, the new territories were created States by the Congress. It was a process which demonstrated that the country belonged after all to the whole people, and that the people could go on bringing forth new commonwealths just as their forefathers had brought forth a new nation back in 1776.

The process of migration and of creating new commonwealths persuaded Americans to think imperially, as it were, to think in terms of a national destiny. Because, outside the South, Americans had so few local attachments, they cherished, all the more ardently, their general attachment; because they were seldom able to develop loyalty to village or county or state, they concentrated all their loyalty on the nation. Where, in the old world, sentiment and affection were customarily centered on a particular patch of ground—a Dorset, a Tuscany, a village in Britanny, a town in Württemberg—in the new world patriotism of necessity attached itself to the country as a whole, "from sea to shining sea." Boys and girls in Florida or Texas sing with rapture,

We love thy rocks and rills
Thy woods and templed hills

though they cannot imagine a rill or a templed hill, and they take for granted that Plymouth Rock and the Pilgrims belong to them just as children in the streets of Boston or New York take for granted that they should play at cowboys and Indians. Popular songs and literature proclaim this generalized passion for the land. The true American folk songs are songs such as "Oh! Susanna," or "Suwanee River," or "My Old Kentucky Home," or modern ballads like "Ole Man River," or "Oklahoma!" or—that favorite of Franklin D. Roosevelt, the Hudson River squire—"Home on the Range." American literature, too, is preoccupied with the land, thus Fenimore Cooper's *Leatherstocking Tales* with their grand sweep of country from the Hudson to the prairies, thus that greatest of American classics, *Huckleberry Finn,* thus modern classics like Willa Cather's *O Pioneers!* or Ole Rölvaag's *Giants in the Earth,* or Margaret Mitchell's *Gone with the Wind,* thus, too, the poetry of Walt Whitman or of Robert Frost.

Consciousness of space, opportunity, and mobility, had another result whose consequences are with us today, and will be for a long time to come. They encouraged Americans to exploit rather than to conserve the seemingly limitless resources of the country. Early settlers in New England and

Pennsylvania did, to be sure, put their roots down deep into the soil. They cleared the land, cultivated it, and cherished it; they built handsome houses that were meant to last and pleasant communities: to this day Americans have produced nothing more beautiful than the eighteenth-century New England town. But a series of events early in the next century introduced an era of exploitation whose consequences are still evident and whose habits are now a part of the American character. First, the area of the nation was dramatically doubled by the purchase of the Louisiana Territory in 1803, and then enlarged as much again by the acquisition of new territories, including Texas, California, and Oregon in the 1840s. Second, such new means of transportation as the steamboat and railroad made it easy to penetrate to the farthest interior, to seek out, everywhere, the best land. Third, wasteful methods of farming ruined the soil in the seacoast states, forcing farmers to abandon their ancient lands and seek out virgin soil in the interior. All this, plus the most rapid growth of population any nation had ever experienced, loosed a flood of immigration into the Ohio and Mississippi valleys and beyond to the Pacific coast. These pioneers had little affection for their temporary homes, and they were in a hurry to be rich. They cut down or burned down the woods, gutted the soil, killed off the wild life. They put up jerry-built houses, threw together frowsy towns, and moved on to new territory as soon as they could sell at a profit. They were inspired, no doubt, by a dream of peace and plenty, and they pioneered with the song of the trailmakers on their lips:

When we've wood and prairie land
Won by our toil,
We'll reign like kings in fairy land
Lords of the soil.

But that wasn't the way it turned out for most of them; most of them could say, with the hero of Stephen Benét's *John Brown's Body,*

—I took my wife out of a pretty house.
—I took my wife out of a pleasant place.
—I stripped my wife of comfortable things.
—I drove my wife to wander with the wind.

Stephen Vincent Benét, *John Brown's Body*
(New York: Holt, Rinehart and Winston, Inc., 1960)

Few of the pioneers did lasting damage to the soil—though collectively the sheepmen and cattlemen of the west may have done so—but they created a habit of mind and of conduct which lingered on into the era of industrial exploitation. Large in scale and dangerously efficient, that exploitation—mechanized lumbering, strip mining, drilling for oil, pouring industrial and chemical wastes into streams and lakes, polluting the very air —did and does lasting damage.

Americans are paying the price for all this now in wasted resources, ugly towns, blighted cities, and a countryside despoiled. While everyone

THE FAR WEST.—SHOOTING BUFFALO ON THE LINE OF THE KANSAS-PACIFIC RAILROAD.

Wood engraving. *Frank Leslie's Illustrated Newspaper,* June 3, 1871. The American bison that roamed the plains was all but exterminated as the settlers moved West, confident that Nature's bounty was inexhaustible.

Landing of Roger Williams. Engraving after painting by Alonzo Chappel. Ca. 1861. Roger Williams, a clergyman, established the first settlement in Rhode Island in 1636 after being banished from Massachusetts for his non-doctrinaire religious beliefs. He maintained good relations with the Narragansett Indians and became known as an apostle of religious toleration and liberal government.

knows that this long tradition of waste must be ended and reversed, the habits of laissez faire and the habits of ruthless exploitation are so strongly ingrained that it is almost impossible for Americans to change their ways— which is another way of saying that it is almost impossible for Americans to stop destroying their own country. Perhaps size was not altogether a blessing to the American people; perhaps if they had had less land and fewer resources, they might have taken better care of what they had.

recommended reading

Bakeless, John E. *The Eyes of Discovery: America as Seen by the First Explorers.* New York: Dover Publications, 1950.

Bromfield, Louis. *The Farm.* New York: New American Library (Signet Books), 1955.

*Brown, Ralph H. *Mirror for Americans: Likeness of the Eastern Seaboard.* New York: Plenum Publishing Corporation (Da Capo Press), 1968.

*Carroll, Gladys H. *As the Earth Turns.* New York: Macmillan Company, 1944.

Cather, Willa. *My Antonia.* Boston: Houghton Mifflin Company (Sentry Editions), 1961.

————. *O Pioneers!* Boston: Houghton Mifflin Company (Sentry Editions), 1962.

de Crèvecoeur, Hector St. John. *Letters from an American Farmer: Sketches of Eighteenth-Century America.* New York: New American Library (Signet Books), 1963.

De Voto, Bernard. *Course of Empire.* Boston: Houghton Mifflin Company (Sentry Editions), 1962.

*Dick, Everett. *Sod House Frontier, 1854-1890.* Lincoln, Neb.: Johnsen Publishing Company, 1954.

Faulkner, William. *The Hamlet.* New York: Random House (Vintage Books).

————. *The Wild Palms.* New York: New American Library (Signet Books), 1968.

Ferber, Edna. *American Beauty.* New York: Avon Books, 1961.

Garland, Hamlin. *Main-Travelled Roads.* New York: New American Library (Signet Books), 1962.

*————. *Son of the Middle Border.* New York: Macmillan Company, 1962.

Glasgow, Ellen. *Barren Ground.* New York: Hill & Wang (American Century Series), 1959.

*Goetzman, William H. *Exploration and Empire.* New York: Alfred A. Knopf, 1966.

*Huth, Hans. *Nature and the Americans: Three Centuries of Changing Attitudes.* Berkeley, Calif.: University of California Press, 1957.

Jewett, Sarah O. *"The Country of the Pointed Firs" and Other Stories.* New York: Doubleday & Company (Anchor Books), 1954.

Jones, Howard M. *O Strange New World: American Culture: The Formative Years.* New York: Viking Press (Compass Books), 1967.

*Lorant, Stefan. *The New World: The First Pictures of America.* New York: Duell, Sloan & Pearce, 1965.

*Marine, Gene. *America the Raped.* New York: Simon & Schuster, 1969.

Norris, Frank. *The Octopus.* New York: Airmont Publishers, 1968.

Phillips, Ulrich B. *Life and Labor in the Old South.* Boston: Little, Brown & Company.

° Hard-cover edition. Titles not so marked are paperback editions.

*Quick, Herbert. *Vandemarck's Folly*. Indianapolis, Ind.: Bobbs-Merrill Company, 1922. OP

Rölvaag, Ole E. *Giants in the Earth*. New York: Harper & Row (Perennial Library).

Smith, Henry N. *Virgin Land: The American West as Symbol and Myth*. New York: Random House (Vintage Books), 1957.

Steinbeck, John. *The Grapes of Wrath*. New York: Viking Press (Compass Books), 1958.

*Suckow, Ruth. *The Folks*. New York: Doubleday & Company, 1934. OP

Thoreau, Henry D. *Cape Cod*. New York: Apollo Editions, 1966.

————. *The Maine Woods*. New York: Apollo Editions.

————. *Walden and the Famous Essay on Civil Disobedience*. New York: New American Library (Signet Books), 1942.

*Turner, Frederick J. *The Frontier in American History*. New York: Peter Smith Publisher.

Twain, Mark. *Huckleberry Finn*. New York: Airmont Publishers, 1964.

————. *Life on the Mississippi*. New York: Washington Square Press (Collateral Classics Series).

Webb, Walter P. *The Great Plains*. New York: Grosset & Dunlap (Universal Library), 1967.

Welty, Eudora. *The Ponder Heart*. New York: Harcourt, Brace & World (Harbrace Paperback Library).

° Hard-cover edition. Titles not so marked are paperback editions.
  OP indicates that the edition is out of print.

Courtesy of The Art Institute of Chicago. Friends of American Art Collection.

American Gothic. Grant Wood. 1930.

2. the people

Americans, like almost all other peoples, are an amalgam of many nations, races, and ethnic groups. For two thousand years, race after race swept over Greece and Italy and Spain: the Germans are a blend of scores of tribes and peoples; the original Britons were successfully overcome by Romans, Angles and Saxons, Danes, Normans; century after century, the Russians—never a single people or race—were inundated by conquering tribes from the steppes of Asia, from the forests of Germany, from Turkey and Greece and the Caucasus, and to this day there are scores of languages and dialects spoken in the many states of that vast country. So, too, India is a vast mixture of people and tongues. There is therefore nothing unique about the racial amalgam in the United States except that it is a product of recent instead of ancient history, and that it is still going on. In most nations outside the new world, a kind of ethnic stability was achieved some centuries back, so that Frenchmen have predominated in France, Danes in Denmark, Japanese in Japan, for a longer time than men can remember. But America has never known ethnic stability; even now, though immigration from Europe has been cut back severely, immigrants pour in by way of Canada as well as from Mexico and Puerto Rico. Thus of the two and one-half million immigrants admitted in the fifties, one million came from the other countries of the Western Hemisphere, a figure which does not include Puerto Ricans, who are U.S. citizens. The census of 1960 recorded over three million Americans of Canadian birth or parentage and one and three-quarter million Mexicans. Ethnically, then—it is an awkward term but we do not seem to have a better one—America is, and has always been, a nation of nations, a people of many peoples.

The first settlers in America found only a sprinkling of Indians along the Atlantic coast; many of these were killed in the numerous Indian wars, many more died of the diseases, chiefly smallpox, the white invaders brought with them and the rest withdrew into the forests. Unlike the French and Spaniards, the English colonists did not intermarry with the native races, either then or later. Yet there was no such thing as ethnic "purity," even at the beginning. English colonists shared the East coast with some thousands of Dutch along the Hudson, with Swedes on the Delaware, with Spaniards in Georgia and Florida. These were absorbed, or driven out, but in their place came hundreds of thousands of settlers from Scotland, Ireland, and

France, from the many states of Germany and the cantons of Switzerland, and a few thousands, chiefly Sephardic Jews, from Spain and Portugal. Some of these, the Germans, for example, tried to carve out their own domains, and live for and to themselves, but except in small areas of eastern Pennsylvania they were unsuccessful; the overwhelming majority of newcomers from Europe blended in and were absorbed by the original English-speaking settlers. That acute observer of the Revolutionary era who called himself "The American Farmer," J. Hector St. John de Crèvecoeur, described the process in one of his famous letters:

> In this great American asylum the poor of Europe have by some means met together. . . . Everything has tended to regenerate them: new laws, a new mode of living, a new social system; here they are become men; in Europe they were as so many useless plants. . . . they withered, and were mowed down by want, hunger, and war; but now, by the power of transplantation, they have taken root and flourished. . . .
> What attachment can a poor European immigrant have for a country where he had nothing? The knowledge of the language, the love of a few kindred as poor as himself, were the only cords that tied him; his country is now that which gives him his land, bread, protection, and consequence. . . . What, then, is the American, this new man? He is neither an European nor the descendant of an European. *He* is an American, who, leaving behind him all his ancient prejudices and manners, receives new ones from the new mode of life he has embraced, the new government he obeys, and the new rank he holds. . . . Here individuals of all nations are melted into a new race of men, whose labors and posterity will one day cause great changes in the world. (*Letters from an American Farmer*, III: "What Is an American?")

Thus the process of absorbing all comers, blending them in with the native population or with other newcomers, winning their loyalty, transforming their language and their very character, went on everywhere with a quiet, almost ruthless efficiency.

One major element of the population, however, was not absorbed: the Negro. It was in 1619 that a Dutch merchantman brought the first boatload of Negroes to Virginia. The new colony (it had been settled only twelve years earlier), like all the American colonies for the next century and a half, was facing an acute labor shortage, and the habit of depending on Negro slaves to work in the tobacco fields caught on and spread. During the seventeenth century not many Negroes were imported, but in the eighteenth century the trickle swelled to a stream, and at the time of independence, Negro slaves numbered between four and five hundred thousand. The first census of the United States, in 1790, revealed 757,000 Negroes in a population of a little less than four million, a proportion of the population perceptibly higher than at any time in the twentieth century. Today twenty-some million Negroes make up roughly one-tenth of the total population.

Even at the time of independence, then, the American population was a mixture of European and African peoples. The pattern thus established became more pronounced as immigration swelled to a flood. Yet because the natural increase of population was so large—incomparably larger than in Europe—the proportions of native and foreign born remained substantially the same all through the nineteenth and well into the twentieth century. For over a hundred years, roughly one-tenth of Americans were foreign born; since immigration restriction in the 1920s and after, the proportion has fallen gradually, and today only one out of every twenty Americans is foreign born and one out of every eight of foreign or mixed parentage. It is certain that the American people will become increasingly homogenous and will, in the foreseeable future, take on the population pattern long familiar in other countries.

During the half century from 1830 to 1880, hard times in the old world—religious discrimination and persecution, poverty and, in Ireland, actual famine, wars and the threat of conscription, and the burdens and miseries of early industrialism—persuaded millions to flee to the new world. Steam transportation on sea and land made migration easy and relatively cheap. Most of those who left Europe headed for the United States, attracted by the promise of cheap land, jobs, social equality, and religious freedom; in time the United States came to be called The Promised Land. Most of the newcomers—Irish, English, Germans, Norwegians, and Swedes —landed in cities along the Atlantic seaboard and either stayed there or moved west along the roads, canals, and railroads to the Ohio Valley. Few went to the South, for they could not compete with slave labor on the plantations, and there were no cities or industries to speak of to provide them with work. The United States, for its part, actively encouraged immigration, for it needed workers to till its soil, and labor in its factories and mines. It made both immigration and naturalization easy, recognized (and defended in international law) the notion that men could voluntarily change their nationality, brought immigrants as rapidly as possible into politics, and their children into public schools. Correspondingly, the nation assumed that newcomers would not only cast off their old allegiance, also language, and culture, but assimilate at once to American society. This is what in fact happened, and it explains the paradox that the most heterogeneous of peoples should have, in many ways, the most standardized of civilizations. It should be added that Americans maintain something of a double standard here: while they expect all newcomers to become American overnight, they themselves, when they live abroad, tenaciously cling not only to American citizenship but to their own language and habits.

The process of large scale immigration, which had set in with the Irish famines of the 1840s, gathered force in succeeding decades. The 1870s brought almost three million immigrants to American shores, the 1880s over five million. In the first decade of the twentieth century the number rose to the astonishing total of eight million, eight hundred thousand: more than twice the population of the United States when Washington was inaugurated President. Beginning in the 1880s, too, there was a

In the collection of the Corcoran Gallery of Art

In the Land of Promise: Castle Garden. Charles F. Ulrich. Throughout the nineteenth century and well into the twentieth, newly arrived immigrants crowded into receiving stations where they were admitted to the United States and a new life.

shift in the source of immigration from western to eastern, and from northern to southern Europe. Immigration from England, Ireland and the Scandinavian countries declined, while that from Italy, Poland, and the Austro-Hungarian Empire soared. The shift was not merely one of ethnic stock—it was also religious, for most of the new immigrants were Roman Catholic, Eastern Orthodox, or Jewish. And it was economic, for the great majority of the new immigrants went not to farms (which they were unable to buy in any event) but to the cities, to the factories, mines, and railroads. It was even in some ways social, for the new immigrants were, for the most part, desperately poor, many of them illiterate, and they were bewildered by the New World in which they found themselves. They tended therefore to cling together in the large cities; and because of language difficulties they blended less readily with the native population than had the earlier immigrants.

Four aspects of this vast immigration that brought altogether some forty million Europeans to American shores catch our attention. The first is that the process of assimilation proved surprisingly easy—an observation that cannot be made of the Germans in Brazil or the Argentine, of Poles in Germany, or, in our own time, of Muslims in India or French in Algiers. The process was easy for a variety of reasons, most of them reflecting the good luck but some of them the good will of the American people. First, as we have seen, Americans welcomed the newcomers, gave them citizenship on easy terms, assured them political equality, elected them to office, appointed them to high rank in the armed services, brought them into their voluntary associations, churches, labor unions (immigrants were chiefly responsible for founding these), farm societies like the Grange, fraternal organizations, and so forth. Second, the immigrants themselves were, for the most part, touchingly eager to cast off their old world character and become part of American society: as Crèvecoeur put it so succinctly *Ubi panis, ibi patriae* (Where there is bread, there is the homeland). Silly Americans worried, from time to time, over what they imagined was the problem of Americanization, and President Theodore Roosevelt—who should have known better—even talked ominously about hyphenated Americans, but there never has been a time when there was difference in the loyalty of native and foreign-born Americans.

In the light of this incontestable fact, the treatment of Japanese Americans by the United States government during the Second World War takes on a lurid character. There was no evidence that the Japanese in California were less loyal to their adopted country than were their white neighbors, nor was any instance of Japanese-American disloyalty or espionage uncovered during the war. Yet, driven by fear, by impatience, by racism, and by cupidity, the government swept up the Japanese of the West Coast and "relocated" them—herded them into prison camps—in the mountain wildernesses of the West.

Third, throughout the nineteenth century the United States very badly needed additional manpower to till her soil, built her railroads, work in her factories, mine her coal and iron ore and copper. For long periods individual states actually competed with each other to drum up emigrants from Europe and bring them to their own domains. During this same period—the latter part of the nineteenth century—railroad and business corporations did everything they could to attract cheap labor to America. Fourth, the American system of universal free public education caught up the children of immigrants in classroom and playing fields and Americanized them—and they in turn Americanized their parents.

This phenomenon of generation after generation of children teaching their parents the American language, instructing them in American manners and customs, in short, Americanizing them, was to have lasting significance. It meant that for millions of families the traditional relationship of parent and child was subtly but decisively reversed. In America it was the child of foreign-born parents who had the upper hand, the child who set the pace, the child who was sophisticated, as his parents were

21

not, the child who held the magic key to the mysteries of American life.

There was, needless to say, a reverse side to this zeal of the newcomers to become Americans almost overnight. For the immigrants themselves it often spelled tragedy, for it cut them off from their roots, their culture, without giving them any satisfactory substitute. It cut them off from their parents and their families, who remained part of the old world, alienated them from their children, who were so defiantly part of the new. Nor was the emotional and psychological problem less difficult for first-generation Americans. They were, almost of necessity, in rebellion against their parents, their families, their language and culture, often their religion as well, for they had somehow to differentiate themselves from the old world and prove their identity with the new. They were, at the same time, not wholly of the new: the family was there, the familiar words, habits, usages, faiths, the old loyalties. All too often these children of German, Norwegian, Polish, Italian, Jewish parents found themselves in a kind of twilight zone—between a world they had never known and a world they had not yet made their own.

Another remarkable feature of Old World immigration to the New is that the world to which the immigrants assimilated, over a period of two centuries, was, quite simply, English. Ethnically the United States was a reproduction of the whole of Europe, and of much of Africa, too, but politically, socially, linguistically, she was a product and a reflection of England. By the mid-twentieth century over one-half the American people were of non-British blood—Blacks, Germans, Italians, Poles, Russians, Spaniards, and others. But while all these people made signal contributions to the society and the economy of their adopted country, they made relatively little impression on its culture or its institutions. The language remained English, with only the faintest dilution from other tongues. The books that Americans read were English, their law was English law, their political institutions were rooted in English history. Even in religion the English influence was enormous. All the major denominations except the Lutheran came to America direct from the British Isles: the Puritan, the Congregational, the Presbyterian, the Anglican, the Baptist, the Methodist, the Quaker. For a hundred years American Catholicism was predominantly Irish: of the seven American cardinals in 1968, six were of Irish extraction. Where there were significant contributions from other elements—in theology or education, for instance—these commonly lost their original character and were blended into an American pattern. In the United States the Lutheran Church, for one, is by now more American than it is German or Danish. At the hands of its American disciples tran-scendentalist philosophy, though rooted in German idealism, has taken on a wholly different character. Schools, though deeply influenced by Swiss and German models, soon took on a native color: Friedrich Froebel, the father of the kindergarten, himself said that only in America had the kindergarten reached its fulfillment.

"The American Farmer," Crèvecoeur, first used the metaphor of the melting pot to describe American society. Here, he said, "individuals of all races are melted together into a new race of men." More than a century later the Jewish poet Israel Zangwill wrote a memorable play about Jewish immigrants in New York City which he called *The Melting Pot*. The term caught on. The idea, though not the phrase, appears in the verse that Emma Lazarus wrote in 1885 for the Statue of Liberty:

Give me your tired, your poor,
Your huddled masses yearning to breathe free,
The wretched refuse of your teeming shore,
Send these, the homeless, tempest-tossed, to me.
I lift my lamp beside the golden door.

All very well, but was the United States in fact a melting pot which fused the miscellaneous ingredients of all peoples into something new and harmonious? Pretty clearly it was, for Europeans; certainly it is difficult now to distinguish white Americans by their racial or national origins. The undergraduate body of a large American university, for example, reveals no discernible ethnic differences; the students look and are alike, in all important respects. Even names provide but a meager clue; over the years foreign names have become Americanized—Schwartz into Black, Jensen into Johnson, Pozzi into Wells—and even where names remain unchanged it does not follow that a Carroll is Catholic, a Campbell Presbyterian, an Andersen Lutheran.

Where the melting pot failed most conspicuously was with the non-white elements of the population.

The Spanish, Portuguese, and French who settled in the New World, amalgamated readily enough with the native races, and in turn, with the Negroes who had been brought in as slaves. But for a variety of reasons the English settlers in the new world and the non-English immigrants who joined them did not. For one thing the early English immigrants—unlike the Spaniards and the French—brought their wives and families with them; for another, the Indians were few in number, and these fled before the oncoming whites. Nor later, did Americans amalgamate with Negroes—not, in any event, in any formal fashion. Intermarriage between whites and Negro slaves was illegal and even after the abolition of slavery many states placed legal restrictions on intermarriage. Only recently have the courts struck down these laws. That a good deal of extralegal amalgamation between white and black took place cannot be denied, but white Americans, who set the standards and made the laws, steadfastly refused to recognize the fact and defiantly insisted that even the smallest infusion of Negro blood made one a Negro. Thus though there was a great deal of fusion of Negro and white, especially in the South, the fusion did not result in absorption and the two races kept—or were kept—apart. Clearly, where Negroes were concerned the melting pot most decidedly did not melt.

Nor can it be said that integration or amalgamation has been successful with other racial minorities, whether Mexicans, Puerto Ricans, or Orientals. Though Puerto Rico is part of the United States, and though both Mexicans and Puerto Ricans are whites, both are exposed to many of the discriminations and indignities that black Americans experience at the hands of the whites. Happily this situation is changing rapidly, and it is a safe prophecy that another generation will see both of these large minority groups—roughly some two million each—assimilated to American society and culture, as the Irish, Italians, and Poles of earlier generations were assimilated.

As for the Orientals—in 1960, 465,000 Japanese, 237,000 Chinese, and 175,000 Filipinos—they tend to live in their own quarters and keep to themselves, and have managed to retain their racial integrity. In other respects, however, they blend readily into the pattern of American life. It is not without interest that a larger proportion of Chinese and Japanese school children go on to university than of any other ethnic group, including native-born whites.

C an it be said, then, that there is an American people, as there is a French, a Danish or a Japanese people? Certainly most Americans, whatever their backgrounds, think of themselves as a distinct people. They speak the same language—with fewer variations of region or class than in England, Germany, or Italy. They eat the same foods, drink the same soft—and sometimes hard—drinks, play the same games, go to the same schools, read the same newspapers and magazines, watch the same television programs, drive the same cars, from one end of the country to the other, even from one end of the social spectrum to the other. If racial amalgamation is far from complete, social and cultural amalgamation has flourished with perhaps fewer inhibitions and difficulties than might have been expected.

Yet we can now see that the impression of social harmony and unity which was a heritage of nineteenth-century optimism and a product of a contrast between old world and new formerly more striking than now, was a misleading one. American society was, in fact, not nearly so unified or so harmonious as most interpreters—statesmen, historians, poets, and novelists—assumed; it required, perhaps, the more dispassionate eye of the sociologist to see this. Today American society seems beset by suspicion, racked by misunderstanding, torn by violence, as it has not been since the Civil War. The divisions in society seem almost fortuitous, as do the issues.

Abraham Hanson. Jeremiah Hardy. Abraham Hanson was a barber who came to Bangor, Maine, in 1825 and became a well-known local personality.

25

To the not unnatural hostility of blacks against whites has been added the unfamiliar hostility of slums against suburbs, of the young against the old, and of incongruous groups—political, military, religious or family—of individuals against authority. The expectation of progress by evolution seems to have given way to a resignation to change by revolution, the deeply ingrained instinct for compromise to an instinct for violence, the comfortable acceptance of familiar truths to the rejection of all truths, the assumption of mutual good will to the presumption of universal malevolence. None of this, it should be added, is confined to the American scene.

Does the current disillusionment with the "establishment" and the widespread resort to violence portend a breakup of American society, a profound change in its internal character? That seems improbable if only because national—like individual—character does not change radically or dramatically. Besides, not all the portents are unfavorable. If there is disillusionment, it can be said that there were illusions that needed to be shattered: the illusion of equality, the illusion of equal justice, the illusion that American prosperity was a triumph of some peculiar virtue rather than of isolation and the abundance of nature, the illusion that America was exempt from the problems and crises that afflict other peoples, the illusion that America could bestride the stream of history and direct it down her own channels, the illusion that American habits and values were all rooted in the cosmic system. The revolt against these beliefs, and against misguided policies based upon them, has been a healthy one. If it can be said that many of the manifestations of the current revolt are aimless and irrational—the "never trust anyone over thirty" kind of nonsense, or the ostentation with which the new sexual freedom is paraded—we must also concede many of its objectives are reasonable and just and must be achieved if American society is to recover its former harmony.

It is relevant, too, to remember that revolutions have their origins not so much in desperation as in impatience born of rising expectations. They are not necessarily a sign of hopelessness or futility, but sometimes of promise. The past quarter-century has seen more progress towards general economic and social equality, more widespread education, broader participation in politics, and a livelier concern for the entire commonwealth than at any time since the Civil War. Alas, none of these developments has gone far enough or fast enough. Much of the almost convulsive discontent that flames out now on every quarter of the horizon is a reassertion, not a repudiation, of earlier ideas of liberty and equality.

recommended reading

Addams, Jane. *Twenty Years at Hull House*. New York: New American Library (Signet Books).

Antin, Mary. *The Promised Land*. Boston: Houghton Mifflin Company (Sentry Editions), 1969.

*Blegen, Theodore C. *Norwegian Migration to America: 1825-1860*. New York: Arno Press, 1969.

*Bok, Edward. *The Americanization of Edward Bok*. New York: Charles Scribner's Sons (Popular Edition), 1923. OP

Cahan, Abraham. *The Rise of David Levinsky*. New York: Harper & Row. (Colophon Books).

Cather, Willa. *O Pioneers!* Boston: Houghton Mifflin Company (Sentry Editions).

Commager, Henry Steele. *America in Perspective*. New York: New American Library (Mentor Books).

*Commons, John R. *Races and Immigrants in America*. 2nd edition. New York: Augustus M. Kelley, Publishers, 1967.

Du Bois, William E. B. *The Souls of Black Folk*. Greenwich, Conn.: Fawcett World Library (Premier Books), 1969. Also in *Three Negro Classics*, edited by John Hope Franklin (New York: Avon Books (Discus Books), 1969).

Ferber, Edna. *American Beauty*. New York: Avon Books, 1961.

————. *So Big*. New York: Avon Books.

Glazer, Nathan, and Moynihan, Daniel P. *Beyond the Melting Pot: The Negroes, Puerto Ricans, Jews, Italians, and Irish of New York City*. Cambridge, Mass.: Massachusetts Institute of Technology Press.

Handlin, Oscar. *The Uprooted*. New York: Grosset & Dunlap (Universal Library), 1957.

Hansen, Marcus L. *The Atlantic Migration: 1607-1860*. New York: Harper & Row (Harper Torchbooks).

Myrdal, Gunnar. *An American Dilemma: The Negro Problem and Modern Democracy*. 2 volumes. Harper & Row (Harper Torchbooks).

*Pochmann, Henry A. *German Culture in America: Philosophical and Literary Influences, 1600-1900*. Madison, Wis.: University of Wisconsin Press, 1957.

*Pupin, Michael. *From Immigrant to Inventor*. New York: Charles Scribner's Sons, 1925.

*Riis, Jacob. *The Making of an American*. New York: Macmillan Company, 1947.

Rölvaag, Ole E. *Giants in the Earth*. New York: Harper & Row (Perennial Library).

*Wittke, Carl F. *We Who Built America: The Saga of the Immigrant*. Cleveland: Press of Case Western Reserve University, 1964.

° Hard-cover edition. Titles not so marked are paperback editions.
  OP indicates that the edition is out of print.

3. how Americans govern themselves

The American people have a longer experience with self-government than any other people on earth except perhaps the Swiss and the Icelanders. In one way or another they have been governing themselves continually since the beginning of the seventeenth century. It is not surprising therefore that it is in the realm of government and politics that they have made their most important and lasting contributions. We can go further and assert that over a period of three hundred and fifty years Americans have been politically the most creative of peoples. As early as July, 1619, twenty-two burgesses, elected by all men over seventeen, met in the straggling village of Jamestown, Virginia, in what may be considered the first representative assembly in the modern world. The very next year Pilgrims on the *Mayflower* drew up the Mayflower Compact, the first written instrument of government in history. From that time to the present America has never been without written constitutions and representative assemblies.

When, in 1776, Americans set up on their own, they contrived, or developed, a whole complex of institutions designed to solve the major problems of government that had perplexed mankind for two thousand years. The principles which animated the Americans of that generation are set forth with incomparable succinctness by Thomas Jefferson in the preamble to the Declaration of Independence, as a set of "self-evident" truths:

> That all men are created equal, that they are endowed by their Creator with certain unalienable Rights, that among these are Life, Liberty and the Pursuit of Happiness. That to secure these rights, Governments are instituted among men, deriving their just powers from the consent of the governed. That whenever any Form of government becomes destructive of these ends, it is the Right of the People to alter or to abolish it, and to institute new Government, laying its foundations on such principles and organizing its power, in such form, as to them shall seem most likely to effect their Safety and Happiness.

Now none of these principles was new, but on the other hand it can be said that none had as yet been translated into practice. From the beginning the American contribution to government and politics, as to so many other areas, was to make real what had heretofore been speculation; as John Adams said, when he presided over the first Massachusetts Constitution, Americans *"realized* the theories of the wisest writers." Thus out of the principles of the Declaration came institutions: the Constitutional Convention as a method of creating, or instituting, government; the written

Constitution; Bill of Rights; separation of powers and judicial review as devices for limiting government; democracy and equality as methods of advancing the happiness of men; federalism as a means of combining national and local governments in a single political mechanism; and a new colonial system which recognized colonies—or territories as Americans called them—as equal extensions of the mother country. To these may be added the first modern politcial parties as instruments of popular government.

Necessity dictated these and other political institutions. The first one, the creation of a nation, was very much a product of necessity for, as old Benjamin Franklin said, "We must all hang together, or assuredly we shall all hang separately." Nothing more urgent than this: to hold together three million people from thirteen independent states in a single nation. We take for granted that, in the words of Abraham Lincoln's Gettysburg Address, "our fathers brought forth on this continent a new nation," but we should not; after all no people had ever "brought forth" a nation before. Heretofore, military conquerors had welded nations together, or royal dynasties, or nobles, but not *people*. The United States was not only the first nation to be "made," it was also the first to be made by the rank and file of the people.

This was by no means easy. Some of the ingredients of nationalism were already present in eighteenth-century America—a common language, a common territory, a common political inheritance. But others, equally important, were absent and had to be invented or contrived. Needless to say the inventions and contrivances did not go on in a vacuum; they were dictated by circumstances and molded by the character of the American people.

The Founding Fathers, as the generation of Washington, Jefferson, Hamilton, and John Adams is known, met the task of creating a nation with the greatest ingenuity. The first problem they faced was that of creating a government which would somehow balance local and national interests, or the principles of particularism and of unity. The people of the thirteen states—soon to be increased by the admission of new states in the West—were not prepared to merge their local character in a highly centralized nation-state. That was one of the things they had revolted against when they threw off the rule of George III and of Parliament. On the other hand it was quite impossible for thirteen governments to try to run foreign or even domestic affairs either individually or on behalf of each other. What the Founding Fathers did to solve this problem was something new under the sun: they set up a *federal* system which divided authority between state and nation on common-sense and realistic grounds. And to make this new kind of federalism work they devised a whole series of new mechanisms, all of them still with us: a written constitution which should set forth precisely the lines of division between state and national governments yet allowed for overlapping jurisdictions; dual citizenship, so that every American was a citizen both of his state and of the nation, and subject to the laws of both; enforcement of the laws on the individual citizen directly by each government, operating through the courts and ordinary legal processes; and a Supreme Court which eventually acquired the authority to settle disputes between the claims of state and nation by ordinary judicial processes, thus avoiding (except in the Civil War) those bloody contests which had heretofore destroyed all efforts to create federal systems.

The Fathers wrought better than they knew. The system set up for thirteen small states hugging the Atlantic coast proved adequate for forty-eight continental states—and eventually two that were noncontiguous —and for a territory many times that of the original thirteen. The great Montesquieu had laid it down in *The Spirit of the Laws* as axiomatic that republics must be small, while a large territory implacably demanded a military despotism. Certainly there was no historical evidence to support the expectation that a republican government could flourish over a territory of continental dimensions. But then Americans had not created a republic like the republics of the ancient Greek city-states, or of medieval Italy, but something quite new under the political sun: a federal republic. The American republic, therefore, did not have the almost intolerable burden of administering the affairs of tens of millions of people, spread over an immense continent, from a single center. Under the federal system, as originally planned, almost everything that concerned the ordinary citizen— marriage and family, law and order, roads, schools, labor, public welfare, and so forth—was taken care of by state and local governments, while the national government was to confine itself to the conduct of foreign affairs, national defense, and such domestic concerns as were common to the whole nation—public lands, for example, or Indian affairs, or the postal system, or the regulation of interstate commerce.

A federal system with the center of gravity in the states worked very well as long as the concerns of the ordinary man were primarily local, and the nation itself isolated from the danger of foreign wars. It worked well as long as the economy was agricultural, and therefore largely local, and problems of law and of social welfare also local. But in the course of the nineteenth century came two fateful developments that changed this pastoral situation dramatically. First was the industrial revolution, which transformed the economy from a local to a national one; second was war and, eventually, world power, which placed immense new duties, functions, and responsibilities on the national government. These chapters in American history are too familiar to permit elaboration.

These two factors, a national economy and the requirements of national security, fix the latitude and longitude of American politics and government today. The American economy is, by now, completely national: transportation, communications, manufacture, finance, even labor and agriculture, cannot be managed, can scarcely even be thought about,

The Declaration of Independence. Lithograph by N. Currier. Below, torchlight parades were a flamboyant part of political parties' campaigns in the nineteenth century. Pictured: a Democratic procession through New York's Union Square in 1856. From *Frank Leslie's Illustrated Newspaper,* September 27, 1856.

except in national terms. And it is obvious that all considerations of the military and of national security—considerations which extend from the raising of armies and the construction of an air force to the research of scientists in laboratories and of sociologists in libraries—are national in scope. Inevitably the center of gravity has moved from state capitals to Washington; inevitably the federal system has become nationalized.

What is true in the economic arena is equally true in the social. The major concerns of American society are no longer local but national— public health, education, race relations, pollution of air and water, poor relief, law and order and the administration of justice. None of these interests can be compressed within the narrow confines of state or local government, or dealt with effectively by these. Everywhere the national government is required to step in, not only with financial aid, but with administrative support and legal control.

Although almost all the problems that vex the American people are now national, the states still have the powers reserved to them by the original Constitution: these are the much-disputed "states' rights." This means that even though the states are incapable of dealing with these problems, they retain constitutional authority and the power, therefore, to hamper and even to sabotage the activities of the national government in these areas.

The conflict between the authority of state and nation is particularly deep, persistent, and virulent in the economic arena. It is, in recent years, the malaise of the economy that has contributed most to the growth of the welfare state, for as the welfare of the entire population of the nation is at stake, only the national government can safeguard this welfare. Clearly a welfare state is easier to develop and administer in a centralized than in a federal system: that is one reason that it came so much earlier in Germany, Scandinavia, and Britain than in the United States and that is one reason, too, why it works better in these nations than in the United States. It is in response to the irresistible demands for national welfare that the national government has gone into every state with programs of social security, housing, conservation, public health, and so forth. It has done this not out of a passion for the aggrandizement of power—there is no evidence that Presidents, Congresses or even bureaucracies have lusted for power—but out of necessity. Had states been either able or willing to legislate effectively in these areas it would not have been necessary for the federal government to invade them. But with few exceptions (and all of these in the North), the states made no serious efforts to solve the pressing problems of modern economy. It is by no means clear that they could have done so had they tried—how after all can a state take care of the problem of floods along the great rivers?—but they did not try very hard.

Yet instead of welcoming federal aid, many of the states have stoutly resisted it, as an "invasion" of their "rights." From the beginning, the resistance was flawed by inconsistency. For the states have never been against federal support in such activities as road building, or agriculture, or even schools; they are merely against the regulation and supervision that inevitably accompanies such support. This is particularly true in the South, where the federal government has sought to assure equality of treatment for Negroes and whites in such areas as education, jobs, and housing. Just as, in the nineteenth century, states' rights were invoked to protect slavery against the forces of freedom, so in the twentieth century it has been, and is, used to protect the doctrine of white supremacy against the principle of equality.

This is an old story. For a century and a half "states' rights" has been the *cri de coeur* of those who opposed progress or change. It was invoked to delay expansion into the West, to defeat the regulation of trusts and of railroads, to frustrate the prohibition of child labor, to put off the grant of suffrage to women, to oppose social security, the conservation of natural resources, national support to public education, and national standards of civil rights. No political doctrine in American history has been more consistently invoked on behalf of privilege and injustice. Yet there is no reason to be astonished at all this. Politics is a matter of power, and under federalism states have power to balance and to counterbalance national power.

If federalism lends itself so readily to abuse, must we conclude that federalism is obsolete? Has it served its purpose, has it run its course? Is the preservation of a federal system, with all its historic values, too high a price to pay for the inequities, injustices, and deprivations that are visited upon the inhabitants of many of our states?

It is not easy to answer this question, for we do not yet know what the alternatives are, nor what price we should have to pay for them. Clearly federalism has history on its side: it was the only way in which the original states could have joined together to make a nation, and it provided a system which still endures. Clearly, too, it still has many advantages. It recognizes that there are in fact differences among the peoples and regions of a nation of continental dimensions, and encourages the expression of these differences. It makes possible experiments in the separate laboratories of the individual states. It moderates the leviathan state by freeing the national government from the intolerable burden of administering the affairs of three thousand counties and additional thousands of towns and cities. By placing responsibility for local government on the people of each community it enlists everyone in politics and administration and thus fosters and encourages grass-roots democracy. After all, almost every American political leader had his training in local and state politics: John and Samuel Adams were products of the New England town meeting, Thomas Jefferson and James Madison of the Virginia county court, and almost every member of the federal Constitutional Convention had seen service in the government of his colony or state. What was true in the

Wide World Photos

Library of Congress

Library of Congress

Library of Congress

Top left, Franklin D. Roosevelt. Campaign photo, 1944. President from 1933 until his death in 1945, Roosevelt, who was elected for four terms, was the only United States President to be elected more than twice. He headed the nation through its worst economic depression and through the Second World War. *Top right,* Theodore Roosevelt. President from 1901 to 1909. He believed in, and exemplified, strong executive power in the office of the President. One of the ways in which he exercised this power was in putting restraints on the industrial and rail monopolists of the day. *Bottom left,* Thomas Jefferson. President from 1801 to 1809. A scholar, educator, and inventor from Virginia, he was the author of the Declaration of Independence. *Bottom right,* George Washington. The first President of the United States, he served from 1789 to 1797.

Abraham Lincoln and son. President from 1861 until his assassination in 1865. Lincoln headed the Union during the Civil War and signed the Emancipation Proclamation freeing the slaves.

eighteenth century is equally true today. Franklin Roosevelt was trained in local politics in New York State before he went to the governorship and the Presidency; Harry Truman was a product of local Kansas City politics; and Lyndon Johnson had long experience as a Texas politician.

Another advantage of federalism is negative rather than positive: it fragments and localizes discontent by confining it within the compartments of the states which serve, as it were, as safety valves. This is what happened, again and again, in the past. Shays's Rebellion of 1786 was localized in western Massachusetts; the so-called Whisky Rebellion of 1794 in western Pennsylvania; the nullification crisis of 1832 was pretty much confined to South Carolina. In more recent times the Populist Revolt, the Farmer-Labor movement, the States' Rights movement of 1948, even Governor Wallace's "American" party of 1968 were funneled into state channels and thereby largely, though not wholly, localized. If a grievance is sufficiently widespread, to be sure, regional concentration can be very dangerous: thus the crusade to defend slavery in 1860, though it used the mechanism of state sovereignty, detached an entire section from the Union. But the secession of the South cannot rightly be attributed to federalism, but to the collapse of federalism.

The obvious alternative to federalism is a national system where all powers are centralized in Washington, just as in France or Sweden all powers are centered in Paris or Stockholm. Such a centralized system works well enough in small countries—though it is interesting that one of the most successful of small countries, Switzerland, boasts a federal government. In any case, the United States is not to be compared with France or Sweden but, as we have seen, to the whole of western Europe, and it is highly improbable that the whole of western Europe could be governed effectively from Berne, let us say, or Bonn. Indeed nothing is more sobering than the spectacle of a western Europe still so divided that it cannot make either a common market or an economic union work except by excluding half the nations of the Continent.

The strongest argument for federalism is, no doubt, the most obvious: that it tends to mitigate the curse of bigness. Every modern nation with far-reaching welfare activities and massive military responsibilities tends to be swamped by the almost insatiable demands of administration and to sink beneath the weight of bureaucracy. Even with federalism, the United States is no exception. In the twenty-nine years from 1940 to 1969 the federal bureaucracy has grown from slightly over one million civilian employees to slightly under three million, and is suffering badly from hardening of the administrative arteries. Suppose there were added to this bureaucracy the millions of state and local employees! Washington could, no doubt, impose efficiency on such an immense civil service, as it imposes efficiency on the armed forces, but a democracy cannot run its schools, its justice and conservation agencies, its agricultural, labor, and social security forces as it runs its armed forces.

It was all very well for the Founding Fathers to set up governments for state and nation, and to assign to them the essential powers to govern. Equally important—to the Revolutionary generation, and to ours—are limits on the power of government.

To the Founding Fathers history taught one clear lesson: that all governments tended towards tyranny; that men in power were always tempted to abuse their power; that no governments or men could be trusted to refrain from the misuse of power. The highest statesmanship, therefore, consisted not in giving power to government but in imposing limits on government. But easier said than done: after all, for two thousand years and more philosophers had talked about limiting the power of government, but so far no people had ever worked out a method of making limits really effective.

One of the most notable achievements of the Founding Fathers was that they did, for the first time, devise ways to limit government; what is more, they wrote these into fundamental law. Indeed, if anything, they overdid the limitations; so fearful were they of the abuse of power that they all but paralyzed their new governments with checks and balances of the most intricate and ingenious character. There was first the written Constitution which *enumerated* the powers that government was permitted to exercise. There was the federal system, which divided up governmental powers, and set state and national governments to balance and check each other. Then came the separation of powers—a really effective separation for the first time in history—between executive, legislative and judicial branches; bicameral legislatures; frequent elections at fixed periods, and—something quite new in history—a judiciary which had authority to pass on the constitutionality of legislation, both state and national, and on the legality of the exercise of executive power as well.

This remarkable practice, which we call simply "judicial review," deserves special consideration, for it is an illuminating example of how Americans took old familiar ideas and transformed them into institutions. Judicial review is a product of two old and accepted principles: one the principle that any act of government contrary to natural or fundamental law ("the laws of Nature and of Nature's God," as Jefferson put it in the Declaration of Independence) is void and of no force, and, second, the principle of the separation of powers and the independence of the judiciary. In the past these principles had been chiefly rhetorical or ceremonial. Americans put them together and produced judicial review—the right and the duty of the courts to review independently the validity of acts passed by legislative bodies, state or national, and to reject as invalid any that did not conform to the Constitution.

What this meant in practice was that when cases came before them in the ordinary course of litigation, courts reviewed the legislation which

John Marshall. Chief Justice of the Supreme Court from 1801 to 1835, he established fundamental principles for Constitutional interpretation.

was challenged in order to determine its constitutionality. In the over-whelming majority of the cases, this meant a review of state laws to see if they were consistent with the Constitution of the United States which is—after all—"the Supreme Law of the Land." If the courts concluded that state acts were not consistent with the federal Constitution, they would declare them void and of no force. Courts could, and sometimes did, review acts of Congress as well and, on rare occasions, pronounced them void. But this happened only twice in all the years up to the Civil War, and less than one hundred times in the whole of American history; mostly judicial review was an instrument for bringing about state con-formity to the federal Constitution.

Judicial review had three striking consequences. First, it meant that the courts came to be accepted as the final and supreme arbiters of the Constitution. Second, it meant that increasingly the courts came to be the umpires of the federal system, harmonizing state legislation with the national constitution. Third—and particularly in the past thirty years—it meant that the courts came to be the expounders and defenders of the guarantees of the Bill of Rights. In recent years fully half of the cases that come to the Supreme Court involve the application of the appropriate provisions of the federal Bill of Rights. All of this gave to the American judiciary a power and prestige not enjoyed by the judiciary of any other country. It also, needless to say, involved them deeply in current affairs and exposed them to the criticism that they were usurping legislative or constitutional functions.

Now this intricate system of limitations on government which seemed almost as if it were designed to produce stalemate came into existence just as the growth of the nation and the immense enlargement of govern-mental activities placed new and inescapable responsibilities on government. So having placed effective limits on the authority of government, limits which still function—Americans had to turn around and find some way of freeing government from these limits and giving it the authority it needed to cope with the vast and complex problems of a modern industrial society. This they achieved in a variety of ways; it will be sufficient to give two illustrations.

First, and most important, as a method of making the governmental mechanisms work was the political party. Here is a characteristic American invention, and one which has gone into every continent on the globe—though not into every country. There had been something like political parties in eighteenth-century England and Sweden, but these British Whigs and Tories, these Swedish Hats and Caps, were not genuine political parties, but factions, cliques, cabals, drawn from the ruling classes, and representing only a small fraction of the people of the country. The American political party came from the people up, not from the top down—and still does. It embraced the whole body politic—which in the United States meant just about the whole white adult population, and now means the whole adult population. It was national, not local or regional—and still is. It divided into two—not as in so many other countries into a dozen or a score fragments—and the United States still boasts a two-party system. The two parties (over the years Federalist-Republican; Whig-Democratic; Republican-Democratic) represented a pretty fair cross section of the whole people. American parties never divided on ideological lines, but on practical and even personal issues. Their objective has never been (with the possible exception of 1860) the triumph of a body of political principles, but the triumph of their candidates at the polls.

This remarkable invention, the political party, quickly became the most important institution of American politics. It was the machinery that ran the government. It took over responsibility for making democracy work: putting up the candidates for office, raising the issues, conducting campaigns and elections, organizing legislatures, bridging the gap between legislative and executive departments, and harmonizing the political organs of local, state, and national governments.

These activities are so important that it is hard to see how government could function without them, and it is clear that a federal system could not possibly function without them. But the contributions of the political party to the commonwealth are even broader. Parties have long been one of the chief instruments of democracy itself—the mechanism which enables the democratic system to work. They are largely responsible for the political education of the electorate. In every election, state as well as national, they debate men and issues on long and elaborate campaigns. They pay most of the costs of elections raising money by voluntary contributions—contributions which parties are, to be sure, expected to repay by favorable legislation or by valuable appointments to office. They harmonize the disparate interests of sectional, ethnic, religious, economic and social groups, providing a safety valve for passion and discontent, and canalizing different interests and passions into peaceful channels. Perhaps the simplest way to realize the importance of the political party is to imagine what American politics and government would be without it.

Just as Americans pay a price for the advantages of federalism, so they pay a price for their party system. Thus because both major parties reject ideological differences and concentrate instead on winning the votes of as many voters as possible, they tend to be much alike in character and conduct. This means that they rarely offer the American people genuine alternatives. It is difficult to see much difference in the administrations of, let us say, Presidents Truman and Eisenhower, or Presidents Johnson and Nixon, just as in the past it was difficult to see much difference in the Presidencies of Democrat Grover Cleveland and Republican Benjamin Harrison. Because parties avoid principles, they concentrate all the more on practical issues, or perhaps on no issues at all but merely on candidates. The contest between Woodrow Wilson and Theodore Roosevelt in 1912

Television brought political campaigning out of the streets and meeting halls into the living rooms of the voters in the U.S., as it has all over the world. Above, John F. Kennedy and Richard Nixon debating during the 1960 Presidential campaign.

was largely one between two brilliant personalities, and that between John F. Kennedy and Richard Nixon in 1960 was one between two candidates with very different styles. With television differences in personality and style have taken on increased importance. Because the country is large and the task of nominating candidates and conducting campaigns arduous, parties tend to fall back upon showmanship and advertising. Nominating conventions are notoriously conducted in a carnival atmosphere, and television is coming to play an ever larger role in campaigns. Because these campaigns are alarmingly expensive—a party will raise as much as fifty or sixty million dollars to elect a President—parties have to reward their generous supporters with jobs, benefits, and favors. All this is distressing, but so far no alternative method of running the political machinery has been devised.

A second illustration of the way Americans overcame the inherent limitations of their constitutional system and provided government with the authority and the tools to adapt itself to the needs of the welfare state and of world power is the history of the Presidency. The evolution of the American Presidency is interesting not only in itself, but as perhaps the best illustration (after the political party) of the growth of an "unwritten" constitution alongside the written Constitution. The Constitution itself has very little to say about the Presidency, and no wonder, for it was a new position, and few of the Founding Fathers had any clear ideas about it. The Constitution simply says that "the Executive power shall be vested in a President." To be sure it specified a few of these powers—Commander-in-Chief of the armed forces, for example, the power to grant pardons, to receive ambassadors, to make certain appointments, such as ambassadors and judges of the Supreme Court—and it required him to "take care that the laws be faithfully executed."

All this provided a very slender foundation for what has come to be the most powerful office in the Western world. For clearly a President who limited himself to the exercise of the powers *specifically* set forth in Article II of the Constitution would be a lamentable failure and would involve his administration and his country in crisis and ruin. Nor is this clear merely in the light of the crises that were aggravated by "weak" Presidents like Madison, Buchanan, and Hoover. It was clear from the very beginning, and George Washington himself established the principle and the precedents which have flourished ever since: that "the Executive Power" is the power successfully exercised by Presidents. Throughout American history, Presidents—especially "strong" Presidents like Washington, Jackson, Lincoln, Franklin D. Roosevelt and Kennedy—have used such executive power as seemed to them essential to the protection and welfare of the nation, and once they had acted, their actions became precedents upon which their successors could build.

Thus—to take a few examples—Washington issued, quite on his own, a proclamation of neutrality in the war then raging between Britain and

France; Jefferson bought Louisiana; Monroe issued the doctrine that bears his name; Lincoln raised armies to put down a rebellion and freed the slaves; Theodore Roosevelt sent the American navy around the globe, "took" Panama, and landed marines in the islands of the Caribbean; Woodrow Wilson sent an expeditionary force into Mexico; Franklin Roosevelt gave fifty destroyers to Britain in exchange for leases on bases in the Caribbean; Kennedy launched an invasion of Cuba; and Johnson conducted for four years an undeclared war in Vietnam.

Almost all of these exercises of Presidential power were in the arena of foreign affairs, and it is in this arena—where the imperatives of emergency and the claims of national security seem to operate most powerfully, that the executive power has lent itself to the greatest expansion. Flexibility obtains in the domestic arena as well: here, too, a strong and bold President, like Lincoln, or Franklin Roosevelt, or John Kennedy, can do a great many things not specified in the Constitution nor contemplated by the authors of that document.

Library of Congress

Parades and public demonstrations historically played, and still play, a major role in special-interest groups' efforts to win public and legislative support for their causes. Above, "suffragettes" march in 1913 to win support for women's right to vote. They won the right through a Constitutional amendment ratified in 1920.

44

What all this means is that Americans have, in a sense, the best of both constitutional worlds: the world of law and the world of custom. They have all the advantages of a written Constitution with its clear and precise arrangements, and its careful limitations; they have most of the advantages, too, of an unwritten constitution, which permits them to adapt their government to the exigencies of different issues and circumstances. All this was foreseen, at the beginning, by the authors of the Constitution, who provided (in the document itself) that Congress shall have power— "To make all laws which shall be necessary and proper" to fulfill the specific provisions of the Constitution.

Because Americans contrived for themselves a constitutional system which was authoritative and binding on most fundamental matters but wonderfully flexible in its mechanics, adaptable in its administration, and dynamic in its resourcefulness, they were able to grow from a small pastoral society of four millions of people scattered over thirteen states along the Atlantic coast, to a world power of two hundred million, occupying fifty states, with only one major constitutional crisis—that of 1860— and with fundamentally the same political and constitutional principles that they had adopted at the beginning of their experiment in independence, constitutionalism, and democracy.

The American nation began with the most democratic political system in the world. By "democracy" we mean, quite simply, popular government. At the very threshold of independence Americans discovered that fundamental principle of democracy set forth in the Declaration of Independence, that governments must derive "their just powers from the consent of the governed." What is more important, they institutionalized this principle in the constitutional convention, an enlarged and sophisticated version of the meetings that had given form to the Mayflower Compact, or the Fundamental Orders of Connecticut of 1639, or the Plantation Agreement of the Providence Plantations of 1640. It was a convention to which all the adult males of a commonwealth elected delegates who were authorized to draw up a constitution of government and submit it, for approval or rejection, to the people assembled in their towns or counties. Massachusetts led the way in 1778 and 1780, and thereafter all the American states followed her example. So, too, did the people of the United States (with some modifications) in 1787.

The constitutional convention, it can be said, was sovereignty organized: a regular and formal method whereby the sovereign people "alter or abolish governments, and institute new ones." It is also revolution legalized: a method of overthrowing government not by violence, but by law. Except in the American colonies and, briefly, in Commonwealth England, nothing like it had been tried before; to this day we have found no way of improving upon it.

So much for the principle. But more than this was necessary if principle was to be translated into practice. Here the important question was What is the body politic? Who are the people that institute government? The body politic of the Revolutionary era was a minority of all the people: free, white, adult, Christian males. Some states narrowed that group even further by requiring property qualifications for voting and officeholding, but there were no such limitations in the federal Constitution.

By modern standards these limits on voting were undemocratic. But two things must be said. First, the proportion, and the numbers, entitled to vote in the new United States were far and away the highest in the world, and remained so for over a century. Second, property and religious qualifications for voting, never very effectively enforced, disappeared altogether within a generation or so of independence. Not until the twentieth century, however, were limitations on suffrage based on race and sex swept away. The Fifteenth Amendment to the Constitution, ratified in 1870, provided that no one should be denied the right to vote on account of color; the Nineteenth Amendment, of 1920, granted the vote to women. The grant of suffrage to women went into effect at once, without opposition or sabotage. Not so the grant of suffrage to Negroes. That had to be vindicated again and again, and is even now frustrated and defeated in many parts of the country.

From the beginning Americans supplemented the formal Constitution by an unwritten constitution. So, too, from the beginning they supplemented formal governmental institutions by informal and unofficial institutions. Of all informal institutions of government, far and away the most important was the private voluntary organization. While these have flourished in all societies at one time or another, it is in America that they have had their greatest growth and their deepest significance. What Alexis de Tocqueville wrote back in the 1830's is still true:

> in no country in the world has the principle of association been more successfully used, or more unsparingly applied to a multitude of different objects, than in America. (*Democracy in America,* tr. by Henry Reeve.)

And he went on to observe that

> wherever at the head of some new undertaking, you see the Government in France, or a man of rank in England, in the United States you will be sure to find an association.

Because in the eighteenth century the new nation started with institutions of government that were simple and weak, Americans from the beginning fell into the habit of providing for their needs by voluntary associations. As they had come together voluntarily in scores of villages and towns to set up their own local governments, so they came together to set up churches, to establish schools and colleges, to provide for defense against the Indians, to form companies that would organize new settlements in the West, to create political combinations and parties, and for scores of other purposes. It is sometimes forgotten that all American political parties are voluntary organizations (in some respects private, in others public), as are all churches, all labor unions, all philanthropic and charitable societies, all scientific, literary, and professional organizations. Equally characteristic are the literally thousands of purely social organizations: brotherhoods and sisterhoods sometimes, as with the Knights of Columbus, connected with churches, sometimes, as with the American Legion, related to military service, sometimes, as with the Rotary or Kiwanis, tied to business, sometimes, as with the Masonic Order, or the Elks, or the Woodmen of the World, purely social. Americans associate for everything: for table tennis and walking, for stamp collecting and photography, for simplified spelling and travel, for celebrating a blizzard or a football game—the list is inexhaustible.

It is easy to explain all this as a silly expression of gregariousness or as a sobering commentary on the atomization of American society. These considerations are, indeed, relevant, and no wonder in a country where everything was new, and people were repeatedly uprooted from familiar surroundings and thrown into communities that were new and unfamiliar. An equalitarian society *is* gregarious; a society that is physically and socially mobile *does* seek to substitute new relationships for those that have been abandoned. But both the explanation and the purposes of the American habit of joining have deeper significance. The basic explanation of the popularity and the effectiveness of private associations is threefold. First, the absence of those formal governmental, religious, and social institutions which dominated and almost monopolized the European scene —a deprivation which forced Americans back on their own resources. Second, the pioneering experience, which forced each new generation of Americans into a state of nature, as it were, and put a premium on cooperation. And third, the habits of democracy which encouraged people to do for themselves whatever they wanted done.

The consequences of the habit of voluntary association were far-reaching, pervasive, and persistent. First, this activity, going on ceaselessly in a thousand communities, was a training ground for democracy—was indeed a form of self-government, for managing the affairs of church, school, labor union, business and professional organization, fraternal order was in a sense governmental, if not political. Second, voluntary associations were training grounds for equality. Thousands of societies of the most miscellaneous character demanded the most miscellaneous talents, and there was room for everyone, even room at the top. Those who could not hope to achieve social distinction or political power or professional prestige, could content themselves with leadership in their local church, their labor union, their farmers' Grange, or their fraternal order. No one, it could be said, was so lacking in intellectual attainment, social grace, wealth, or popularity, that he could not achieve some kind of position in one of the voluntary associations of his own choosing. Third, the voluntary organization encouraged and strengthened national unity. Vast distances, regional interests, ethnic and linguistic differences, the demands of federalism, all threatened to fragment American society. But the voluntary associations stretched across political lines, spanned geographical differences, transcended distance. Masons and Elks from South Carolina and Massachusetts could be brothers socially if they were not politically; members of agricultural Granges and labor unions learned to know and understand each other across state and regional lines; stamp collectors in New York and Texas, fishermen in Maine and Montana, Mormons or Christian Scientists in Utah or Pennsylvania, alumni of Harvard or Ohio State universities, living in every state, yet boasted a common denominator and discovered common interests. In a country where so much threatened to fragment, the voluntary association unified.

recommended reading

Agar, Herbert. *The Price of Union.* Boston: Houghton Mifflin Company (Sentry Editions).

*Binkley, Wilfred E. *American Political Parties.* New York: Alfred A. Knopf, 1963.

Boorstin, Daniel. *The Genius of American Politics.* Chicago: University of Chicago Press (Phoenix Books), 1953.

*Bowers, Claude. *Party Battles of the Jackson Period.* New York: Octagon Books, 1965.

Bryce, James. *The American Commonwealth.* 2 volumes. New York: G. P. Putnam's Sons (Capricorn Books), 1959.

Burns, James M. *Deadlock of Democracy: Four-Party Politics in America.* Revised edition. Englewood Cliffs, N. J.: Prentice-Hall (Spectrum Books).

Chafee, Zechariah, Jr. *Free Speech in the United States.* New York: Atheneum Publishers, 1969.

Corwin, Edward S. *The President: Office and Powers.* 4th edition. New York: New York University Press, 1957.

*Cushman, Robert E. *Civil Liberties in the United States.* New York: Johnson Reprint Corporation, 1956.

*Ernest, Morris L. *The First Freedom.* New York: Macmillan Company, 1946. OP

*Graham, George A. *Morality in American Politics.* New York: Random House, 1952. OP

Hamilton, Alexander, Madison, James, and Jay, John. *The Federalist Papers.* Edited by Clinton Rossiter. New York: New American Library (Mentor Books), 1961.

Hartz, Louis. *Liberal Tradition in America: An Interpretation of American Political Thought Since the Revolution.* New York: Harcourt, Brace & World (Harvest Books).

Hofstadter, Richard. *The American Political Tradition*. New York: Random House (Vintage Books).

*Holcombe, Arthur N. *Our More Perfect Union: From 18th-Century Principles to 20th-Century Practice*. Cambridge, Mass.: Harvard University Press, 1950.

*Josephson, Matthew. *The President Makers, 1896-1916*. New York: Frederick Ungar Company, 1964.

Key, Vladimir O., Jr. *Southern Politics*. New York: Random House (Vintage Books).

Kohn, Hans. *American Nationalism: An Interpretative Essay*. New York: Macmillan Company (Collier Books), 1961.

*Konvitz, Milton R. *Fundamental Liberties of a Free People: Religion, Speech, Press, Assembly*. Ithaca, N. Y.: Cornell University Press, 1957.

La Follette, Robert M. *La Follette's Autobiography: A Personal Narrative of Political Experiences*. Madison, Wis.: University of Wisconsin Press, 1960.

*McLaughlin, Andrew C. *Constitutional History of the United States*. New York: Appleton-Century-Crofts.

*Roosevelt, Theodore. *Autobiography of Theodore Roosevelt*. New York: Charles Scribner's Sons, 1958.

Rossiter, Clinton. *The American Presidency*. Revised edition. New York: New American Library (Mentor Books).

————. *Conservatism in America: The Thankless Persuasion*. New York: Random House (Vintage Books).

Schlesinger, Arthur M., Jr. *A Thousand Days: [John F. Kennedy in the White House]*. Greenwich, Conn.: Fawcett World Library (Crest Books).

Steffens, Lincoln. *Autobiography of Lincoln Steffens*. 2 volumes. New York: Harcourt, Brace & World (Harvest Books), 1968.

de Tocqueville, Alexis. *Democracy in America*. New York: New American Library (Mentor Books).

*Warren, Charles. *The Supreme Court in United States History*. 2 volumes. Boston: Little, Brown & Company, 1960.

*White, William A. *Autobiography of William Allen White*. New York: Macmillan Company, 1946.

*Whitlock, Brand. *Forty Years of It*. Westport, Conn.: Greenwood Press, 1969.

*Zink, Harold. *City Bosses in the United States*. New York: AMS Press. OP

° Hard-cover edition. Titles not so marked are paperback editions.

OP indicates that the edition is out of print.

4. the American economy

For almost two hundred years it has been common for foreign visitors —and not visitors alone—to assert that America had a "business civilization." The phrase itself is ambiguous, but there is little doubt that in America business does enjoy privileges and exercise power denied it elsewhere. It plays a dominant role in government and in the military; it commands distinction in society; it controls most forms of communication and education, such as newspapers, journals, and television; it permeates and perhaps dominates the cultural scene. Most Americans take for granted that businessmen should run government and sit on the boards of trustees of universities, libraries, museums, and orchestras; they accept as natural, and even inevitable, the subordination of social, cultural, and aesthetic interests to the interests of business. Thus, they have heretofore accepted with little protest the subordination of public health to the interests of the cigarette industry, of the natural beauty of the countryside to the billboard industry, of public interest in the airwaves to the television and advertising industries, of town planning to the interests of private landowners and real estate operators. Needless to say this habit of conceding priority to the interests of business is not confined to the United States, but the phenomenon itself is usually ascribed to the United States, and when it appears in France or England or Brazil it is stigmatized as "Americanization."

The explanation of the special role of business in America is rooted in American history.

When, in the late seventeenth and eighteenth centuries, the industrial revolution began to develop in England and France, the pattern of government and economy was pretty well fixed. Business and industry did not have a clean slate on which to write their own terms; on the contrary they had to fit, as best they could, into the existing pattern of control. The crown was there, the church was there, the great landed aristocracy was there, the guilds and the merchant adventurers were there, the army and the navy were there, and the law, largely fashioned by these interests over many centuries, was there too. Business and industry were in no position to dictate terms or to demand special consideration; rather they had to be content with what the existing interests of government, church, and society would allow them. In the old world business enterprise therefore took for granted, for a long time, that it occupied a subordinate position in society,

51

that it could not have its way in all matters that concerned it, but was bound by ancient law, prescriptive rights, and by other interests more powerful than those it represented.

But in the new world all was different. Here there was no fixed pattern into which business had to fit, no powerful interests to which it was required to adjust. Here there was no crown, no church, no landed aristocracy, no army or navy, no guilds, no prescriptive rights, and few legal regulations or restraints. What is more, the new governments that Americans set up in the Revolutionary era were, as we have seen, weak. From the beginning the federal system played into the hands of the business community. The federal government, which had only those powers granted to it, was reluctant to exercise far-reaching economic power and for a long time contented itself with a kind of benevolent patronage. Thus it is illuminating that though the Constitution granted the federal government power to "regulate commerce among the States," the first timid regulation of such commerce came in the Interstate Commerce Act of 1887—precisely a century after the original grant. Not indeed until the New Deal of the 1930s did the federal government use its power to supervise the American economy in any vigorous or comprehensive fashion.

As for the states, they were not strong enough to regulate great national business interests like steel or oil or railroads, nor did they display any lively desire to do so. Quite the contrary. For the most part they competed with each other for industry, railroads, and business. Far from imposing effective regulation upon these, the states more commonly tempted them with special privileges and seduced them by promises of exemption from restrictive laws and burdensome taxes.

For here was a vast continent to be settled, limitless resources to be exploited, and it was private enterprise—not government—that was allotted the gratifying task. Thus here, in the New World, business could in fact pretty well write its own ticket, to use a very American phrase. And that is what business proceeded to do, with the enthusiastic support of most of the public.

Out of this background came the principle—obsession, fetish, call it what you will—of "private enterprise." Put most simply, the principle of private enterprise has meant that progress and prosperity can best be achieved by allowing private enterprise to conduct the economy with a minimum of governmental supervision or interference.

This principle was rooted, originally, in a simple economy where in

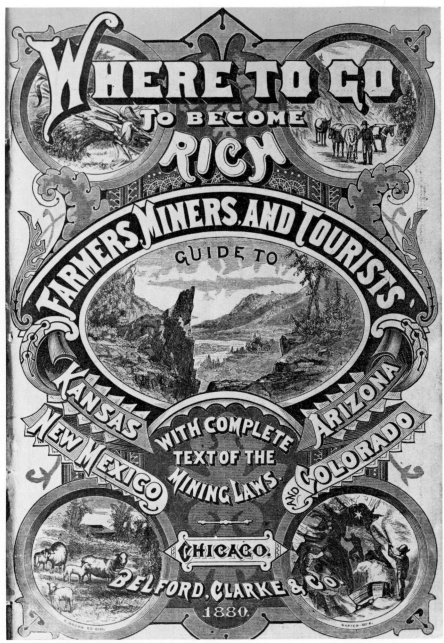

WHERE TO GO TO BECOME RICH

FARMERS, MINERS, AND TOURISTS'

GUIDE TO

KANSAS

NEW MEXICO

ARIZONA

AND COLORADO

WITH COMPLETE TEXT OF THE MINING LAWS.

CHICAGO.

BELFORD, CLARKE & CO.

1880.

The Kansas State Historical Society, Topeka

The lush promise of the frontier shaped the American economy — and the American character — throughout the nineteenth century.

53

fact the individual farmer, the fisherman, the merchant, the craftsman, could fend for himself. The farmer could grow what he pleased, and if the soil wore out he could sell and move west to better land and begin all over again. The fisherman could build his own boat, sail out to the Newfoundland Banks or hunt whales in the North Pacific. The merchant—often a sailor boy who had worked his way up from the deck—could sail his own ship to the Mediterranean or the China seas and come home to Salem or Boston with a fortune from a single trip. The craftsman, too, could fend for himself, if not in Philadelphia or Baltimore, then in Cincinnati or Chicago or San Francisco. They did not need government subsidies; they did not want government interference.

Yet the whole notion of private enterprise was, from the beginning, something of an illusion. It was an illusion because the assumption that the American economy could flourish without government, or wholly outside government, was quite fallacious. Government legalized incorporation and limited liability on which the whole of American corporate development rested; government gave patents and copyright and provided protective tariffs to "infant" industries and to others; government disposed of land, supervised the building of railroads and telegraph and telephone; government enforced laws of contract, wills, promissory notes, and bills of exchange; government created coinage and directed banking and finance; government erected the courts which pronounced the law, and governmental authority enforced the law. Government indeed provided both the foundation upon which the entire economy rested and the mechanisms through which it functioned. This was true in Alexander Hamilton's time; but the role that government played in the economy in the early days of the Republic was increased a hundredfold by the time of Franklin Roosevelt, or Lyndon B. Johnson.

Thus the notion that the economy was a product of private enterprise and therefore independent of government control was, and remained, an illusion. It became, in the twentieth century, a myth. For increasingly the economy came to be dominated by giant corporations that left little room for individual or private enterprise. As late as the 1860s the majority of Americans probably lived on farms or in villages, and pretty much fended for themselves. A century later the economy was almost wholly urban, industrial, and corporate. Individual corporations, like General Motors, or the American Telephone and Telegraph Company, employed more workers and enjoyed more revenues than many individual states. The great majority of Americans did not work for themselves, but for corporations or government—neither of them very private: thus by 1968 farm employment had declined to less than four million, while more than twelve million men and women worked for government, at all levels, and nearly fourteen million for industrial corporations.

More and more, as the nineteenth century merged into the twentieth, giant corporations came to control the American economy and to play an

Fractionators. Phillips gasoline plant, Borger, Texas, 1942. Photo by John Vachon. Below: Today complex machines harvest the grain on America's vast prairies. The men and women who used to do the work they do have crowded into the industrial cities.

55

ever-larger role in American politics. Starting late in the 1890s industrial consolidation came to be the order of the day, and out of this concentration came, in the end, something close to monopoly. Federal laws prohibited "combinations in restraint of trade," but these were hard to enforce; besides, as combinations and concentration brought both efficiency and prosperity, the zeal for enforcement of prohibitions evaporated. Two world wars greatly accelerated the process of consolidation, for during time of war governments are interested only in getting ships, airplanes, and tanks as fast as possible, and on almost any terms. By mid-twentieth century the telephone business—incomparably the largest in the world—was dominated by one corporation, automobile manufacture by three, the aircraft industry by six, the steel industry by five or six, the aluminum industry by two, tobacco by three or four, and the oil industry, the most complex of the lot, by perhaps a dozen. All of these could be called "private" enterprise, in the sense that they were not, after all, governmental, but the notion that they somehow provided more opportunity for individual enterprise, or that they were less bureaucratic than government, was fallacious. Few enterprises, indeed, were now private in the eighteenth-century sense. The corner grocery store had given way to supermarkets which were, in turn, cogs in a vast national chain; the independent newspaper of Benjamin Franklin's day was a giant enterprise that cost tens of millions of dollars in initial financing; and only multimillion dollar corporations could hope to finance television networks. Thus while American television was doubtless "private" as contrasted with the British which is "public," it would be a mistake to suppose that American television is therefore more "enterprising" than British, or even more independent. The contrary is probably true. Here and there in corners of the economy, it was still possible for the individual to create a new business and come out with a fortune, but for the economy as a whole the day of individualism —certainly of President Hoover's "rugged individualism"—was a thing of the past.

The privileges and powers of business, the tradition of corporate enterprise and of private aggrandizement of natural resources and even of public utilities all were the consequence of deep-rooted historical conditions; they in turn bred attitudes of mind that rose to the dignity of principles and crystallized into policies of historical significance. The first of these was the policy of laissez faire, or hands off!; the second the policy of government support to business enterprise.

It would be tedious to trace the operation of these two policies— policies which seem at first glance contradictory but which in fact proved to be complementary. Laissez faire itself had its roots in both principle and experience. The principle was (as we have seen earlier) that government itself was dangerous, because government inevitably abuses power; therefore—in Jefferson's phrase—that government was best that governed least. Experience appeared to reinforce this elementary conclusion. After

56

all, in the circumstances of the late eighteenth and the early nineteenth centuries, the average American could manage for himself without governmental interference. He did not need government to do things for him; he could do better for himself. All he wanted was to be left alone—left to take up land where he chose, to cultivate it as he pleased, to sell his produce where and as he would, left alone from the exactions of church, of taxation, the burdens of war, the meddling of bureaucrats. Together with his neighbors, who were like-minded on this matter, he could build his own schools, erect his own churches, defend himself against Indians, stake out claims on public lands, and even enforce home-made law against those who stole cattle or tried to cheat him out of his land.

This was all very pastoral, to be sure, but it was born not out of a reading of Rousseau, but out of experience. With the coming of industry, railroads, and cities, the experience changed, but the theory lingered on. After the Civil War it was reinforced by what has come to be called Social Darwinism—the assumption that the Darwinian principle of the survival of the fittest worked just as well in the realm of human society as in the realm of nature. Thus, just as in nature the failure of the weak and the unfit and the survival of the strong and the fit make for the gradual improvement of species, so in human society and economy the weak will go under and the fit will survive—but only if there is no outside interference in the process. Banish therefore all governmental interference in the operation of the economy, and let "nature" take its course! Only if we resolutely reject all artificial interferences in the processes of society and economy can we be sure of progress.

The second widely held economic principle was not logically consistent with the first, but looked to the same end—the prosperity of business as a necessary basis for progress. This was the principle that what was good for business was, ipso facto, good for the country, and that it was therefore the clear duty of government to contribute in every possible way to the prosperity of business and industry. Some of this thinking, to be sure, had its roots in old world mercantilism, and it is interesting that the first and greatest American economic statesman, Alexander Hamilton, was also the leading American mercantilist. For the most part, however, this politico-economic policy recommended itself not on grounds of theory, but of common sense. For a new country clamored for development. Farmers could not sell their produce without access to markets, and that depended on canals and railroads. They could not finance improvements without loans, and that required banks. They could not develop their villages into cities, or exploit their resources of coal or iron ore or oil, or attract those newcomers who would multiply the value of their lands, without industry. Every community therefore regarded the businessman, the manufacturer, the railroad builder, the banker, as a benefactor.

How natural therefore that a people who regarded rapid economic growth as an unmitigated blessing should insist that their government speed such development. Every new community needed a railroad: let governments therefore—state and national alike—subsidize railroad construction with gifts of public lands and lavish loans. Countless new industries—"infant industries" as Americans fondly called them—clamored for assistance and protection: let local governments then give subsidies in the form of land or tax exemption, and let the national government provide protection through tariff legislation which would keep out foreign competition. Farmers, too, needed help, for was not farming socially and morally the most advantageous of all occupations? Let government then give freely of its vast public lands to farmers—*give,* not sell; let it provide the farmers with tariff protection and low-cost loans, and all the products of scientific research.

Thus almost every interest in the American economy—farming, manufacture, transportation, banking, even education—believed in laissez faire in principle, but made an exception for its own interest. What they wanted was both simple and natural: a policy of hands off! when it came to regulation or supervision, but a policy of aggressive activism when it came to protection and special favors.

The twentieth century saw a challenge to these shibboleths and a reversal of these policies. For increasingly it was clear that vast industrial organizations made a mockery of private enterprise and that corporations had taken advantage of the doctrines of laissez faire to aggrandize the natural resources of the country, create shocking extremes of riches and poverty, and bend government—which was meant to serve all the people, future as well as present—to their will. As early as the 1890s a newly formed People's party had demanded a vast expansion of governmental regulation and economic activities, but not until the Woodrow Wilson administration of 1913-1917 was anything effective achieved in this arena. The Wilsonian program, admirable as it was, was still in large part negative: it put an end to some of the graver abuses of big business but did not substantially expand welfare activities of the government itself. After the First World War the collapse of farm prices, ever swifter progress towards concentration of corporate control, and the rapid exhaustion of natural resources inspired demands for governmental intervention far more effective than that of the past. It was, however, the great depression of the thirties that dramatized the futility of mere "regulation," and the necessity of active interposition by the government in the economy—in short, the creation of a welfare state.

River Rouge Plant. Charles Sheeler. 1932. River Rouge is near Detroit, home of America's vast automobile industry.

There was nothing new about the welfare state except in America. It was the natural, almost the inevitable, product of the industrial revolution and had its beginnings in the Germany of Bismarck in the late nineteenth century, and in Scandinavia, Britain, and some of the Commonwealth nations early in the twentieth century. It came late to the United States because here resources were so abundant that they long cushioned the shock of industrialism, because labor was not organized politically, or even political-minded, and because the tradition of laissez faire was so strong. The basic welfare state legislation was enacted as part of Franklin

59

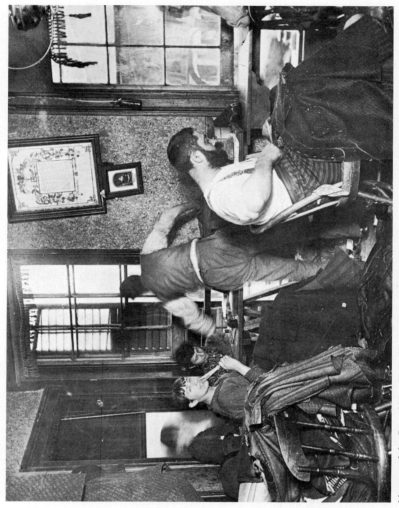

Museum of the City of New York. The Jacob A. Riis Collection.

Sweatshop in Ludlow Street Tenement. Photograph by Jacob A. Riis. Immigrants to American cities lived in slums and worked in dismal sweatshops, in the expectation that their children would have better lives. Almost invariably, they did.

D. Roosevelt's New Deal in the 1930s: unemployment compensation, social security, guarantees to labor, enlarged support to farmers, federal development of hydroelectric power (TVA), firmer control over banking and investments, and conservation of natural resources. This body of legislation was greatly enlarged in subsequent administrations, particularly those of Harry Truman and Lyndon B. Johnson, to embrace such things as medical care, federal aid to education at all levels, federal guarantees of civil rights, urban relief and rehabilitation, and a large-scale attack on air and water pollution. By the decade of the seventies it could be said that the American welfare state did most of the things for its people that the welfare states of Britain, Scandinavia, France, Holland, and Germany did for theirs, and did them reasonably well. But where generally throughout the world the welfare state was socialist or communist, Americans—like the peoples of the British Commonwealth—managed to assimilate the welfare state to the existing political system and economic order, and to create what might be called welfare republicanism or welfare capitalism.

T he natural resources of the new world were almost limitless—soil, timber, water and water power, coal, iron ore, precious metals, oil and gas; what it lacked, from the beginning, was labor. Never, until the twentieth century, could it be said that there were enough workers to do the tasks that needed to be done. This lack of enough workingmen had interesting and far reaching consequences. It meant that during the long colonial period the mother country provided, and the colonies welcomed, labor in the form of indentured servants (who worked their passage to America by five to seven years' servitude) and Negro slave labor. It meant that once Americans were independent they would, inevitably, set up a system which encouraged immigration, and made it easy for immigrants to be absorbed not only in the economy but in society as well. And it meant, in a very broad way, that in America labor, certainly white labor, would have the upper hand, at a price: that it ceased to be a distinct economic or social body but rather merged with the great mass of American society and thus lost its identity.

If the availability of natural resources was the central fact of American economic history, immigration has been the central fact of American labor history. Altogether, over a period of three and a half centuries, something like forty-five million immigrants came, or were brought, to that part of the new world which became the United States. Many of these were Negro slaves, especially during the colonial period.

Not all of the others joined the labor force in any literal sense. If women and children did not commonly become workers, the women did the necessary domestic labor and produced children who grew up to be workers. Nor should we assume that only those immigrants who worked on farms, built railroads, mined coal, or became factory hands, were workers; after all, every preacher, teacher, journalist, writer, musician, soldier, and sailor was part of the labor force, and contributed to the American emonomy. And the new world attracted these just as it attracted the Swedish farmer, the Hungarian coal miner, and the Jewish peddler.

What this meant is something Americans themselves do not fully appreciate: that all through the nineteenth and well into the twentieth century Europe conducted a vast foreign aid program for the United States. This was certainly not conscious or deliberate. Most European countries, indeed, did their best to discourage emigration to America. But whatever the motives, the fact is that over the years Europe raised, nourished, and—after a fashion—trained, millions of young people who then took their strengths and skills to America. What was true for the farmer and the laborer was doubly true for the skilled mechanic, the artist, and the intellectual. We hear a great deal now about the "brain drain" from Britain, and some other countries, to the United States; needless to say the brain drain—and the character drain and the talent drain—began with the emigration of the Puritans and the Pilgrims and persisted down to our own day.

Because the United States needed this work force, it facilitated both immigration and naturalization. For a hundred years the United States took all comers, without any kind of selection or restriction. In the 1880s came restrictions on immigration from the Orient, and the exclusion of what some thought "undesirable" on account of health or morals. This early legislation did nothing to stem the tide of immigration; the decade of the eighties brought over five million immigrants to the United States, and the next three decades over eighteen million more. Not until the 1920s, when the prospect of tidal waves of immigrants from war-stricken Europe alarmed both organized labor and businessmen, did Congress write effective limitations on immigration into law.

Labor therefore commonly had the upper hand in the sense that (except during periods when the economy was depressed) it was in demand and could demand—and usually obtain—good wages and working conditions. All through the eighteenth and well into the nineteenth century the average free workingman in the United States enjoyed a standard of living substantially higher than his counterparts enjoyed in Britain or Germany or—in the second half of the century—in Italy and Poland. There was usually ample food on the table; there was shelter which, though often cramped and cold and mean, was usually better than what was available to him in Europe. If the hours of labor were long and conditions harsh, so it was everywhere in the industrial world. Best of all he could change jobs; he could move away; he could—if he were either clever or lucky—better himself. And he could confidently expect what few workingmen or farmers anywhere else could expect—that his children would be better off than he was. They could go to school—and did. They could take any job that was available, enter any trade or any profession for which they were fitted. They could work their way up; they could go, as the phrase had it, "from rags to riches." Not all American titans of industry or masters of capital started as poor boys, just as not all American Presidents were born in log cabins, but it happened often enough so that there was some substance to the otherwise romantic myth. After all, this was the history of John Jacob Astor and Stephen Girard, two immigrant boys in the early years of the nineteenth century; it was the history of John D. Rockefeller and Andrew Carnegie, of James B. Duke and Meyer Guggenheim, of James J. Hill and Henry Ford, in later years. Even in a day when, as the sociologists constantly point out, it helps to have rich parents and go to one of the more exclusive eastern schools, boys who were born poor have made great fortunes: the banker A. P. Giannini, the oilmen Paul Getty and H. L. Hunt, the aircraft manufacturer Howard Hughes, the film producer Spyros Skouras, and scores of others.

But the open society and the open economy meant that it was very hard for the working man to develop class solidarity or for labor to organize into unions or to play a dominant role in politics. Where the workingman assumed that he would always have the same job, in the same place, and that his children, after him, would work at the same trade or in the same shop, it was inevitable that there should develop a working class psychology, that workingmen should form guilds and trade unions and develop a class solidarity. That is what happened in the industrial countries of Europe. But in America, laborers and farmers and tradesmen and others did not think of themselves as a separate class, nor did they expect to stay in the particular job in which they happened to find themselves. Farm laborers became farm owners—and so did factory workers when they chose to. Workingmen shifted jobs as they shifted from one city to another, one state to another. Peddlers and shopkeepers branched out and became merchants, money-changers became bankers, teachers became preachers, and lawyers became businessmen. Even to this day there is considerably greater mobility in American labor and professions than can be found in any other nation. Thus nearly every student in Europe knows what he is going to study, and what he is going to be, when he enters university; most American students do not know what career they will adopt until they are ready to graduate.

One consequence of this is that labor unions were slow in developing in the United States and that when they did come, in the eighties and nineties of the last century, it was in a form that tended to divide rather than to unite labor. Early projects of the Knights of Labor in the 1870s, for "one big industrial union," or of the Populists for a union of workers and farmers in the 1890s failed to materialize. What did materialize were craft unions of carpenters, bricklayers, plumbers, railroadmen, automobile workers, and so forth, representing only skilled labor. This meant in turn that unskilled labor, which was long the majority of the labor force, was not organized and did not share the benefits of organization. What was particularly unfortunate was that unskilled labor was largely Negro and newly arrived immigrant labor. Thus a kind of race and class division grew up inside the ranks of labor. Even today, at a time when the number of unskilled workers is dropping and the number of skilled workers increasing, the members of the two, now-merged, great labor organizations —the American Federation of Labor and the Congress of Industrial Organizations—number less than a fourth of the total labor force and less than one-half of agricultural, industrial, and clerical labor, and they still discriminate against Negroes.

In almost all other western countries a Labor party represents the interests of the workingmen and, presumably, others, and competes, often successfully, for control of the government. But in the United States labor has always shied away from direct participation in politics. There has never been a national Labor party in the United States. Labor has preferred to do its own collective bargaining, and to achieve its legislative programs not by acting directly in the political arena, but by bringing pressure to bear on both the major parties. To be sure there is no such thing as a "labor vote" in general, any more than there is a farmer vote or a Catholic vote. But where the interests of labor are directly involved, the labor vote is decisive, and there are few Congressmen who would risk their political careers by systematically opposing the wishes of organized labor.

Perhaps the most striking fact about the American economy since the Second World War is the avoidance of an economic depression and the steady growth of general, though not universal, prosperity.

What chiefly distinguishes the American economy today is quite simply prosperity—a prosperity greater and more widespread than at any previous period of American history. Previous wars—the Civil War, and the First World War—had been followed by depressions that ravaged the social well-being of the American people; and there had been lively fears that when the twelve or thirteen million men and women in the armed services and the equal numbers in war industries were demobilized after the Second World War, history would repeat itself with a vengeance. Nothing of the kind happened. The economy absorbed the millions of military and war workers without embarrassment, and the nation was caught up in a spiral of expansion and prosperity which has lasted for a longer period than at any previous time.

Almost all statistics tell the same story. While unemployment lingered on among unskilled workers, particularly Negroes, there is something like full employment in all other ranks. By 1969 the number of employed had passed seventy-six million. Almost all indices of production doubled, and the value of the gross national product rose from $285 billion in 1950 to $860 billion in 1968. Personal income marched with production, increasing from $228 billion to $685 billion in the same years. This income was perhaps more widely distributed than at any period since the Civil War; per capita income rose, from $1,500 in 1950 to $3,410 in 1968. Some of this increase was a bit spotty, to be sure. Between 1958 and 1967, the wages of industrial and service workers rose a good deal more, proportionately, in the same period than professional salaries did. While farmers' and farm workers' per capita income almost doubled in a decade, farming remained the lowest-paid work in the U.S. in terms of individual cash earnings. Meanwhile, the over-all earnings of business and corporations achieved spectacular heights.

Some of the increased earnings, too, were counterbalanced by inflation and high taxes, which struck especially at the poor and the middle classes: thus in the sixties "real" wages of factory workers went up hardly at all. Yet the evidence is persuasive that in terms of what he could buy for a day's work, the average American was better off than he had been for a hundred years. And it was relevant, too, that social security, medical care, old age pensions, and other contributions from the welfare state cushioned the shock for the less fortunate.

For there were still large pockets of American society that did not share the general prosperity, and it was the presence of these, stubbornly lingering on in every area of the country, that made something of a mockery of the American claim to the highest standard of living in the world. For if we consider the general well-being of all members of society rather than the wealth of the more fortunate, it is clear that countries like Sweden, Denmark, Holland, and Switzerland enjoy a higher standard of living than the United States. In the eighteenth century it was possible for Benjamin Franklin to write that nowhere in the world were there so few extremes of wealth and poverty; no commentator on the American scene of 1970 could say the same.

Poverty lingered on among the blacks of the deep South, in Appalachia, among the Mexicans of Texas and California, and everywhere in the great cities—poverty with all of its somber associations. Back in the midst of the Depression, Franklin Roosevelt had said that one-third of the nation were ill-fed, ill-clad, and ill-housed. Now, in the midst of great prosperity, that proportion had declined to perhaps one-tenth the population. But one-tenth was twenty million people—twenty millions in the rat-infested slums of great cities, the derelict farms of the Appalachian

Mountains, the cotton plantations of the deep South, the truck farms of Colorado and California—without adequate medical care, their children condemned to inferior schools or, after the age of fourteen, to no schools at all, their old people cast off by an industrial society interested chiefly in efficiency. Millions of these, to be sure, were on "relief" of one form or another, and federal and state governments had launched ambitious programs not only for relief but for rehabilitation. The "war on poverty" had become to the new generation what the New Deal had been to the previous generation. So far it has not been as successful, for poverty continued to glare at the American people from every corner of the horizon, and neither the American democracy nor the American economy, for all their triumphs, had yet learned how to deal with it.

recommended reading

Arnold, Thurman. *The Folklore of Capitalism*. New Haven, Conn.: Yale University Press, 1937.

Berle, Adolph A., Jr. *The 20th Century Capitalist Revolution*. New York: Harcourt, Brace & World (Harvest Books).

*Bromfield, Louis. *The Green Bay Tree*. New York: Grosset & Dunlap, 1927. OP

Cochran, Thomas C., and Miller, William. *The Age of Enterprise: A Social History of Industrial America*. New York: Harper & Row (Harper Torchbooks).

Commager, Henry Steele, editor. *Lester Frank Ward and the Welfare State*. Indianapolis, Ind.: Bobbs-Merrill Company (Liberal Arts Press), 1966.

*Dorfman, Joseph. *The Economic Mind in American Civilization 1606-1933*. 5 volumes. New York: Augustus M. Kelley, Publishers, 1946-59.

*Douglas, Paul H. *Ethics in Government*. Cambridge, Mass.: Harvard University Press. OP

Dreiser, Theodore. *The Titan*. New York: New American Library (Signet Books).

Dulles, Foster R. *Labor in America: A History*. 3rd edition. New York: Thomas Y. Crowell Company.

Fine, Sidney. *Laissez Faire and the General-Welfare State*. Ann Arbor, Mich.: University of Michigan Press (Ann Arbor Books), 1964.

Galbraith, John K. *The Affluent Society*. 2nd edition. Boston: Houghton Mifflin Company, 1969.

———. *The New Industrial State*. New York: New American Library (Signet Books), 1968.

Giedion, Siegfried. *Mechanization Takes Command*. New York: W. W. Norton & Company, 1969.

Hacker, Louis M. *The Triumph of American Capitalism*. New York: McGraw-Hill Book Company, 1940.

Hamilton, Walton. *The Politics of Industry*. New York: Random House (Vintage Books).

Harrington, Michael. *The Other America*. New York: Penguin Books (Pelican Books), 1962.

*Heilbroner, Robert L. *The Quest for Wealth: A Study of Acquisitive Man*. New York: Simon & Schuster, 1956. OP

Howells, William D. *A Hazard of New Fortunes*. New York: New American Library (Signet Books).

————. *The Rise of Silas Lapham*. New York: Macmillan Company (Collier Books), 1962.

*James, Henry. *The Ivory Tower*. New York: Charles Scribner's Sons, 1917.

Jones, Peter D. *The Consumer Society: A History of American Capitalism*. Revised edition. New York: Penguin Books (Pelican Books), 1965.

Mills, C. Wright. *The Power Elite*. New York: Oxford University Press (Galaxy Books), 1959.

Mumford, Lewis. *Technics and Civilization*. New York: Harcourt, Brace & World (Harbinger Books).

*Mund, Vernon A. *Government and Business*. 4th edition. New York: Harper & Row, 1965.

*Nevins, Allan, and Hill, Frank E. *Ford*. 3 volumes. New York: Charles Scribner's Sons, 1954-63.

Sinclair, Upton. *The Jungle*. New York: New American Library (Signet Books).

*Tannenbaum, Frank. *A Philosophy of Labor*. New York: Alfred A. Knopf, 1951.

Twain, Mark. *The Gilded Age*. Indianapolis, Ind.: Bobbs-Merrill Company (Liberal Arts Press), 1969.

Veblen, Thorstein. *The Theory of Business Enterprise*. New York: New American Library (Mentor Books).

*Wright, Chester W. *Wool-Growing and the Tariff: A Study in the Economic History of the U. S.* Harvard Economic Studies Series. New York: Russell & Russell, 1968.

* Hard-cover edition. Titles not so marked are paperback editions.
  OP indicates that the edition is out of print.

5. religion in America

Religion plays a larger, if not a deeper, role in American society than in most countries of the world and certainly than in the predominantly Protestant societies of the Old World. No less than one hundred and twenty-six million Americans are members of some church—two-thirds of the population—though membership is often merely nominal. Protestant churches count some sixty-six million members, Roman Catholics forty-eight million, Eastern Orthodox Catholics over three million, and Jewish synagogues perhaps five million. A faithful public supports not only some three hundred and twenty-five thousand churches and perhaps four hundred thousand clergymen, but, in addition, scores of divinity schools and theological seminaries, hundreds of colleges, and numerous flourishing charitable and missionary activities. The Roman Catholic Church maintains, entirely at its own expense, parochial schools with over ten million pupils, plus innumerable colleges, universities, and seminaries.

Do these statistics demonstrate that the Americans are a deeply devout people? It is difficult to answer this question, for we have no criteria by which to judge the depth of religious feeling or the intensity of religious conviction. Certainly by the not-superficial test of economic and social support, Americans appear deeply religious, for no people contribute more to the support of their churches, or support them more lavishly: contributions to churches come to more than $3.6 billion a year. By the superficial test of formal and ceremonial recognition, Americans also appear to be religious. "Protect us by Thy might, Great God our King" Americans sing in what is still their favorite national anthem, "America," and "In God we trust" is stamped on every coin. The President takes his oath of office on a Bible, sessions of Congress are opened with prayers, and there is a special Prayer Room in the Capitol. Jurors are customarily sworn on a Bible, school children repeat, sometimes daily, a pledge of allegiance to the flag and to "one nation, under God," and almost all colleges and universities have chaplains and open all their formal ceremonies with prayer. By the somewhat more substantial test of church attendance, too, Americans appear to be a religious people, for almost half of all adults attend church—irregularly—Sundays and holy days.

On the other hand, by the test of spiritual or intellectual contributions, America does not seem devoutly religious. Not since Jonathan Edwards

Farm Security Administration (New York Public Library Collection)

Gospel Bus. Photo by Dorothea Lange. 1938. In early America, the circuit-riding preacher visited frontier settlements on horseback. In the twentieth century his conveyance, though not his message, changed.

(1703-1758) has America produced a religious thinker of major importance, unless it is Reinhold Neibuhr in our own day. The great religious leaders in America have been, for the most part, not theologians or saints but popular preachers: evangelists like Peter Cartwright, reformers like Theodore Parker, popularizers like Henry Ward Beecher, revivalists like Billy Sunday or in our own day, Billy Graham. Puritanism was an intellectually exacting religion and in colonial New England it encouraged critical thought and scholarship, but with the evaporation of Puritanism towards the end of the eighteenth century, American religion lost much of its intellectual toughness and spiritual force.

The two dominant strains in American religion—by no means exclusive but intertwined—are emotionalism and practicality. A people uprooted from their traditional institutions and familiar surroundings (as most Americans were and continue to be) and flung into wholly new environments, physical and social, needed emotional reassurance. Such reassurance Americans found, generation after generation, in religious revivals, and since the "Great Awakening" of the mid-eighteenth century the revival has been a distinct, though not a unique, American institution. In the early days of the Republic religious revivals swept up and down the frontiers. Thousands of men, women, and children would foregather from isolated farms and scattered settlements, and listen, day after day, as revivalist preachers exhorted them to confess their sins, and come to Jesus. These so-called "camp meetings" were not only religious exercises but safety valves for the emotional starvation of life on the isolated frontiers. They also provide, like the fairs of the Middle Ages, opportunities to see old friends and to make new ones, to rejoin society, as it were. The revival did not die out with the frontier, it filled a need for the new industrial urban society as well. It flourished among the Negroes of the South, and among the poor of the great cities: to both it provided a sense of fellowship and solidarity, an emotional outlet, an escape from the burdens and frustrations of life on earth and a promise of everlasting happiness in the life to come.

The practical strain in American religion has been even more prominent, and pervasive.

One of the oldest controversies in the history of religion—certainly of American religion—has been that between the doctrines of salvation by faith and salvation by works. In the United States it can be said that it is the doctrine of salvation by works that has triumphed and American religion, in the nineteenth and twentieth centuries, can almost be defined as the religion of good works. American churches—certainly the Protestant ones—attract communicants and command support principally for their social and community activities rather than for theological or dogmatic reasons. A large church—like the Riverside Church in New York City—combines the functions of a church, a university, and a social service agency as would no church elsewhere. It carries on literally scores of activities, most of them secular. It maintains a library and a nursery school; conducts classes in nonreligious subjects; provides lectures on literature or politics; supports social service activities among the poor, among nearby university students, and overseas; caters to the young with games and outings; and is a force in civic and community affairs.

All this is a natural product of American history and of American experience. In the old world the church traditionally concerned itself with the poor and with education, but beyond this it did not customarily go. Some government official, some lord or lady of the manor, some guild of craftsmen or of merchants, would be the center of social life in village or city. The new world had none of these, nor did the rich, when they emerged in the early nineteenth century, take on themselves the social duties of the old world aristocracy—though they did perform many of its civic functions. The church was the one institution—often the only one— that embraced all members of the community, women and children as well as men, immigrants as well as native born, blacks as well as whites. It was, in the social arena, the agency that Americans used to do the things that no other agency was prepared to do.

But did not denominationalism counterbalance, and even counteract, the social service function of the American church?

Denominationalism was, and still is, the most ostentatious, though by no means the most important, feature of religion in America. Altogether the Census Bureau lists some three hundred religious denominations; of these perhaps one hundred are sufficiently large to demonstrate that they have both individuality and drawing power. Of Protestant denominations the traditional and orthodox are the largest: there are, in all, some sixteen million Baptists, fourteen million Methodists, nine million Lutherans, four and a half million Presbyterians, and three and a half million Episcopalians. Some of the smaller denominations, like the Friends (Quakers), Unitarians, and Jehovah's Witnesses, play a larger role in American intellectual and social history than might be expected from their numbers. Two relatively new denominations, the Latter Day Saints (Mormons) and Christian Science, number respectively two million and one million adherents and are growing rapidly. The Eastern Orthodox Church, too, is fragmented into a score of independent churches, the largest of which is the Greek Orthodox; and Jewish synagogues are divided into Reformed, Conservative and Orthodox. Only the Roman Catholic Church preserves its unity unbroken.

But this pattern of denominationalism in American religion is somewhat deceptive. Just as an impressionist painting, made up of hundreds of daubs of paint, achieves unity and harmony, so the many American religious denominations manage somehow to combine into a fairly harmonious pattern. Certainly anyone who, contemplating the statistics of American churches, concluded that American society was really fragmented by religious differences would be deeply mistaken. The first thing

Spanish colonial influence is evident in this eighteenth-century church in
Trampas, New Mexico.

to note is that many denominational divisions are quite misleading, for they represent not religious but linguistic and geographical differences. After all, most immigrants brought with them their churches, preachers, Bibles, and hymnbooks and tried to reproduce all of these in the new world. Thus the twenty or so Lutheran Churches in America represent Danes, Swedes, Norwegians, Finns, Germans, and others rather than religious groups. Denominations were regional too: witness the Missouri Synod of the Lutheran Church, the Cumberland Presbytery, and the Oregon Meeting of the Friends. Indeed, the largest single Protestant denomination in America is still the *Southern* Baptist Convention.

More important in mitigating the ravages of denominationalism are two other considerations. First, because the American religion is good works, rather than dogma, Americans generally are not much interested in dogmatic differences. In fact the average American—certainly the average Protestant—neither knows nor cares very much about the theological tenets that distinguish his particular denomination from its competitors. Second, religious and denominational differences have not, certainly among white Americans, reflected social or political differences. As there is no "Church" in America, so there is no "chapel." From time to time in the past, to be sure, religion reflected or proclaimed social position: thus the planter class of the Old South was predominantly Episcopalian, the Boston aristocracy of the nineteenth century largely Congregational or Unitarian, and the first families of Philadelphia Quaker. But these affiliations gradually disappeared, and today it is quite impossible to detect religious or denominational affiliations by speech, accent, education, or wealth. It should be added, however, that ancestry is a pretty fair index to religious loyalty: the Irish, Italians, and Poles have remained Roman Catholics, Scandinavians still tend to be Lutherans, and Scots to stay in the Presbyterian fold.

The most interesting feature of religion in America is the sharp separation of church from state. Even today most countries in the old world, Latin America, and the Middle East maintain an "established" church which is more or less official and which enjoys support from the government. In England it is the Church of England, in Scandinavia the Lutheran Church, in France, Spain, Italy and the states of Latin America the Catholic Church, in Israel the Jewish religion, in the Arab states the Muslim that is thus established. But in the United States no church is "established," either in the states or in the nation and no church receives

Gershom Mendes Seixas, religious leader who rallied the New York
Jewish community to support the American Revolution. He was one of the
clergymen who officiated at George Washington's inauguration and was one of the
first trustees of Columbia University, which had been King's College before the war.

support from public funds. All churches are independent and all are
supported voluntarily by their members.

History accounts for this remarkable situation.

The Spanish and French colonies in the new world were founded by
governments and were, therefore, extensions of the mother countries. Not
only did Spain and France extend the Catholic religion to their American
colonies and thus "establish" that church in America, they excluded all

Above, **Preacher.** Charles White. 1952. Below, **Baptism in Kansas.** John Steuart Curry. 1928. Rural America found social opportunities in religious occasions.

other churches and religions. Just as there was no room for "heretics" in Spain, Portugal, or France in the seventeenth and eighteenth centuries, so there was no room for them in their colonies. But the English colonies in America were not the creations of government, but were planted by private enterprise—by joint stock companies (which we could call simply corporations) like the Virginia Company; by religious groups like the Pilgrims and the Puritans; and by great proprietors like William Penn and Lord Baltimore. The Anglican Church was, to be sure, established in the southern colonies, though even there dissenters were allowed to have their own churches. Elsewhere there was a miscellany of churches and religions: Puritans and Separatists in New England, Quakers in Pennsylvania, Catholics in Maryland, and Presbyterians almost everywhere. Long before the Revolution there was complete religious freedom in Pennsylvania and Rhode Island, and in the other colonies a far larger degree of toleration than was to be found elsewhere in the western world.

Religious freedom and equality and the separation of church and state were leading objects of the American Revolution. Everywhere the Anglican Church was overthrown and—following the example of Virginia —many states provided in their new constitutions for the separation of church and state. What this meant in practice was that no church could receive state support or impose its religious principles on its members by law, that no one denomination of the Christian church would be favored over others, and that there would be complete toleration of all beliefs and unbeliefs. The further implications of the separation of church and state were left to the future to work out.

The principle thus embraced by the states was shortly incorporated into the federal Constitution. Originally the Constitution simply said nothing about religion whatsoever, and as it was a document of "enumerated powers" this meant, quite clearly, that the new government had no power over matters of religion. But even that negative assurance was not enough for the American people, and the very first article of the new Bill of Rights added to the Constitution in 1791 provided, in sweeping terms, that "Congress shall make no law respecting an establishment of religion, or prohibiting the free exercise thereof."

This was, to be sure, a limitation on the Congress rather than on the states, and, theoretically, the states could have preferred and supported one church over any other. But the pressure of opinion was all the other way. Early in the nineteenth century the New England states got rid of the last remnants of any connection between the state and the Congregational Church, and all the new states that came into the Union after 1790 kept church and state wholly separate. The provision of the Fourteenth Amendment to the Constitution (1868) that no state shall "deprive any person, of . . . liberty . . . without due process of law" has been interpreted in our own time to mean that states may not interfere in any way with the liberty to worship, or not to worship, as one pleases.

Freedom of religion and separation of church and state are not, however, entirely products of either constitutional or religious principle. They are in part the products of circumstances, even of necessity. In a country whose population numbered millions of Protestants, Catholics, and Jews, and where Protestants were fragmented into scores of competing denominations and Catholics and Jews into major competing groups, not only toleration but equality was necessary. To have discriminated against one religion in favor of another, to have given one church privileges denied another, would have produced perpetual turmoil and even religious wars.

Americans take their immunity from religious antagonisms and wars pretty much for granted, but should not. In the old world, after all, religion has for centuries whipped up tempestuous storms in politics and society—thus the religious wars of the seventeenth century; thus in the nineteenth century the struggle over Catholic emancipation in England, the *Kulturkampf* in Germany, the pogroms against Jews in Poland and Russia, the turbulence of the Dreyfus case in France; thus in our own time the extermination of the Jews by the Nazis, and the religious wars that tore India asunder when she achieved her independence. By contrast, religion has rarely ruffled the waters of American politics. There have, to be sure, been sporadic outbreaks of religious prejudice. Back in the 1840s Mormons were persecuted and driven out of Illinois and Missouri, but more on account of their practice of polygamy (now long since abandoned) than on religious grounds. Hostility to Catholicism flared up in the Know-Nothing movement of the 1850s, and again in the activities of the so-called American Protective Association in the 1890s and of the notorious Ku Klux Klan in the 1920s. But anti-Catholicism was never strong enough to find expression in legislation, and as Catholics increased in numbers, and came to play an ever increasing role in politics and society, early prejudices died out. It is true that John F. Kennedy was the first Catholic ever to become President, but too much can be made of this; after all Warren G. Harding, in 1921 was the first Baptist ever to be made President, and the Baptists had long been the largest Protestant denomination. Anti-Semitism emerged in the 1890s with the large-scale immigration of Polish and Russian Jews, but there was never a time that Jews did not enjoy all the rights of other citizens of the United States, and during the present century they have been fully absorbed into the fabric of American life. Now and then there are manifestations of anti-Semitism—curiously enough chiefly among belligerent blacks, today—but these have no discernible effect on either politics or society. In a broad way it is fair to say that though American society acknowledges a heavy burden of guilt for racial prejudice and intolerance over the years, it has been, and is, largely innocent of religious prejudice and intolerance.

Religion plays no active part in American politics, nor are religious issues generally permitted to enter the political arena. But political parties usually try to appeal to the support of major religious groups by balancing

Addison Gallery of American Art, Phillips Academy, Andover, Massachusetts
Portrait of Rev. Nathaniel Taylor. Ralph Earl.

their "ticket" with Protestant, Catholic, and, in a city like New York, Jewish candidates. Earlier in American history it was possible even for avowed freethinkers to get elected to office—though Tom Paine suffered from his reputation as an "infidel"—but no political party today would take the risk of nominating an avowed atheist for elective office, and most candidates are ostentatiously respectful of church and religion. In this, as in some other respects, the American people are probably more orthodox than they were in the eighteenth century.

The effective elimination of religion from American politics has had one unexpected advantage that can be appreciated only against the background of centuries of European history. In the old world liberalism almost everywhere had to fight the church—if on no other issue than that of freedom of religion, of speech, and of press. Thus anti-clericalism came in time to be the hallmark of liberalism. Voltaire, the very symbol of liberal thought in the eighteenth century, crusaded all his life against the obscurantism of the church in France, and his battle cry was *Ecrasez l'infâme!* while Edmund Burke, the very symbol of conservatism in the same century, based his conservative philosophy squarely on the preservation of religion and of the church. This alliance of liberalism or radicalism with anti-clericalism and of conservatism or reaction with the church persisted into the nineteenth century even in countries like Britain and Germany, and can be found today in Italy, and in many of the countries of Latin America. Nothing of this kind happened, or could happen, in the United States. Here, from the beginning, it was possible to be orthodox and devout and still be politically radical: witness Franklin D. Roosevelt and John F. Kennedy. It was equally easy to be heterodox in religion— or indifferent to religion—and be politically conservative: witness the careers of avowed agnostics like Robert Ingersoll, or of a Unitarian like President William Howard Taft. Liberalism was not burdened with the supposed necessity of attacking some religious establishment; conservatism was not paralyzed by the supposed necessity of defending some religious orthodoxy. All this has given a freedom of maneuver and of choice to liberalism and conservatism in the United States that cannot be found in equal measure anywhere else.

There is one aspect of the problem of religion—or of the Church— that has long agitated American politics and constitutional law. That is the precise nature of the "separation" of church and state. Separation in its more obvious sense is taken for granted: no established church.

But just what is meant by "established," and how nearly absolute is the separation between church and state?

Earlier generations were not greatly worried by this problem. They took for granted that there was to be no state church, but they took for granted too that the United States was a Christian nation, and that it was quite all right to permit special favors to the churches and to give official approval to the moral principles associated with Christianity. This permissive attitude obtains to the present day. Thus, though there is no direct support to churches, every state and local government provides indirect support through the exemption of church property from taxation. This is, to be sure, justified not primarily on religious grounds, but on the same broad principles of social expediency that justify tax exemption to private colleges and universities, and to philanthropic foundations. Yet it cannot be doubted that tax exemption is a form of aid to religion. Again, indirectly rather than directly, legislation has reflected religious views and principles. Thus temperance legislation, and legislation regulating sexual morals, reflected and indeed responded to the views of churches. So too with strict divorce laws, laws dealing with birth control, and censorship laws: these are often a response to church pressures of one kind or another.

Indirect aid to religion has raised a number of difficult constitutional questions. If government may not support religion, may it support—or aid—parochial schools? The British and Canadians see nothing wrong with such state support to church schools, but American law has heretofore not authorized such support, certainly not in any overt form. What of a less overt form, such as free textbooks for children in parochial as in public schools, or the extension of the free lunch program and school-bus transportation to children in church schools? Or, in another area, may public schools provide religious instruction of any kind? May they even permit public prayers or any other form of religious exercise or observance? What of the requirement of a religious oath for jury duty, of a loyalty oath for school children whose religion does not permit taking oaths? What, for that matter, of legal limitations on polygamy or faith healing when these are practiced as an expression of religious dogma? What right do parents have to forbid the vaccination of their children on religious grounds?

There are no easy answers to these and similar questions. Courts—for sooner or later all these questions get into the courts—have worked out governing principles case by case, trying to hold an even balance between the interest of society in advancing the education of the young, or preserving public health and morals, and the interest of individuals and churches in enjoying the greatest possible extent of freedom. On the whole the courts seem to prefer to take a chance even on the vagaries of religious freedom, rather than encourage the state to expand its control in the realms of faith and morals.

81

recommended reading

*Beasley, Norman. *The Cross and the Crown*. New York: Duell, Sloan & Pearce, 1952.

*Brodie, Fawn M. *No Man Knows My History*. New York: Alfred A. Knopf, 1945.

*Burton, Richard F. *City of the Saints*. Edited by Fawn M. Brodie. New York: Alfred A. Knopf, 1963.

*Clebsch, William A. *From Sacred to Profane America: The Role of Religion in America*. New York: Harper & Row (Harper Religious Books), 1968.

Commager, Henry S. *Theodore Parker: Yankee Crusader*. Boston: Beacon Press, 1960.

Edwards, Jonathan. *Jonathan Edwards: Basic Writings*. Edited by Ola Winslow. New York: New American Library (Signet Books).

*Garrison, Winfred E. *The March of Faith: The Story of Religion in America Since 1865*. New York: Harper & Brothers, 1933. OP

*Gladden, Washington. *Recollections*. Boston: Houghton Mifflin Company, 1909. OP

Howe, Mark D. *The Garden and the Wilderness: Religion and Government in American Constitutional History*. Chicago: University of Chicago Press (Phoenix Books), 1965.

James, William. *The Varieties of Religious Experience*. Introduction by Reinhold Niebuhr. New York: Macmillan Company (Collier Books), 1961.

Lewis, Sinclair. *Elmer Gantry*. New York: New American Library (Signet Books).

Maritain, Jacques. *Reflections on America*. New York: Doubleday & Company (Image Books).

*Maynard, Theodore. *Story of American Catholicism*. New York: Macmillan Company, 1941. OP

*Miller, Perry. *The Life of the Mind in America: From the Revolution to the Civil War*. New York: Harcourt, Brace & World, 1965.

————. *Roger Williams: His Contribution to the American Tradition*. New York: Atheneum Publishers, 1962.

Morgan, Edmund. *Roger Williams: The Church and the State*. New York: Harcourt, Brace & World (Harvest Books), 1968.

*Pfeffer, Leo. *Church, State, and Freedom*. Revised edition. Boston: Beacon Press, 1967.

*Reimers, David M. *White Protestantism and the Negro*. New York: Oxford University Press, 1965.

Santayana, George. *Character and Opinion in the United States*. New York: W. W. Norton & Company, 1967.

Schneider, Herbert W. *Religion in 20th-Century America*. Revised edition. New York: Atheneum Publishers, 1964.

*Stokes, Anson P., and Pfeffer, Leo. *Church and State in the United States*. New York: Harper & Row, 1964.

*Sweet, William W. *The Story of Religion in America*. Revised edition. New York: Harper & Row, 1950.

White, Morton. *Social Thought in America*. Boston: Beacon Press, 1957.

Wilder, Thornton. *Heaven's My Destination*. New York: Popular Library.

° Hard-cover edition. Titles not so marked are paperback editions.

OP indicates that the edition is out of print.

6. equality—and inequality—in America

In the very heart of American social history nestles a paradox. A fundamental and pervasive characteristic of American society has been, from the beginning, equality. But at the same time the fundamental and pervasive problem of American society is, and has been for over a century, inequality. It is not possible to reconcile these two social traits, but it is possible to trace each of them to its origins to explain it, and to follow out its implications and consequences.

The very first of the truths which the Declaration of Independence asserts is "self-evident," is that "all men are created equal." What did Thomas Jefferson mean by this phrase, which was to become immortal? He meant, no doubt, a great many things, things which were in fact so self-evident that he did not feel under any compulsion to explain them. He meant that men were equal in the sight of God and equal in a state of nature. Himself a slave owner, he could not be blind to the inequalities in his own society. But these were imposed not by nature, but by man-made laws.

As far as Negroes were concerned, equality was a philosophical myth: they may have been equal in a state of nature, or in a future world, but they were not equal in fact, or in this world. As far as white people were concerned, however, equality was not at all a myth but a reality—a social, legal, political reality. Equality was, indeed, the most striking feature of white American society, the social condition that distinguished it most sharply from European and even more from other societies.

Everywhere in the old world society was divided into classes which were distinct not only socially and economically, but legally. There was, at the top, an hereditary nobility; there was, in the middle, a bourgeoisie; there was a yeoman or independent farmer class and a large peasant class; and there was, in the more advanced industrial countries, a proletariat or working class. In most countries these broad classes were divided into subclasses, each with its legal rights, privileges, and, sometimes, duties. Take, for example, the Hungarian aristocracy, which happened to be the most numerous in eighteenth-century Europe. They had the right to all offices in state and church; they had the privilege of exemption from taxation; they had the duty to fight. They insisted on their rights, enjoyed their privileges, but failed to fulfill their duties. One generalization applied to almost every other nation in the world: that the vast majority of mankind belonged to the peasant, or labor, or servant class and enjoyed no privileges whatever. Now and then a boy of great talent could rise out of his class—usually via the church, but sometimes through learning or music or art—but almost all people were condemned to live and to die in the class in which they were born. They could not hope to shift from serf to landowner, from servant to master, from private to colonel, from workingman to merchant prince. They could not expect to marry out of their class. They were denied any part in politics or, with rare exceptions, in public life. They were not expected to learn how to read or write—except here and there, in Scotland or Holland or in some German states—or to enter the professions. They did not even enjoy equality before the law.

This class system, a burden everywhere, was less burdensome and more flexible in England than on the continent. By great good fortune, the English colonies in America were planted by members of the middle and lower classes from the mother country. No members of the nobility emigrated to America—after all, why should they?—no great landowners, no rich merchants. Those who came over were farmers, craftsmen, apprentices, indentured servants, debtors and refugees from prisons, deserters from the army and the merchant marine, and along with these a sprinkling of clergymen and scholars and some younger sons of the aristocracy who hoped to carve out a fortune for themselves in America. These original settlers were followed by a stream of crofters from Scotland and Ireland, peasants from Germany, a scattering of Huguenots from France (most of these from the middle classes), deserters from the Hessian and Brunswick regiments that fought under the British flag during the Revolution and quietly slipped away to join their fellow Germans in Pennsylvania or Virginia. Clearly it was impossible to transplant a class system to a new world society of this nature, and none was provided for, either by law or by custom. Nor were the circumstances of life in the new world propitious for the creation of a new class system. Quite the contrary. "There was no worse market," as Benjamin Franklin observed, to which to bring birth, title, or social distinction for "in America people do not inquire of a Stranger, 'What is he?,' but 'What can he do?'" In America everybody could start fresh. It was, from the beginning, what it remained for over two centuries in the European imagination, the land of second chance.

Where it was easy for anyone to move from country to town, from colony to colony, and later from state to state, and almost as easy to move from job to job; where labor was everywhere in demand and could pretty much set its own terms; where there were no legal barriers to the intermarriage of young men and women of different faiths, different languages, different backgrounds; where some frontier was always open and new settlements welcomed all comers on equal terms without asking awkward questions about social credentials; where some kind of schooling

Tombstones. Jacob Lawrence. 1942. Although economic opportunity has always been one of the primary attractions of the United States, the general affluence does not reach into every corner of American life.

was available to all children and illiteracy was almost unknown; where every white man could participate in town and county affairs, serve in the militia, and vote; where land and work were easy to come by, and almost everyone had enough but few too much: where such conditions obtained equality was simply the common sense of the matter.

Dual Hamburgers. Claes Oldenburg. 1962. The pop artist's irony applied to what is a staple of American cuisine from Maine to California.

Thus geography, economy, the social order, religion, voluntary associations, education, politics, law, all dictated equality among whites. There were, of course, social distinctions—distinctions between old families and new, between native born and immigrants, between the highly educated, the partly educated, and the uneducated, between the rich and the poor. These differences, more ostentatious than deep, have persuaded some sociologists to assert that there are indeed "classes" in the United States and even to distinguish, by various tests of background, schools, jobs, residence, and income, different categories of upper, middle, and lower classes. But this is a superficial view. Questioned as to their class status, most Europeans readily identify themselves as upper, middle, or working class, but when Americans are similarly questioned over 90 per cent of whites identify themselves as middle class and only 1 or 2 per cent have the temerity to admit that they are upper class. And it is relevant that Americans lack even the vocabulary of class. Like all societies, the American has the rich, has businessmen, workers, farmers, clergymen, and academics. But it has no aristocracy, no bourgeoisie, no proletariat, no peasantry, it does not even have an ecclesiastical class or an intelligentsia; it just has people.

In the old world class is legal and hereditary; in the United States it is neither. In the old world, too, it is quite impersonal: you are what you are, and that is the end of it. In America it is almost wholly personal; each individual carves out his own social position, as he carves out his own economic position, nor is the job ever finished once and for all—as the individual can move upward on the social scale, so he can move downward. Here neither wealth, family, nor formal position provides any guarantee—though collectively they do provide indications—of social standing. In Europe and Asia a government official, an officer, a professor has a kind of automatic right to deference and prestige, and he is deemed worthy of distinction until proved otherwise. But woe betide the American who operates on that principle. He cannot command respect or honor merely by virtue of his title and if he is wise he will not use his title; it is well to remember that the title of the President of the United States is "Mr. President," and that all Harvard professors are called "Mister." A judge may be "Your Honor" and a clergyman "Reverend," but the judge will not receive honor nor the clergyman reverence unless he merits it. Money can, of course, buy special favors—the best seats in a restaurant, the best service in a hotel, publicity in the press—but it cannot buy deference. In other lands, too, class commonly has visible stigmata: dress, manners, speech, accent, school and church affiliation. These indices are of little or no importance in the United States, and anyone who tried to apply them would go badly astray. It is characteristic that Americans— almost all of them—drive the same cars. The car is a very good index of social standards. In Britain, and in Europe generally, the difference between cheap, or workingmen's, cars and expensive or upper-class cars is visibly impressive. No one could possibly mistake a Volkswagen for a Mercedes, a Morris Minor for a Rolls-Royce. But in the United States the differences between cars are almost invisible; all cars are about the same size, all cars look alike, and all cars appeal equally to all classes. The United States does not produce a Rolls-Royce or a Lagonda for its rich, a Volkswagen or a Fiat for its working class; these—with all that they proclaim about wealth and class—are imported.

The habit of equality, more a habit than a principle even, carries over into almost every relationship in life. It means that distinctions are blurred, even individuality is blurred. The Constitution itself forbids titles of nobility, and no others are used, or if they are it is in a semihumorous fashion: thus southern governors create honorary "colonels"; thus almost every clergyman is called "Doctor," and so, too, in the South, almost every druggist or apothecary. In addressing each other, Americans now commonly use first names. Thomas Jefferson and James Madison knew each other intimately for fifty years, yet in their voluminous correspondence it was always "Mr. Jefferson" and "Mr. Madison." Today you may well be encouraged by a total stranger to "Call me Bill." Outside a few great cities where the standards of public school education are low, everybody, rich and poor alike, goes to public (that is, state) schools, and there is no social and, for that matter, no academic difference between public and private colleges and universities. Nor is there any generally accepted social hierarchy of religion, or if there is, it is local, and varies sharply from town to town.

In one respect this pervasive acquiescence in the forms and habits of equality is deceptive, for if it can be said that all Americans are equal, it can be said too that some are more equal than others. The American is, probably, the most competitive society on the globe. Cultural anthropologists assure us that in America children compete for parental love and parents for their children's approval, and we do not need the anthropologists to remind us of the ardent competition for "dates" that begins in the secondary school and ravages every adolescent community. And where else do colleges and universities compete so fiercely in athletics, where else does business engage in such cut-throat competition, where else does competitive advertising so dominate the economic scene?

This competitiveness, too, is rooted in history, and indeed in equalitarianism itself. In the old world—certainly in the eighteenth and much of the nineteenth centuries—there was no point in being competitive: no matter what you did you were not, in fact, going to get out of your class or marry the boss's daughter: you were going to go on in your father's and your grandfather's footsteps. But in the New World everything was, from the beginning, wide open: the sky, as Americans said, was the limit. Here, with industry, talent, and a little bit of luck, everything might be achieved. Here it was, in very fact, possible to go from rags to riches, from log cabin to White House. Where everything could be accomplished by zeal, there was a tremendous premium on zeal. Every child learned, from his school days, that by hard work he might excel all others. And where there were so few formal recognitions of merit—no titles, no robes, no academies—merit came quite simply to be associated with success, and the index of success was inevitably statistical: to win the most games, to have the most dates, to make the most money. That some ended up as world champions (it was always "world," for Americans were not content with being mere national champions), as chairmen of boards, as millionaires, was not at all a violation of the principle of equality, but rather evidence of its wonder-working.

One of the consequences of equality is conformity.

The process of leveling up and down (and it was mostly up) affected not only such things as speech, dress, conduct, and manners, but ideas as well. Just as Americans tend to be suspicious of eccentricity in speech, dress, or conduct, so they tend to be suspicious of eccentricity in ideas. All Americans are expected to enjoy the same television, the same popular music, the same cartoons or—as they are called—"comic strips," just as they are expected to belong to the same churches, political parties, and fraternal orders. Ordinarily something like 98 per cent of all votes go to the Democratic and Republican parties, and less than 2 per cent to the splinter parties; almost all Americans belong to the major orthodox churches, while "independent" churches like the Unitarian or the Quaker count less than two hundred thousand members. Almost all Americans read the same middle-class magazines like *Look* or *Life* or *Reader's Digest* or *Sports Illustrated;* no airline hostess, no doctor's waiting room, would think of offering high-brow magazines like the *New Republic* or the *New York Review of Books.* Almost everybody watches—and talks about —professional football and baseball, and there is no class division, as in England, between different kinds of games or sports.

This is not, in itself, of great importance, but its implications in the realm of social and political thought are significant. Pressure for intellectual conformity—for the uncritical acceptance of such notions as the odiousness of socialism and the superiority of private enterprise, the superiority of private over public control of television and radio, the superiority of the American form of government over all others and of the "American way of life" over any other way, the advantages of fraternal organizations, the uncritical acceptance of advertising, the notion that progress is material and can in fact be translated into road building or new inventions—is strong everywhere and in some sections of the country irresistible. This pressure is not necessarily overt, and it is rarely legal; it is rather a voluntary response to the weight of public opinion. In a class society individuals can always fall back on the consciousness of their own superiority, or on the support of members of their own class who share their views and habits, but in an equalitarian society the non-conformist has no such support. He is judged by the common standards—standards which he himself was brought up to respect and approve. The American is therefore uncomfortable and vulnerable when he departs from the social or intellectual norm.

The principle and habit of equality inspired and encouraged the principle and habit of standardization, which is equally characteristic of American life. Standardization as a technological principle is indeed something of an American invention, for it was the Connecticut Yankee, Eli Whitney (inventor of the cotton gin) who first originated it by manufacturing rifles with interchangeable parts, just as it was Henry Ford who revolutionized the automobile industry by mass producing cars on an assembly line. Technology and standardization has made for uniformity almost everywhere—not in the United States alone. Where all the common material things are made to a pattern—houses, furniture, china, clothes, even decorations—people themselves tend to look alike and to act alike. Older societies, with deep-rooted and built-in character, where individuality persists (the Italian, for example, where each city has its own architecture, food, and wine) can resist the pressure for standardization with some success. But the United States has never had communities with deeply rooted traditions and indelible character (though Boston, Salem, Charleston, have always had some of this) and Americans have lacked, too, any desire to resist standardization. Quite the contrary. An equalitarian society where everybody *seemed* to live alike, was more comfortable even if they in fact did not—for standardization, in appearance or in reality, vindicated equality. The American landscape has infinite variety, but over a stretch of three thousand miles the towns and cities of America look more like each other than do the towns and cities of little Switzerland or Denmark. Americans have the best and most abundant meats, fish, fruits and vegetables in the world, yet the result is not a series of distinctive cuisines but a cuisine of monotonous similarity: packaged in the same way, processed in the same way, and sold in the same supermarkets or dished up in the same chain restaurants. France has two hundred wines and three hundred cheeses, while Americans have perhaps a dozen of each, and these hard to obtain. Almost all Americans watch the same television programs, and producers worry themselves into an early grave if some opinion poll shows that the "rating" of a show has gone from forty-five to forty-four million viewers.

Many other countries are on the escalator to standardization: supermarkets, glass skyscrapers, washing machines, and laundromats, a television in every home and a copy of *Reader's Digest,* in the appropriate language, on every table. But many, too, have a long tradition of resistance to centralization and standardization. It is interesting that though Germany was almost totally destroyed in the Second World War and has been almost wholly rebuilt with glass skyscrapers and supermarkets and four lane highways, Bavaria, Baden, the Rhineland, Mecklenburg, and other sections of Germany have retained their ancient individualism, and so have such cities as Munich, Hamburg, Frankfurt, and Stuttgart. But there is little to resist standardization in the United States.

Still it is easy to exaggerate the significance of standardization in America. Doubtless you find it everywhere, but you find everywhere, too, individuality and experimentation. If television and radio networks seem to provide but a single program, there are still thousands of small independent stations providing a far wider choice of program than can be found in any other country. If the plays on Broadway all seem headed for Hollywood, the off-Broadway theatre is as lively and as experimental as any on the globe. If all Americans seem to read the same magazines, the United States supports more "little" magazines, more experimental presses, and more independent newspapers than does any other country. Public food may taste the same everywhere, but domestic cooking is both varied and imaginative, and more cookbooks are sold, read, and followed in the United States than elsewhere: indeed the cookbook industry is by now one of the major branches of American publishing! It is true that American cars do look alike, but it is true too that Americans buy more foreign cars than do any other people. American colleges and universities all seem to conform to the same educational pattern, but an American student has an incomparably wider choice of subjects to study than any student elsewhere, and if the classification systems of American libraries are all pretty much the same—either Library of Congress or Dewey Decimal—the selection of books is far richer and the services far more varied than in any foreign academic community.

The United States is, in fact, so big and so complex that there is nonconformity to match every conformity—indeed there is some danger that nonconformity itself will yield to a conformist pattern. There is no conclusive evidence that the workings of democracy and of technology will inevitably produce the kind of society imagined by George Orwell in *1984* or Aldous Huxley in *Brave New World,* and it is not without interest that neither of these two prophecies of social doom is in fact American. Just as the United States produced in the same generation, a Mark Twain

The Battle of Gettysburg. Engraving by Sartain. One of the key battles in the Civil War, which ended slavery in the Southern states. A century later, however, Negroes still suffer *de facto* discrimination, although the law guarantees them equal rights with whites.

92

and Henry James, a Carl Sandburg and Elinor Wylie, the skyscraper and the horizontal houses of Frank Lloyd Wright, the educational ideas of John Dewey and Robert Hutchins, the political styles of Adlai Stevenson and Dwight Eisenhower, so she still has resources for experimentation and variety within the larger framework of uniformity and standardization.

Hovering over the bright landscape of equality is the shadow of inequality, and it has darkened American society for over a hundred years. When Jefferson lived, the doctrine of equality was not supposed to embrace Negroes: they were slaves and, in the melancholy words of Chief Justice Taney in the Dred Scott case (1857), had no rights "which the white man was bound to respect." Chiefly for economic reasons, slavery disappeared quickly in the North, though not the habit of regarding blacks as somehow inferior to whites—and it was formally prohibited in all the territory west of the Appalachians and north of the Ohio River. In the South, however, thanks chiefly to the spread of the Cotton Kingdom, slavery grew stronger year by year, and by the mid-nineteenth century it dominated the society, economy, politics, and culture of the South. With every passing year southern whites, even the great majority, who did not own slaves, became more deeply committed to the principle of white supremacy and the corollary of black inferiority—a principle they tried to buttress by an appeal to history, social philosophy, anthropology, and religion.

Yet through it all, millions of Americans knew that slavery and freedom could not flourish side by side, that, in the words of Abraham Lincoln, "a house divided cannot stand." They knew perfectly well that slavery repudiated the principle of the Declaration of Independence, that it made a mockery of the boast, in the national anthem, that America was "the land of the free." And all through the first half of the century agitation against slavery deepened and spread.

But slavery could not be ended by agitation: it was too deeply entrenched for that, too much part of the economic and social fabric. Criticism and attack merely encouraged the South to close ranks to protect her "peculiar institution," and this is what she did. And when the election of 1860 went against the South, and appeared to doom slavery, southern states chose to break up the Union and set up as an independent nation rather than expose slavery to erosion. The war that ensued was a war to preserve the Union but it became, in the process, a war to end slavery as well. Lincoln proclaimed the emancipation of

World Wide Photos

Dr. Martin Luther King, Jr., center, leads the 1963 March on Washington, in which
hundreds of thousands of black and white Americans joined in demanding
equal rights for blacks.

slaves as a war measure; the Thirteenth Amendment to the Constitution, ratified in 1865, legally abolished slavery for four million Negroes. A few years later came two other Amendments to the Constitution—the Fourteenth and Fifteenth—which were designed respectively to assure the Negro protection against any and all discrimination on account of race, and the right to vote.

Alas, these amendments were neither observed nor enforced. The Negro was no longer a slave, but he was not wholly free and certainly he was not yet equal. The myth of white supremacy persisted, and Southerners closed ranks against making any concessions on jobs, schools, or politics that might threaten the myth with reality. The Negro was legally a citizen but he was almost everywhere a second-class citizen— treated as a social inferior; condemned to work in the cotton fields or to menial jobs, and to live in slums, urban or rural; fobbed off with wretched schools; denied political rights or power; denied even that equal protection of the laws solemnly guaranteed to him by the Constitution.

Over the years a growing body of public opinion, not in the North alone, demanded an end to this long chapter of exploitation, violence, and injustice, but in vain, for prejudice was deep and inertia stubborn. It was not until the Franklin Roosevelt administration of the thirties that the national government was able to make the first dent in this façade of discrimination. But it was the Second World War, rather than legisla- tion, that began the process of undermining racial discrimination and injustice that is still going on. President Roosevelt tried to put an end to discrimination in the armed forces, and Negroes and whites served in the same battalions and companies, or on the same ships, sometimes (though not often) commanded by Negro officers. A Fair Employment Act outlawed racial discrimination in government jobs and in industries that were bound by government contracts, and soon many States passed similar legislation.

More important by far was the dramatic change in the position of the Negroes themselves and the role they now assumed in the struggle for racial equality. The hundreds of thousands of Negroes who had fought in the armed services in all parts of the globe were not prepared to return to civilian life as inferiors. Not only had they experienced the equality of the uniform—they had seen and experienced the equality that was taken pretty much for granted in Britain, France, Italy, and occupied Germany, and in the islands of the Pacific. Second, there was a massive shift of Negro population from cotton and tobacco fields to the city and factory and from the South to the North and the West as well. By the end of the 1960s over half of all the black population lived outside the South, and over two-thirds lived in cities, while from one- to two-thirds of the population of great cities like Washington, Baltimore, Philadelphia, Detroit, and Newark was Negro. Third, the war, and the shift to the North, meant that the Negro now had far greater political leverage than he had ever had in the past, for now he held the balance of political power between Democratic and Republican parties in most northern cities and in all the great industrial states. Both parties therefore catered to the Negro vote by attractive legislative programs and by nominating Negro candidates to elective office. Finally, prosperity and improved education now provided the Negro with his own leadership—leadership not alone in politics, but in many areas of American life.

The campaign for equality is waged on five fronts: the political, looking to equal rights in voting and officeholding everywhere in the Union; the educational, looking to the end of segregation in schools and colleges and equal access to learning; the economic, looking to equality in jobs, pay, and union membership; the legal, looking to an end to discrimination in jury duty, in the enforcement of law and of penalties and punishments for crimes, in marriage and family relations, in access to professions, and in other areas where the law has allowed inequalities to creep in; and the social, looking to "open" housing—that is, to an end to segregated neighborhoods and streets, and equal access to all scenes of social activity such as theatres, swimming pools, railway cars, restaurants, and so forth.

In all these areas the Negro—that is to say, the whole country—made significant progress during the fifties and sixties. Congress at last put teeth into the enforcement of the Fifteenth Amendment, designed to assure the Negro the right to vote, and during the sixties the traditional barriers to Negro voting collapsed, even in the South. In the election of 1968 more than five million Negroes were registered to vote in the eleven Southern states, and most of them apparently did. For the first time since Reconstruction, a Negro sat in the United States Senate—Senator Brooke of Massachusetts—and for the first time in the whole of American history a Negro sat on the Supreme Court—Thurgood Marshall. The great Negro leader W. E. B. DuBois had been right, after all, when he had argued, back at the beginning of the century, that the Negro would have to win political rights before he could win any other, because only political power would give him any real leverage for reform in other areas.

The first great leader of the free Negroes, Booker T. Washington, had been above all an educator; like Thomas Jefferson a century earlier, he was persuaded that all progress ultimately depended on education. But given the climate of opinion in the South in his day—roughly the fifty years after Reconstruction—there was little he could do to improve the educational level of the Negro. The trouble was in part the general poverty of the South, but deeper than that, it was the indifference of the South to Negro education, an indifference amounting at times to downright hostility. Everywhere after the 1880s, Negroes were forced to go to "segregated," or all-Negro schools, and while in theory these were "separate but equal," in fact they were separate and shockingly unequal, inferior in facilities and teaching. Few Negro children learned more than the most elementary reading and writing, and only a tiny minority of them went on from grade school to high school, let alone college. The South spent less on education than any other section of the country, but it spent four or five times as much on each white child as on each black child. Nor were conditions much better in the North. There, to be sure, legal segregation very quickly disappeared in most communities, but something very like segregation persisted because Negroes had no choice but to live in their own quarters of town and to have their own schools. Even in the North, few Negroes remained in school beyond the age of fourteen or sixteen years, the legal requirement of schooling, and many of those who started in high school dropped out within a year or two. School-leaving age has been raised to eighteen in most states of the Union, but the problem of Negro dropouts is as acute as ever.

In 1954 the Supreme Court gave one of the most important decisions in its long history—and one of the most controversial. Brown *vs.* Board of Education of Topeka, Kansas, declared that separation of the races in public schools was inherently unequal, and that it was therefore contrary to the Fourteenth Amendment of the Constitution, and must be ended "with all deliberate speed." The South resisted and continues to resist this revolutionary decision, but gradually the walls of separation came tumbling down everywhere. No less important: states and communities everywhere—even where there was no legal segregation of the races—were awakened to the inadequacy of black education, and launched programs designed to enable Negro children to catch up with white. More and more Negro children were persuaded to stay in high school until they graduated, and more and more, too, were encouraged to go on to college and university. The decade of the 1960s saw a nationwide effort to improve Negro colleges, to bring larger numbers of Negroes to the best colleges and universities in the land, and to train Negroes for public life and the professions. In late 1969, after fourteen years of "deliberate speed," the Supreme Court ruled that all separate black and white school systems must be integrated immediately. In principle Negroes had won the battle for equality in education by 1970, but much remained to be done before the principle could be translated into practice.

The struggle for racial equality was less successful in other areas, where the law could not operate effectively because of deeply entrenched local resistance. Nothing is more important than employment, for economic equality was basic to the struggle for Negro rights. Here there was discrimination, everywhere but in the federal civil service. Negroes worked as porters on trains, but not as engineers; as janitors in office buildings, but not as clerks or managers; as maids or cooks in domestic service, but not as receptionists or head waiters in hotels. They had relatively few jobs in teaching or in libraries, and a Negro in the police force was unusual. Labor unions, which should have extended a helping hand to Negroes who were struggling for job security even as white unionists had struggled fifty years earlier, were on the whole suspicious and unfriendly, and for a long time many of them excluded Negroes from membership.

Beginning in the 1930s state after state passed laws designed to end racial discrimination in jobs and discriminatory practices by unions. At the same time, the New Deal welfare legislation provided a kind of cushion for the shock of unemployment. This was, and remained a most serious problem. Partly because he was a black, partly because he had less training and less education than his white competitor, the Negro was generally the last to be hired and the first to be fired. No wonder that even during times of prosperity, as in the 1960s, Negro unemployment was two or three times that of white.

The Kennedy and Johnson administrations made herculean efforts to close the gap between black and white workers, and the sixties saw substantial progress in the economic position of the Negro. Yet the position of the Negro tenant farmer in the South, of the Negro inhabitant of the slums of northern cities, remained precarious and disgraceful. At the close of the decade the economic gap between white and black remained deep, and dangerous.

The problem of housing was as closely connected with poverty as with race. Indeed, it was impossible to separate these factors, so often were they but two sides to the same coin. It was not merely Negroes who were condemned to live in the slums of the great cities; so were all the poor. But Negroes were the poorest group in American society, and the great urban slums in New York, Los Angeles, Philadelphia, Detroit, Cleveland, Chicago, came to be almost entirely Negro or Puerto Rican slums. There was, in addition, widespread racial discrimination in housing, but what kept Negroes out of middle-class neighborhoods and suburbs was not so much overt discrimination, something that legislation might deal with, but simple poverty. Legislation requiring "open housing" and prohibiting discrimination in either public or private rentals or sales of housing made little impression on this situation. And, as more and more middle-class whites moved out of the cities to the suburbs thus depriving the cities of their business and taxes, a vicious circle was set in motion. As the cities got poorer and poorer, the schools got worse and worse, police protection, fire services, sanitation, more and more incompetent, and as this process continued, more and more middle-class whites moved out of the cities, leaving them to blacks and Puerto Ricans who could afford nothing better. Thus in the cities, as earlier on the farms, the Negroes got the worst of all worlds.

Most difficult to overcome were the deep-seated and habitual racial prejudices, that revealed themselves, often unconsciously, in manners, speech, and social relationships, of a private or semiprivate character, in the North and the South. The law, the Supreme Court had solemnly asserted back in 1896, "in the nature of things could not abolish distinctions based on color, or enforce social as distinguished from political equality, or a commingling of the two races upon terms unsatisfactory to either." And though that particular decision had been overthrown, the cliché lingered on: the law could address itself to public but not private manifestations of discrimination. These private expressions of prejudice persisted almost unrebuked.

But beginning somewhere in the 1930s the courts, and public opinion, began to modify the view that private prejudice could not be reached by law. The change came not in any dramatic reversal of the past, but in a gradual modification of the concept of what was public and what was private. Back in 1877 the Supreme Court had modified the concept of "private" business by ruling that all property became "clothed with a public interest when used in a manner to affect the community at large," and that "when one devotes his property to a use in which the public has an interest, one in effect grants to the public an interest in that use and must submit to being controlled by the public for the common good." Under this ruling, the area of private interest contracted and the area of public interest expanded to embrace almost the whole of business. In the past generation the same thing has happened with respect to the allowable limits of the expression of private prejudice: the concept of what was permissible, as purely private, has contracted and the concept of what is impermissible, because public, expanded. And so conscious was the American public of the errors of the past, and of the prejudices that persisted into the present, that it conceded to the Negroes themselves substantial power to determine what manifestations of racialism were affected with a public interest. Thus a great many things long tolerated, fell under the ban: exclusion of Negroes from college fraternities, for example, or the derogatory references to Negroes in Mark Twain's *Huckleberry Finn,* or the neglect of Negro history and literature in the schools.

T he years since the close of the Second World War which have seen the most rapid progress in the vindication of the political and legal rights of the Negroes, and the greatest improvement in their social and economic position, have also been the years of greatest protest, turmoil, and conflict in the racial arena. This is natural enough: revolution almost always comes not when conditions are at their lowest ebb but when they are improving. It is a product not of desperation but of rising expectations. The Negro has now discovered his power in politics and the economy and has discovered, too, how easily he can disrupt American society by open defiance and violence. He has taken over from white liberals not only the leadership but the actual conduct of his own crusade. And he is getting results. There is of course a danger that his campaign for an equal place in the sun of American democracy and prosperity will get out of hand and become violent—as it has in many of the large cities of the country— or that it will provoke counterviolence, as it also has. This is a chance the Negroes seem prepared to take; after all—so they reason—they have little or nothing to lose. But the Negro is not confronting today a stubborn or intransigent Bourbon upper class: the kind of blind hostility that brought on violent revolution in France in 1789, in the American South in 1861, in Russia in 1917. He has won his case philosophically and morally and, to a large degree politically. Full equality is now both constitutional law and official policy and has the support of the great majority of the American people, especially the young, in all parts of the country.

United States Department of the Interior

The First Reading of the Emancipation Proclamation. Engraving by A. H. Ritchie of the painting by Francis Bicknell Carpenter. President Abraham Lincoln (third from left) reads the proclamation that ended slavery in the United States.

recommended reading

Baldwin, James. *The Fire Next Time*. New York: Dell Publishing Company (Laurel Editions).

Brogan, Denis W. *The American Character*. New York: Random House (Vintage Books), 1956.

Commager, Henry Steele, editor. *The Struggle for Racial Equality*. New York: Harper & Row (Harper Torchbooks).

Dollard, John. *Caste and Class in a Southern Town*. New York: Doubleday & Company (Anchor Books), 1957.

Du Bois, William E. B. *The Souls of Black Folk*. Greenwich, Conn.: Fawcett World Library (Premier Books), 1969. Also in *Three Negro Classics,* edited by John Hope Franklin (New York: Avon Books (Discus Books), 1969).

Ellison, Ralph. *The Invisible Man*. New York: New American Library (Signet Books).

Frazier, E. Franklin. *The Black Bourgeoisie: The Rise of a New Middle Class in the U. S.* New York: Macmillan Company (Collier Books), 1962.

*————. *The Negro in the United States*. Revised edition. New York: Macmillan Company, 1957.

Harrington, Michael. *The Other America*. New York: Penguin Books (Pelican Books), 1962.

Lerner, Max. *America as a Civilization*. 2 volumes. New York: Simon & Schuster (Clarion Books), 1967.

Myrdal, Gunnar. *An American Dilemma: The Negro Problem and Modern Democracy*. 2 volumes. New York: Harper & Row (Harper Torchbooks), 1962.

*Perry, Ralph B. *Puritanism and Democracy*. New York: Vanguard Press, 1944.

de Tocqueville, Alexis. *Democracy in America*. New York: New American Library (Mentor Books).

Washington, Booker T. *Up From Slavery*. New York: Dell Publishing Company (Laurel Leaf Library). Also in *Three Negro Classics,* edited by John Hope Franklin (New York: Avon Books (Discus Books), 1969).

Woodward, C. Vann. *The Strange Career of Jim Crow*. 2nd revised edition. New York: Oxford University Press (Galaxy Books), 1966.

Wright, Richard. *Native Son*. New York: Harper & Row (Perennial Classics).

° Hard-cover edition. Titles not so marked are paperback editions.

The Capture of a Texas Town by Cowboys. Sketch by Frenzeny. In the frontier Southwest, off-duty cowboys would dash through a town robbing "every store of importance," according to a contemporary account.

7. law and lawlessness

The United States is at once the most law-respecting and the most lawless nation of the western world. This paradox, like so many other American characteristics, is rooted in history and experience.

Historically Americans were the first people to make a constitution which was, by very definition, "the supreme law of the land." What is more they contrived a constitutional system which depended on and worked through the courts; certainly in no other constitutional system do courts play so large and so decisive a role as they do in the American. No other nation has developed the institution of judicial review to anything like the extent to which Americans have taken it, and nowhere else can it be said, as it can be said with confidence of the American system, that while all three departments of government are equal, the judicial is "more equal" than the other two. In no other nation, not even India, have lawyers played so important a role for so long, and nowhere else would it be possible to speak of an "aristocracy of the robe"—the term which Tocqueville, borrowing from a very different French experience, applied to the American scene back in the 1830s. The term is still not entirely invalid.

These aspects of law in the American system are sufficiently important to justify some elaboration.

The Constitution itself is a legal document, a kind of super contract, drawn up by men who for years had sharpened their wits on legal arguments over the nature of government, federalism, and colonialism. Thus Madison, the chief architect of the Constitution, and next to him James Wilson were lawyers; the three authors of the famous Federalist Papers (Madison, Hamilton, and Jay) were all lawyers, and so too were Thomas Jefferson and John Adams, the one the chief architect of the legal system of Virginia, the other the author of the constitution of Massachusetts and at one time chief justice of that state. At least half the members of the Constitutional Convention which drew up the Constitution were lawyers and all of them were familiar with the doctrines and principles of public law, which was, in the eighteenth century, a gentleman's study. The solutions which their generation contrived for the problems that confronted a new society were legal and constitutional: a written constitution to fix the boundaries of government; a federal system to distribute powers among governments; a Bill of Rights to guarantee the rights of men; covenants and contracts to make clear the rights of territories and

103

of the people who settled them, and so forth. No wonder the constitutional document which this generation fashioned fulfilled Locke's ideal of "a standing law to live by."

It is entirely natural, then, that the study of law should command great influence and prestige in the United States. While no doubt the position of President is more powerful than that of Chief Justice of the Supreme Court, it is nevertheless the judiciary branch of the government that is most respected. The Supreme Court is probably the most exalted judicial body in the world today. It is to most Americans what the royal family is to the English or the Catholic Church to Spaniards. Its prestige is not always equally high, nor its influence equally strong. From time to time, when it gives decisions that adversely affect the interests or prejudices of large segments of the population—as it did, for example, on the issues of racial equality in the decades of the fifties and the sixties—it excites acrimonious criticism. But it is illuminating that over a period of a century and a half only one attack on the Supreme Court has been successful: that written in 1798 into the Eleventh Amendment to the Constitution, limiting the jurisdiction of the Court in special cases involving suits against states. Since that time the Court has weathered every crisis, even the crisis of 1937 when Franklin Roosevelt, one of the most popular of American Presidents, at the very height of his power, had to acknowledge failure in his attempt at "court reform."

It is in large part for these reasons—respect for the Constitution as a legal document, respect for the Supreme Court as the authoritative expounder of the Constitution—as well as from the necessities of a federal system which implacably requires an umpire that Americans of all ranks have come to accept the practice of judicial review almost as a matter of course. It is, of course, no such thing; nowhere else on the globe do courts habitually review acts of the legislative and executive bodies and pronounce them void when they think proper to do so; nowhere else, certainly neither in systems parliamentary nor totalitarian, would the executive or the legislative meekly accept the verdict of the courts as final.

This habit of submitting great issues of public policy to the chance of private litigation is sometimes called the "adversary system." What it means in many instances, is that issues are not settled in any systematic manner, by open discussion and debate, but only when some individual or corporation challenges a law and takes its case to court. Then a kind of gladiatorial combat takes place. Attorneys for the government and attorneys for private litigants confront each other, arguing not issues of public law and policy (though this cannot of course be excluded) but of law, and often of highly technical law. This method of settling issues has the advantage of removing heated problems from the arena of party controversy to the cool atmosphere of the courts, where decisions of an authoritative and final character may be reached. It has the disadvantage of submitting important national problems to the chance of private litigation, causing serious delays in the solution of these problems and risking a decision less on merits than on technicalities.

This preference for settling issues by the adversary method is one manifestation of the highly developed competitive spirit that pervades in American society. In a sense, individuals and government are pitted against each other as in a game—perhaps a chess game—while the whole country looks on.

The habit of referring great questions of public policy to the courts has another danger: it encourages a tendency to substitute constitutional for social or political considerations in the formulation of policy. Not "Is this legislation wise and useful?", but "Is this legislation constitutional?" comes, far too often, to be the crucial question. As Tocqueville wrote over a century ago:

> Scarcely any question arises in the United States which does not become, sooner or later, a subject of judicial debate; hence all parties are obliged to borrow the ideas, and even the language usual in judicial proceedings in their daily controversies. . . . The language of the law thus becomes, in some measure, a vulgar tongue; the spirit of the law . . . gradually penetrates beyond their walls into the bosom of society, where it descends to the lowest classes, so that the whole people contracts the habits and the tastes of the magistrate. (Tocqueville, *op cit.*, I, pp. 284-85)

That in itself would not be deplorable. What is deplorable is that problems primarily economic or social are discussed and decided not in social or economic but in legalistic terms. This in turn places upon American courts burdens heavier than those borne by any other judicial bodies in the world; the responsibility for making great decisions of public policy; questions of the nature and reach of the treaty power, or of the government's power to deal with depressions, even of the constitutionality of wars in which the nation is engaged. And the court is required to dispose of these great questions not on their merits but on the basis of legal precedents and principles.

In the light of all this it is not surprising that law and the study of law occupy a very special position in public life. In America, as Edmund Burke observed two centuries ago, every man is a lawyer. It was prophetic that more copies of Blackstone's *Commentaries on the Laws of England* were sold in the American colonies than in the mother country. Americans invented the "law school": a hundred law journals testify to the degree to which they cultivate the study of law. Americans invented too—just a century ago—the case method of the study of law, a method which has spread widely to other countries, and other fields of study.

To this day most Americans retain a simple faith in the efficacy of law that is at once astonishing and absurd. In many states, constitution makers tried to anticipate everything and provide for everything. Thus some constitutions, like that of Oklahoma, run to one hundred thousand words or more. Congress grinds out hundreds of laws every year; so

Justice's Court in the Backwoods. Tompkins H. Matteson. 1850. Law and the concept of due process were integral to American life from the beginning.

do the fifty state legislatures, displaying an almost lawless passion for lawmaking. Confronted by a phenomenon like student rebellion, Congressmen prepare scores of different laws to deal with the problem and every state boasts its two or three score laws for the same purpose. Only a people confident that the solution of all problems was to be found in making laws about them could enact so many. And if Americans no more expect all these laws to be obeyed, or enforced, than they expect their religious professions to be applied, it comforts them to know that the laws are safely on the statute books, just as it comforts them to know that the churches are open every Sunday. Americans, so often inclined to take the word for the deed in the matter of loyalty oaths, or in the gesture of "Mother's Day" or "I am an American" parades, find a curious satisfaction in going on record publicly in favor of virtue.

So deeply have Americans revered the law that they have customarily insisted that their revolutions be strictly legal. In the 1770s they argued the constitutional and legal issues of their relations with England with matchless skill before they took to arms, and when they did revolt it was as self-professed champions of the British constitution. What, indeed, was the Declaration of Independence but an elaborate justification of the American constitutional position, and of the legal right as well as the moral necessity of revolution? In 1860, just seventy years after the new nation was inaugurated, Southerners justified secession from that Union not on the right of revolution but on strictly legal and constitutional grounds.

A symbol of the pervasive reverence for the law—and also for indulgence in lawlessness—is the role that "due process" plays in American thought and conduct. "Due process of law"—a concept that appears first in Magna Charta—loomed large even in the colonial era, and the term itself appears twice in our Constitution—once in the original Bill of Rights as a limitation on Congress, and again in the Fourteenth Amendment as a limitation upon the states. Due process of law meant originally a fair trial or a day in court, but with the passing of time it took on an ever larger meaning, until it came to encompass the notion of fairness in every step of the process of lawmaking and of the administration of justice. It means, therefore, not only fairness in the court room—the right of an accused person to have counsel, to be assumed innocent until proved guilty, to a jury trial, to call and confront witnesses, to be free from self-incrimination, and so forth—but in addition, fairness in the process of lawmaking, of decision-making by regulatory commissions. It means, in short, fairness in administration. It is, for example, not merely a Negro who may claim that due process has been violated if there were no blacks on the jury that tried him in a criminal case; a civil servant, suspended from his job for something vaguely called "disloyalty," who may invoke due process in the hearing on that suspension; a public utility corporation with rates that have been fixed by a public commission who may charge that due process has been violated if it has not had an opportunity to

Dr. Martin Luther King, Jr. Nobel Prize-winning Negro leader assassinated in 1968 in Memphis, Tennessee, where he had gone to give support to a garbage-collectors' strike against the city of Memphis. More than any other one man, he provided the leadership that helped Negroes begin to win truly equal rights, a century after the Civil War.

present its side of the argument. An immigrant threatened, for one reason or another, with deportation to his native country, may invoke due process to stop repatriation proceedings. Even a soldier can plead due process against the operation of military law if his alleged misconduct is outside the military jurisdiction. A young man drafted into the armed forces may claim that due process was violated if his draft board ignored his claim to exemption on moral grounds. In each of these cases, and a hundred others, those who feel that some injustice is done them may take their case to court, and the court will decide whether the trials, the job hearing, the rate fixing, the repatriation proceedings, the draft, have been fair. In no other country, perhaps, is there so elaborate a mechanism for achieving fairness in justice and administration.

All this is not to say that fairness is always achieved—merely that the ideal of fairness is embedded in the legal system. But much of government and law as well is extralegal, and Americans, like others, often disregard the principle in their practice: witness, for example, the injustice heaped upon blacks in the South for over a hundred years. In the United States as elsewhere, officials put themselves above the law. Police defy the law, usually with impunity; administrators enforce the letter rather than the spirit of the law; politicians help their friends to evade the law; corporations, too powerful to be easily controlled, flout the law; the public, excited whether by fear or vindictiveness, takes the law into its own hands. Thus along with law there is lawlessness.

I t is a commonplace now that the United States is the most lawless of western countries. The spectacle of American lawlessness, from the assassinations of President Kennedy and Martin Luther King to racial riots in Watts, Cleveland, and Washington, or police brutality at the Democratic nominating convention of 1968 in Chicago, is familiar to the world through television, films, and newspapers. To Americans it is familiar through daily experience. They know that they can walk safely in the streets of London, Paris, Rome, Hamburg, or Vienna, but they fear to walk at night in the streets of New York, Washington or Los Angeles, and they fear not only the breakdown of law but a rupture of the very fabric of their society. It is a reflection on the state of mind of Americans that in 1968 Mr. Nixon could conduct a successful campaign for the Presidency largely on the issue of "law and order," and that a former chief of police, whose only issue was "law and order" could in 1969 win the mayoralty of a great city like Minneapolis by a two-to-one majority.

The story of violence in America is too familiar to require elaboration. The murder rate in the United States is some fifty times that of Britain or West Germany; the lesser crimes of violence are almost too common-place to record. There is no effective control of the sale of firearms. Anyone can buy a rifle or a pistol, and almost everyone does: in 1967 alone over four and a half million firearms were sold by mail or over the counter. Between 1960 and 1968 robbery and burglary increased by almost 100 per cent, and so, too, auto theft. Something of the dimensions of crime can be gathered from the statistics of arrests (the majority of crimes are not followed by arrest) in 1967: various forms of robbery and theft accounted for three-quarters of a million arrests. In the same year were reported over six hundred thousand auto thefts—far from the total number.

Needless to say, "formal" crime represents only a small part of violence in America. Violence has been a constant in the warfare between organized labor and corporate industry. It has been familiar, too, within the ranks of labor itself. Violence is one of the generally accepted techniques of police interrogations—the infamous "third degree" familiar from so many crime stories and films. Violence has presided over race relations for a century. Now, for almost the first time, Negroes are themselves resorting to violence in their struggle against discrimination and injustice. Violence has moved onto the university campus and becomes an almost standard weapon of student protest. Nor can we forget that familiar and continuous violence which accounts for more casualties now than in any war the nation has ever been engaged in—violence on the highways with its toll of over fifty thousand lives a year and a total, over the last generation, of over one million.

Yet it is a mistake to interpret American lawlessness merely in terms of violence, of the current scene. Lawlessness itself is deeply rooted in

The Passion of Sacco and Vanzetti. Ben Shahn. 1931-32. Sacco and Vanzetti were two Italian-born shoemakers who were executed for murder in Massachusetts in 1927. Many believed they were, in fact, executed for their radical political views, and the case aroused world-wide indignation.

Collection of the Whitney Museum of American Art, New York.
Gift of Mr. and Mrs. Milton Lowenthal in Memory of Juliana Force.

American history and society and finds expression not so much in violence as in the systematic evasion of the law. Nor is it merely the poor and oppressed who are guilty of lawlessness and of violence. Disrespect for laws that get in the way of private or group objectives is endemic and pervasive. Corporations, university students, government officials, the legislators particularly in the southern states—these and others of comparable social standing are quite as guilty of flouting the law as are those the nineteenth-century preacher Theodore Parker called the "dangerous and perishing classes of society." In one way or another lawlessness finds expression in every segment of American society.

Negroes do not feel any deep obligation either to accept or obey laws that they did not help make and that they regard—with considerable justice—as instruments designed by the white community for their exploitation. As most of them long have felt themselves excluded from the protection of the law, they naturally look upon law and the police as the enemy. Law, in their eyes, is something designed for the benefit of whites; order is just another name for property that belongs to whites. There are of course large elements of the Negro community that are sincerely law abiding; it is unavoidable, notwithstanding, that many blacks regard breaking the law as a gesture of independence with some moral justification.

The poor, especially the urban poor, do not feel any compelling obligation to the supremacy of the law. With considerable justice, they regard the legal system as designed chiefly to protect property. Like the blacks, they tend to think of the police as the enemy, and of the law as a kind of barbed-wire entanglement in which they are hopelessly enmeshed and badly hurt.

Many university students—there are over six million of them in the United States—acknowledge no obligation either to the university, which they assert, rather wildly, is corrupt, or to society, which they characterize as vicious. They consider themselves, therefore, as exempt from both the academic requirements of the university and the legal restrictions of their society. More perhaps than any other group, they sublimate their lawlessness by giving it a veneer of civil disobedience against a system that they think depraved and a government that they consider a tool of the establishment.

Business corporations are vast, impersonal enterprises whose managements usually feel their primary obligation to stockholders—and themselves—rather than to the public. They prefer not to violate laws openly, though they take a rather cavalier attitude towards such things as anti-trust or pollution laws; they maintain large lobbies to shape the laws to their interests and spend a great deal of money to get their friends into high office. Disillusionment with the ethics of business is an important ingredient in the current lawlessness of American society: with, for example, the tobacco industry, that denies or ignores the relationship of cigarette smoking to cancer; with the drug industry that makes profits of 1,000 per cent or more on several medicinal drugs; with chemical industries that presume they have the right to pollute lakes and streams, Providence having provided them just for their benefit; with the vast conglomerate of industries tied to the armed forces that recognize no obligation to inquire into the use to which their products are put; with the television industry that appears to have no compunction about exploiting violence or sex for profit, or about the corrupting impact of its product on children; with the advertising enterprise that is prepared to exploit any emotions of fear, jealousy, envy, lust, or sadism to sell its products. Needless to say all this is not unique to the United States, but corporate ruthlessness and irresponsibility have probably gone further in the United States than in other western countries.

The police, the immediate law enforcement agents, are themselves often guilty of lawlessness and violence. American police, unlike the British, are armed, and not reluctant to use their weapons. Alarmed and frightened by growing violence, the police often react by counterviolence, their answer to demonstrations and riots larger and more sophisticated armaments. Police brutality is not presented in English and French crime stories as a commonplace, but it is almost a required feature of American crime stories and films. One of the considerations that contribute greatly to hostility against the whole social order is the discriminatory character of much of police violence: you rarely hear of police brutality in the prosperous suburbs; almost always it is in the slums.

Not only the police but government itself sets an example of lawlessness. Thus the federal Constitution clearly specifies that no Negro shall be denied the right to vote because of his color, but for a century state legislatures, chiefly in the South, did in fact prevent the Negro from voting. Thus though the Constitution provides that any state to deny the Negro a right to vote because of his color shall lose a proportionate part of its representation in Congress, no state has ever been so penalized. Thus, too, the Constitution provides for full equality before the law, and equal protection for all by law, yet for a century states—again, chiefly in the South—have ignored this constitutional requirement and denied the Negro the equal protection of the laws. Thus though some fifteen years ago the Supreme Court ruled that there must be an end to segregation in public schools, segregation still flourishes almost everywhere in the South, much as it did a generation ago. Thus, in another area, though the Supreme Court has ruled that wiretapping—listening in on telephone conversations—is illegal, the FBI and other agencies of the government go right on with their wiretapping, claiming to be a law unto themselves.

Finally, it is society as a whole, not just special segments of it, that is guilty of lawlessness. It is the millions of automobile drivers who fail to observe the speed laws and inflict almost two million casualties every year. It is the vast public that seems to take pleasure in vandalism and destruction, to assume that what is common property is nobody's property. It is the corporations who use up natural resources that should be preserved for future generations—resources of soil, water, timber, flora and fauna. It is Everyman, who ignores the no-parking signs on the streets, the no-smoking signs in buildings, the no-litter signs in parks—who, in fact, assumes that he is exempt from the law and the requirements of mutual decency.

The explanation for much of the lawlessness in America can be found in history. Let us consider, briefly, some of the relevant historical factors and experiences.

First, Americans are, by their very nature, uprooted. The settlement of America was a product of the unsettlement of Europe; almost every immigrant who crossed the Atlantic had broken with the past—with his society, his family, his work, his language; he had broken that cake of custom which confined and restricted his life and provided him with moral and social guidelines. Nor did the subsequent experience of immigrants, and their descendants in America, make for a stable, orderly, and homogeneous society. The shattering of the cake of custom continued and became almost routine, the uprooting and transplanting, a continuous experience. The ancestral church was often a thing of the past—perhaps more with Protestants than with Catholics—and with it the moral and spiritual world it had constructed for its communicants. The old laws, too, were a thing of the past, and while the English common law was transplanted to America, many communities, especially those on distant frontiers, were, except for such law as its members chose to write, almost without law.

Second, and equally important, many familiar laws, like familiar social and economic activities, proved irrelevant to the American scene. Thus with inheritance laws providing for primogeniture; thus with land and water laws suitable enough for a small island with little available land but wholly unsuitable for a vast continent like the American; thus with a penal code designed to protect property from the depredations of the poor; and thus—more important perhaps—with a great deal of public law that had grown up over the centuries as an instrument of royal or aristocratic rule and had little relevance to the needs of an equalitarian society. If American society was to flourish and prosper, it was necessary to disregard much of this inherited law and to contrive new practices and laws. Inevitably, disregard of much of this inherited law and custom became the price of survival. It became almost honorable to flout land laws that sought to preserve the resources of the American continent to absentee proprietors, or to flout commercial laws that hedged in American trade with a hundred restrictions, all for the benefit of the mother country, or totally to reject religious laws that created a privileged church in the American colonies and established intolerance as a public policy. These, and many other laws inherited from the old world, could be considered as not only irrelevant but tyrannical, and from this attitude it was only a step to the Jeffersonian motto: Rebellion to tyrants is obedience to God.

Third, much of the American frontier experience put a premium on what appeared to be lawlessness. When pioneers went out to successive frontiers they carried laws with them, or not, pretty much as they chose. If old laws did not fit new circumstances, they readily made new laws, and if there were no laws, they enforced what came to be called Vigilante Law. Just as their forebears had been impatient with English laws that did not fit the needs of the colonies, so they were impatient with laws drawn up in the East for a settled society but quite unsuitable to the frontier or the open lands of the West: land laws that denied the right of settlers to take such land as they cultivated; mining laws that preserved to eastern corporations title to precious metals miners had found; Indian laws that seemed to protect Indians more than they did the whites. Many frontiersmen went to the extreme of identifying freedom with the total absence of law, or at least with all law that interfered with their independence.

Fourth, slavery encouraged not so much lawlessness as violence, but that violence inevitably came to embrace disregard for the law. Slavery, as Jefferson said, was "a perpetual exercise of the most boisterous passions, the most unremitting despotism on the one part, and degrading submissions on the other." This was true not of slavery alone, but of the whole principle of white superiority and Negro inferiority on which it rested and from which it drew sustenance. Much of slavery itself was born in defiance of the laws prohibiting the slave trade after 1812. There were of course laws—called Black Codes—which purported to regulate the institution of slavery, but as might be expected these were designed primarily to protect slaveowners, not slaves, and were customarily so drawn as to give the master practically total power over his slaves. While the Black Codes made some gestures towards protecting slaves from cruel or vicious masters, these provisions were in the nature of things quite unenforceable. Masters did, with impunity, work their slaves at their own pleasure, flog them, indulge "the most boisterous passions" at their expense, and break up slave families with little concern for the affections of black husband and wife, mother and child. Nor did the situation improve with the end of slavery; indeed in some respects Emancipation brought more rather than less violence. For now the Negro was exposed to the whole of white society, and without the protection that formerly

The Haymarket Riot in Chicago, 1886. The labor movement in the United States was marked with violence throughout its early history. Above, a bomb thrown at Chicago police who were breaking up a meeting of leftist labor leaders resulted in a slaughter that became known as the Haymarket Massacre.

his master could give him. Now whites of every class thought they had to combine to "keep the Negro in his place," which was, of course, at the bottom. Now white men without any experience with Negroes or any respect for them could vent their wrath, or resentment, on them with impunity. There were to be sure laws to protect the Negro—federal and state—but these were ignored, and the habit of ignoring both morality and law in relations with the Negro accentuated the existing tendency of the South to lawlessness.

Fifth, equality itself, as Tocqueville pointed out, has a tendency to aggravate—or perhaps we would say to glamorize—lawlessness. An equalitarian society has little respect for either authority or discipline. Its members look with suspicion on government, prefer the authority of the individual to that of the official, and think discipline somehow a limitation on the free expression of individualism. They know that *they* are the ultimate source of the law and the ultimate repository of power, and they are tempted to confuse this philosophical principle with the practical notion that they should be the judge of a law's propriety.

So much for the historical roots of violence in America. What is the explanation of the current crescendo of violence in American life? First, it is to be remembered that a generation has now reached maturity which knows only violence in the conduct of international relations—the unparalleled violence of the Second World War, the intellectual and moral violence of the Cold War, the violence of the Vietnam war. It has seen a major part of the energies of government organized for the production of superweapons and superarmaments. It has had before it, for a decade now, the spectacle of a war in Vietnam both senseless and immoral that provides a daily portrayal of violence against a small and helpless people. It sees on the television screen the bombing of villages, the destruction of forests and farms and dams, the razing of cities, the mistreatment of civilians. As government itself seems to have no solution to problems, in part of its own making, but violence, the new generation assumes that violence is the natural and accepted solution to all problems, or if it does not really so assume, it defies the government by thus using its own weapons against it.

Moreover, television—and other media too—provides a portrayal of violence, day and night, to young and to old. It is no wonder that the young, especially, are numbed by the ceaseless parade of beatings and sluggings and shootings, by the deafening shouts of hatred and violence, that pour over them. Television teaches them that violence is the normal and accepted solution for all problems—the natural reaction when you do not have your way, the natural response to opposition. It is not, as some critics of television assert, that children who watch television are inspired to go out and imitate the more extreme displays of violence; it is rather that they come to take for granted that violence is indeed the normal way of life.

117

Also, there is violence as the expression—the not unnatural expression—of the desperation of the perishing classes of society, the violence of those who have nothing to lose. They are not afraid of getting hurt: they are used to getting hurt. They are not afraid of losing their jobs: they have no jobs. They are not afraid of the destruction of the houses they live in or the stores they trade in: they have no affection for either home or shop. Filled with hopelessness and helplessness, they strike out blindly against their enemies—and they regard the whole of society as their enemy.

Some of these considerations operate in the old world as in the new; how then explain the special bitterness and the special violence of the American scene? There are two obvious explanations. First is the consciousness that the United States is today the most militaristic of nations, the one engaged in wars, hot and cold, throughout the globe; for all its traditional commitment to peace, it seems today committed to war. Second, a livelier sense of responsibility than is traditional in many other nations, and therefore a heavier sense of guilt: Americans know that they are supposed to be responsible for what their government does, yet feel that they are unable to exercise that responsibility. Much of current violence and desperation comes out of this feeling of frustration with the apparent breakdown of the democratic processes.

The spectacle of lawlessness in America is a sobering one. But it would be an exaggeration to assert, as so many Americans themselves now do, that American society is demoralized or in process of disintegration. The record of lawlessness is alarming, but there is no general repudiation of government or law, no general breakdown of morality. Nothing that has happened so far in the United States compares with the revolutionary lawlessness of the Nazi and Fascist regimes of Europe a generation ago nor, except for the prolonged injustice to the Negro, has there been anything comparable to the mass violence, destruction, and murder that totalitarian governments perpetrated against Jews and dissenters in the decades of the thirties and forties.

recommended reading

Adamic, Louis. *Dynamite: [The Story of Class Violence in America]*. New York: Random House (Vintage Books).

Aptheker, Herbert. *American Negro Slave Revolts*. New York: International Publishers Company (New World Paperbacks).

Arnold, Thurman. *Symbols of Government*. New York: Harcourt, Brace & World (Harbinger Books).

Baldwin, Leland D. *Whiskey Rebels: The Story of a Frontier Uprising*. Pitt Paperback Series. Pittsburgh: University of Pittsburgh Press, 1968.

Bryce, James. *The American Commonwealth*. 2 volumes. New York: G. P. Putnam's Sons (Capricorn Books), 1959.

Cahn, Edmond. *The Sense of Injustice*. Bloomington, Ind.: Indiana University Press (Midland Books), 1964.

Cash, Wilbur J. *The Mind of the South*. New York: Random House (Vintage Books).

Corwin, Edward S. *American Constitutional History: Essays*. New York: Harper & Row (Harper Torchbooks).

*————. *Court over Constitution: A Study of Judicial Review as an Instrument of Popular Government*. Magnolia, Mass.: Peter Smith Publisher.

*————. *John Marshall and the Constitution*. Yale Chronicles of America Series. New York: United States Publishers Association.

————. *The President: Office and Powers*. 4th edition. New York: New York University Press, 1957.

Frankfurter, Felix. *Mr. Justice Holmes and the Supreme Court*. New York: Atheneum Publishers, 1965.

*Franklin, John Hope. *The Militant South, 1800-1861*. Revised edition. Cambridge, Mass.: Harvard University Press (Belknap Press), 1970.

Graham, Hugh D., and Gurr, Ted R. *Violence in America: Historical and Comparative Perspectives*. New York: New American Library (Signet Books), 1969.

*Grodzins, Morton. *Americans Betrayed: Politics and the Japanese Evacuation*. Chicago: University of Chicago Press, 1969.

*Harris, Frank. *The Bomb: The Haymarket Riot*. Introduction by John Dos Passos. Chicago: University of Chicago Press, 1963.

Holmes, Oliver Wendell, Jr. *Common Law*. Boston: Little, Brown & Company.

*Horn, Stanley F. *Invisible Empire: Story of the Ku Klux Klan, 1866-1871*. Stratford, Conn.: John E. Edwards, 1969.

*Kefauver, Estes. *Crime in America*. Westport, Conn.: Greenwood Press, 1968.

Kohn, Hans. *American Nationalism: An Interpretative Essay*. New York: Macmillan Company (Collier Books), 1961.

*Lane, Roger. *Policing the City: Boston, 1822-1885*. Cambridge, Mass.: Harvard University Press, 1967.

*Laski, Harold J. *The American Democracy: A Commentary and an Interpretation*. New York: Viking Press, 1948. *Out of print, but scheduled to be reissued in 1970.*

Lerner, Max. *America as a Civilization*. 2 volumes. New York: Simon and Schuster (Clarion Books), 1967.

London, Jack. *The Iron Heel*. New York: Hill & Wang (American Century Series), 1957.

*Mason, Alpheus T. *Brandeis: A Free Man's Life*. New York: Viking Press, 1956.

*————. *Brandeis and the Modern State*. Washington: National Home Library Foundation, 1936.

* Hard-cover edition. Titles not so marked are paperback editions.

*————. *Harlan Fiske Stone: Pillar of the Law*. Hamden, Conn.: Shoe String Press (Archon Books), 1968.

McCloskey, Robert G. *The American Supreme Court*. Chicago: University of Chicago Press, 1960.

Merriam, Charles E. *American Political Ideas: Studies in the Development of American Political Thought, 1865-1917*. New York: Johnson Reprint Corporation, 1969.

*————. *History of American Political Theories*. New York: Johnson Reprint Corporation, 1968.

Miller, Perry. *The Legal Mind in America: From Independence to the Civil War*. Ithaca, N.Y.: Cornell University Press.

*————. *The Life of the Mind in America: From the Revolution to the Civil War*. New York: Harcourt, Brace & World, 1965.

Myrdal, Gunnar. *An American Dilemma: The Negro Problem and Modern Democracy*. 2 volumes. New York: Harper & Row (Harper Torchbooks), 1962.

Pound, Roscoe. *The Formative Era of American Law*. Boston: Little, Brown & Company, 1938.

Stampp, Kenneth M. *The Peculiar Institution*. New York: Random House (Vintage Books).

*Tannenbaum, Frank. *Darker Phases of the South*. New York: G. P. Putnam's Sons, 1924. OP

de Tocqueville, Alexis. *Democracy in America*. New York: New American Library (Mentor Books).

Walker, Daniel. *Rights in Conflict: [Chicago's Seven Brutal Days]*. New York: New American Library (Signet Books), 1969.

*Warren, Charles. *The Supreme Court in United States History*. 2 volumes. Boston: Little, Brown & Company, 1960.

Wright, Richard. *Native Son*. New York: Harper & Row (Perennial Classics).

° Hard-cover edition. Titles not so marked are paperback editions.
  OP indicates the book is out of print.

120

8. the family, youth, and sex

The American family is the European family transplanted—a generalization that applies to Negroes almost as much as to whites, for Negroes have been part of American society rather longer than most other Americans. The transplanting was important—the original transplanting to America, and the successive transplantings within the New World—and so, too, was the New World environment.

It is clear that the family plays a less significant role in American than in most other societies, both culturally and socially. Americans are not, on the whole, family conscious, not in the European sense of the phrase and certainly not in the Oriental. Outside of places like Boston, Massachusetts; Richmond, Virginia; and Charleston, South Carolina, few Americans can trace their ancestry back further than their grandparents, and few see any reason why they should. It was said of the first settlers of Virginia that "they had no need of ancestors, they themselves were ancestors," and this has remained true of Americans generally down to the present day. There are, to be sure, scores of societies such as the Colonial Dames, the Daughters of the American Revolution, the Order of the Cincinnati, all designed to advertise ancestral connection with earlier eras in American history and to demonstrate the distinguished lineage of their members, but only the members themselves take the matter seriously. On the whole Americans look with indifference or disdain on the claims of either ancient or distinguished ancestry; as their most popular writer, Mark Twain, observed, "We are all descended from Adam." They have, too, a healthy skepticism about most genealogical claims, for they know that a distinguished Revolutionary ancestor is only one of 128 potential ancestors of that generation. And they know, too, that over the years resounding British names like Black, Stone, and Gordon often emerged from Schwartz and Stein and Gordonowitz. And they remember that though Franklin Roosevelt could show an ancient American lineage, Presidents Truman, Eisenhower, Kennedy, and Nixon all made the White House without benefit of distinguished ancestry.

Family plays a lesser role in another and more important area. Because so many Americans started fresh in the New World—started quite literally without any family—they lacked the sense of family solidarity that is still so familiar in older societies. The industrial revolution, urbaniza-

The Birches. Waldo Peirce. 1937. More than in other Western countries, the child is the focus of the American family.

tion, and mobility have atomized the family everywhere, but nowhere has this process of atomization gone further than in the United States, where families were separated by a broad ocean and where mobility was social as well as physical. Few American children, outside New England and parts of the South, grow up with anything even remotely like the sense of family connections and continuity so familiar in France or Italy, Japan or Thailand. This is not merely because Americans are always on the move, or because modern houses and flats do not lend themselves to old-fashioned family life, as did the sprawling houses of the Victorian age. If Americans wanted a European or a Victorian family life they would build their houses accordingly. But beyond the impact of environment is a sociological factor: Americans were expected, from the beginning, to break their ties with the past, to set up on their own, to be truly independent. The obvious demonstration of this was the move across the Atlantic, or from settled region to frontier. More often than not that move involved the breakup of family: sometimes of husband and wife, more commonly of parents and children. A hundred novels and auto-biographies testify to the traumatic nature of this experience, none perhaps better than Ole Rölvaag's *Giants in the Earth* or the classic memoir by Hamlin Garland, *A Son of the Middle Border*. What these and countless others make clear is that the burden of this uprooting fell most heavily upon the women. As Garland wrote in his autobiography, he had meant to "tell the truth" about life on the Middle Border.

> But I didn't. Even my youthful zeal faltered in the midst of a revelation of the lives led by the women of the farms of the middle border. Before the tragic futility of their suffering, my pen refused to shed its ink. Over the hidden chamber of their maternal agonies I drew the veil.

The modern American family is less communal than it was in the nineteenth century or than it still is in most other parts of the old world. There is no room in the average house or flat for parents, maiden aunts, uncles, cousins, or old family retainers; the average household is reduced to the lowest denominator of parents and children, and the children are expected to leave home and strike out for themselves when they get a job and certainly when they get married. Keeping house is no longer a communal affair, but rather a solitary one: the shared work of the kitchen, the laundry, the nursery, and the garden so familiar from the paintings of Pieter Brueghel or Eastman Johnson, or in the Currier and Ives prints which excite such nostalgia in Americans today—all belong to the past.

It is of course an exaggeration to say that America is a matriarchy, but it is probably true that more than in other western societies, American women set the standards of morality, conduct, and culture. In the average household it is the mother who is expected to maintain the standards of good manners and cleanliness, herd the family off to church on Sundays, encourage and support community culture (by which is usually meant music and art), and take an interest in schools and civic welfare. The famous and powerful League of Women Voters is an American contrivance; there is nothing quite its equivalent in other countries. It is the mother's duty to keep up the house, and often the garden; to maintain connections with both sides of the family; to improve the speech and perhaps even the morals of husband and children. And it is the mother who spends the household money—an elementary fact recognized by all advertisers who direct their campaigns chiefly to women.

Teachers, too, exercise an influence in all of these areas during the most impressionable years of the life of the young, and the overwhelming majority of teachers are women—a situation which is changing now. So, too, with others whose functions are cultural or moral—librarians, for example, or Sunday school teachers. What this meant during most of the nineteenth century, and what it still means to some extent is that what passes for "culture" in America has a distinctly feminine stamp on it, and has, perhaps for that reason, been relegated to the domestic sphere. The concluding lines of the most famous of American novels—*Huckleberry Finn*—embody much of American folklore: "I reckon I got to light out for the territory . . . because Aunt Sally she's going to adopt me and civilize me, and I can't stand it." It was a prophecy of what the American male was to do for the next half century when threatened by culture.

In all this, however, there has been something of a revolution in the past twenty-five years or so—a revolution which owes much to the example and the leadership of John F. Kennedy. Young men are turning with enthusiasm to high school teaching, librarianship, social welfare, and their elders are devoting themselves to the arts with the same zest that their fathers and grandfathers showed for business. Names like Whitney, Mellon, Guggenheim, and Lehman now conjure up not great business tycoons but great patrons of art.

The reverse side of the indifference to family and ancestors is what has always appeared to outsiders an exaggerated concern for children and a tendency to indulge them in all things. The explanation of this goes back to the beginnings of settlement in the new world: after all, one might say, that is what the move to the new world was about—children. Emigrants left their old homes for many reasons, but the most pervasive of them all was that they expected to find in America a future for their children. Each newcomer was confident that, whatever happened to him,

The Family. George H. Story. 1872. The American family was the European family transplanted.

his children would be better off than he or his parents had been—and he was usually right. In this new world children were not a curse, but a blessing, for there was food enough to go around and that made all the difference. Here children would not be condemned to toil in the fields or at the loom from the time they were eight years old; they would go to school and perhaps even to university. Here they would not be bound to some lord's domain or to their father's shop, but could acquire land of their own, find whatever work suited them, become doctors or lawyers or preachers. Here they would be free of the oppressions and superstitions and tyrannies that bedeviled them in the old world—free to work out their own destinies.

The special good fortune of children in America was confirmed by legal innovations. In the mother country, as in Europe generally, the rule of primogeniture—that is, the inheritance of the estate by the eldest son— still flourished. Estates, as well as titles, dignities, and position, passed to the eldest son, and the other children, sons and daughters alike, were fobbed off with a lesser share or expected to fend for themselves. Americans early rejected the principle of primogeniture, and when the states became independent, outlawed it in their new Constitutions. In the United States the idea of equality extends quite naturally to the entire family; the wife is equal to the husband, children to parents, girls to boys. Where, in most parts of the world even today, a family that has only limited means will concentrate them on the education of the eldest son, or on the sons generally, in the United States the tendency would be rather to take care of the daughters, confident that the sons would somehow manage to take care of themselves. So, too, where in most societies it was long customary to provide a daughter with a dowry at marriage—a kind of payment for taking the girl off her parents' hands— the idea of a dowry never caught on in America.

No wonder the new world became something of a paradise for children, or that adulation for them and even deference to them became a habit or that the center of gravity of the family shifted unmistakably from parents to children. There was sound sociological basis for this revolution in the family. In the African, Asian, or European family, it could be taken for granted that parents had more wisdom, better judgment, more skill, than their children; in America the situation was reversed. Here it was clear that each new generation was taller, stronger, and healthier than the preceding one, that each generation was better educated and more sophisticated than its parents. The children of illiterate immigrants went to elementary school; the children of parents with a common school education went to high school; the children of a high school generation went on to university. Even more important psychologically, the native-born children of immigrant parents knew the American language, American mores and habits, could cope better with the new environment. Finally, children who were restless under the weight of parental restraint could strike off on their own—there was land in the West, there were jobs in the city, there were husbands and wives to be acquired even without parental consent. Inevitably the young took advantage of this situation to impose their wills, desires, standards, and culture upon their elders.

Certainly the relations of American children to their parents (as to elders generally) contrast sharply with those common elsewhere. In the United States children take for granted that they are the center of attention, and that the great objective of society and economy is to satisfy their wants. They do not stand in awe of parents; often they do not appear to respect them. They take for granted that they have a right to the family car, that they have a right to preempt whatever space is available for entertainment, that they have a right to make as much noise as they please in public as in private. In the middle classes they take for granted that their parents will finance them through four years of college, and beyond, if necessary. They take for granted, too, that society will cater to their needs and television to their interests; that newspapers and magazines will provide them with the reading they want; that vast industries—the sports industry, the music and juke box industry, even the automobile industry, will adapt their wares to them. They assume that they are exempt from most of the restrictions and limitations which their elders must observe, that conduct is permitted them that is not permitted those who have the misfortune to be either younger or older. These attitudes are sometimes attributed to the influence of the famous Dr. Benjamin Spock, who preached, to millions of mothers, a policy of "permissiveness," but in fact the roots of these attitudes are far deeper.

Youth—as a thousand novels remind us—is always "alienated" from its elders; in the United States the alienation is, if not deeper, certainly more ostentatious than in most other societies. "Never trust anyone over thirty" is the cant phrase of the new generation, and it expresses, for all its extravagance, a widespread mood among the young. What is the explanation of the peculiar alienation of the youth of the sixties? It is, of course, the sense of outrage against the evils for which the young hold their elders responsible: the Vietnam war, the waste of billions of dollars on armaments while social services starve, the dominance, and even predominance, of the military in the conduct of domestic and foreign affairs, the spectacle of racial injustice on all sides, the ever-sharper contrast between affluence and poverty in what calls itself the richest of nations, the blight of the cities, the destruction of the environment by corporate greed and technological irresponsibility. Much of this has, however, been familiar for many years. What gives cogency and thrust to the current revolt is the sense of frustration and impotence produced by bigness and by the impersonality of science and technology. As the young cannot control or humanize either government or technology, they prefer—many of them—to destroy them as the Luddites of nineteenth-century England smashed the new textile machinery which had deprived them of their jobs in protest against the

127

The Jacob A. Riis Collection, Museum of the City of New York

Pietro Learning to Write. Photograph by Jacob A. Riis. For immigrants, the United States became a place where traditional expectations were reversed, and the old learned from the young.

readiness of a heartless society to discard human beings and replace them with machines.

In the eighteenth century it was universally conceded that the standards of sexual morals were higher in America than in the old world, and few French or English visitors failed to remark, with varying degrees of gratification, that in America girls went everywhere unchaperoned without danger or loss of character and that infidelity in marriage was almost unknown. The first of these characteristics persists—the chaperone is still unfamiliar on the American scene—but divorce statistics suggest that in the incidence of marital infidelity the United States has caught up with the rest of the world.

Investigation into the general patterns of sexual conduct in the United States and western Europe indicates that sexual mores are determined by religion, class, and education rather than by nationality or geography. There are, however, cultural variations, and perhaps—as suggested by Russia and China—ideological ones. Religion seems to play a less significant role in conditioning sexual conduct in the United States than in many other countries: Protestants, Catholics, and Jews all conduct themselves about the same way. Thus, too, there are fewer "class" patterns in sexual conduct in America than in, let us say, Britain, and the Kinsey reports on the sexual conduct of Americans—the most nearly scientific that are available—simply substitute the criterion of "education" for that of "class" in distinguishing categories of sexual conduct.

It is in the psychological rather than the physiological arena that an American pattern of sex relations emerges. Thus Americans developed a more complex "dating" pattern in the subculture of the young than was to be found elsewhere. Not physical but social sexual relations begin earlier here than in Europe. There is no attempt to keep boys and girls apart during the adolescent years as is so common in middle-class European societies; on the contrary it is assumed that they should be thrown together as much as possible. Thus while adolescent boys and girls go to separate schools in Europe and Latin America, here coeducation (as it is quaintly called) is all but universal in both high school and college: the few colleges that had been reserved for students of one sex are now rapidly shifting over to coeducation. More than elsewhere, sex is social rather than sentimental or erotic: a contest in, or a demonstration of, success, rather than of sexual prowess. As Margaret Mead puts it:

> . . . the boy who longs for a date is not longing for a girl. He is longing to be in a situation, mainly public, where he will be seen by others to have a girl, and the right kind of girl, who dresses well and pays attention. He takes her out as he takes out his new car, but more impersonally because the car is his for good but the girl is his only for the evening. (*Male and Female.*)*

*© 1949 Margaret Mead.

This pattern is changing now, for the young, who apparently mature one or two years earlier than they did in the nineteenth century, also seem to form permanent attachments, both sentimental and sexual, at an earlier age. But for the older generation it is probably still true that the pattern is not Don Juan but the Jay Gatsby of F. Scott Fitzgerald's *Great Gatsby* whose girl was a social ornament and, in a curious way, evidence of respectability. It is suggestive that though American men probably have as many extra-marital affairs as do those of other countries, the institution of "a mistress"—an institution rooted in a class society—has never been accepted. Where, in the eighteenth century, and even in the nineteenth, it was taken for granted that monarchs and princes maintained mistresses, such conduct would have been fatal to an American President or to any man with political ambitions.

Sex plays a more prominent role in the American economy than in the economy of other countries: the omnipresence of sex in advertising is almost conclusive evidence of this. Nowhere else is sex so generally exploited, and it is an exploitation that is taken for granted by the American public. It intrudes from every page of popular magazines and every television screen; it sells cigarettes, automobiles, books, and vacations to Florida or the Caribbean; and every item that goes to make up the consumer's paradise is supposed to be enhanced when related, however vaguely, with beautiful girls and virile young men.

In an age when moral habits and standards are undergoing convulsive change, the most conspicuous is in the realm of sexual relations. Doubtless some of the new permissiveness in sex was a reaction to the long background of Puritanism and repression: thus Americans seem to take the practical abandonment of censorship harder than do most other peoples, and American paperback and magazine shops now purvey a greater variety of salacious literature than can be found elsewhere outside Denmark or Sweden, while magazines preaching sexual emancipation have become almost required reading in colleges, and perhaps in high schools too. Nudity is taken for granted now in the theatre and in films, and even on the beach and the college campus, where it is rather a technique whereby the young can assert their freedom from the hypocrisies of their elders and their contempt for the establishment than an indulgence in license. Earlier sexual maturity, the practical disappearance of parental (and academic) controls, the rejection of traditional standards, and the efficacy of "the pill" have combined to make chastity seem very old-fashioned indeed, and to put a premium on sex as an exercise in individuality and freedom.

A thousand sex and marriage manuals, a thousand college and university courses in sex and the family, testify to the fact that for all their seeming sophistication, sex is, for a good number of Americans, as much problem as pleasure. Certainly no other people talk so much about sex, probably no other worry so much about it, as the Americans.

Collection of the Whitney Museum of American Art, New York.
Gift of the Howard and Jean Lipman Foundation, Inc.

Love. Robert Indiana. 1968. Aluminum sculpture.

131

One explanation of this is deeply rooted in the American character: the all but universal expectation of happiness and the assumption of the right to happiness. Americans have traditionally confused the real and the ideal, just as they have traditionally substituted the future for the past. Not the dreary flat in the city, but the white clapboard house with green shutters and half an acre of lawn; not the monotonous clerical job, but the executive suite in some great office building; not the little teachers' college in some rural backwater, but Harvard or Oxford; not the drab round of neighborhood life, but the high society that shimmers out of every television program; not the distrust and the prejudice of relations with other races, but perfect equality—these are what many Americans, especially those of the older generation, take for reality. So in sex and marriage: the reality may be the perfectly ordinary girl next door, but in films and television and advertisements—the things that make up so much of the American world—it is some glamour girl who ends up in Hollywood; the reality may be a perfectly ordinary wife and children, but the ideal remains the dazzling charmer who paves the way for her husband's success, the girl who is going to be another Katharine Hepburn, the boy who will surely grow up just like Eisenhower. And all this has happened often enough so that the ideal cannot be dismissed as a dream.

In the United States marriages are supposed to be made in Heaven— unlike those in the rest of the world where they are arranged by parents. This is a myth but there was, at one time, some truth in the myth. Young Americans had, in the past, a far wider choice in marriage (as in jobs and careers) than other youth. They were not confined to the boy or girl on the same farm, in the same village, or—what is more important— of the same social class and the same religious faith. Not at all. They could—and can—range widely over the whole country, and neither class, wealth, nor religion has presented any institutionalized barriers to love, though race very definitely has.

Marriages which are thus "for love" should presumably be more permanent than those "of convenience." It does not, however, work out that way. On the contrary, statistics show that the American divorce rate is rather higher than that of western Europe. In nineteenth-century America, marriage was a pretty permanent affair, but in the last two generations divorces have increased fourfold: the year 1967 recorded slightly less than two million marriages and somewhat over half a million divorces—a ratio of more than one divorce for every four marriages. The explanation for this high divorce rate is a complicated one: earlier marriages, the emancipation of women, an affluent society, changing social attitudes towards divorce, easier divorce laws, and so forth. One important ingredient is the familiar American conviction that nothing is ever final. If one college does not work, there are hundreds of others to which one may transfer; if one job, or career, proves disappointing, there are always other jobs and other careers, and access to them is easy. If life in New York or Chicago is difficult, there is always Texas or Florida or California, where you can start over again under better auspices. Americans are not bound by fate, or by their mistakes—that is the lesson of history: they can find a new country, enter a new profession, make a new life. They apply, many of them, the same reasoning to marriage—not only those who divorce and re-marry, but the society which condones this and, more, regards it as unexceptionable.

This notion that one is not the victim of one's own mistakes is part of the larger notion that everyone has a right to happiness and to success. Just as the road to public success is always open—the path to the executive suite, to the professional chair, to television stardom, the governor's mansion—so the path to private success is always open. Americans are not the victims of fate, or of a closed social system; they are not even the victims of their mistakes, for America is the land of the second chance.

recommended reading

*Anderson, Elin L. *We Americans: A Study of Cleavage in an American City*. New York: Russell & Russell, 1967.
*Bromfield, Louis. *The Green Bay Tree*. New York: Grosset & Dunlap, 1927. OP
*Calhoun, Arthur W. *Social History of the American Family*. 3 volumes. New York: Barnes & Noble, 1960.
Erikson, Erik H. *Childhood and Society*. Revised edition. New York: W. W. Norton & Company (Norton College edition), 1964.
Farrell, James T. *Studs Lonigan*. New York: New American Library (Signet Books).
*Furnas, Joseph C. *The Americans: A Social History of the United States, 1587-1914*. New York: G. P. Putnam's Sons, 1969.
Gorer, Geoffrey. *The American People, a Study in National Character*. Revised edition. New York: W. W. Norton & Company, 1964.
Hechinger, Grace and Fred M. *Teen-Age Tyranny*. Greenwich, Conn.: Fawcett World Library (Premier Books), 1964.
*Hsu, Francis L. *American and Chinese: Two Ways of Life*. New York: Abelard-Schuman, 1953.
Kinsey, Alfred C., et al. *Sexual Behavior in the Human Female*. New York: Pocket Books.
*———. *Sexual Behavior in the Human Male*. Philadelphia: W. B. Saunders Company, 1948.
Lerner, Max. *America as a Civilization*. 2 volumes. New York: Simon and Schuster (Clarion Books), 1967.
Lynd, Robert S. and Helen M. *Middletown*. New York: Harcourt, Brace & World (Harvest Books).
———. *Middletown in Transition: A Study in Cultural Conflicts*. New York: Harcourt, Brace & World (Harvest Books).
Mead, Margaret. *Male and Female*. New York: Dell Publishing Company (Laurel Leaf Library), 1968.
Myrdal, Gunnar. *An American Dilemma: The Negro Problem and Modern Democracy*. 2 volumes. New York: Harper & Row (Harper Torchbooks).

° Hard-cover edition. Titles not so marked are paperback editions.
  OP indicates the book is out of print.

Riesman, David. *Individualism Reconsidered and Other Essays*. New York: Free Press, 1954.

———— et al. *The Lonely Crowd: A Study of the Changing American Character*. Revised edition. New Haven, Conn.: Yale University Press, 1950.

Roth, Philip. *Portnoy's Complaint*. New York: Bantam Books, 1970.

*Schlesinger, Arthur M., Sr. *Learning How to Behave: A Historical Study of American Etiquette Books*. New York: Cooper Square Publishers, 1968.

*Scudder, Townsend. *Concord: American Town*. Boston: Little, Brown & Company, 1947. OP

Tarkington, Booth. *Alice Adams*. New York: New American Library (Signet Books).

Thrasher, Frederic M. *The Gang: A Study of 1,313 Gangs in Chicago*. Chicago: University of Chicago Press (Phoenix Books), 1963.

West, James. *Plainville, U.S.A.* New York: Columbia University Press, 1945.

Whyte, William F. *Street Corner Society: The Social Structure of an Italian Slum*. Revised edition. Chicago: University of Chicago Press, 1955.

* Hard-cover edition. Titles not so marked are paperback editions.
  OP indicates the book is out of print.

9. education—lower and higher

> Today education is perhaps the most important function of the state and local governments. Compulsory school attendance laws and the great expenditures for education both demonstrate our recognition of the importance of education in our democratic society. It is required in the performance of our most basic public responsibilities. It is the very foundation of good citizenship. Today it is a principle instrument in awakening the child to cultural values, in preparing him for later professional training, and in helping him to adjust normally to his environment. In these days it is doubtful that any child may be expected to succeed in life if he is denied the opportunity of an education.

So said Chief Justice Earl Warren in his epoch-making decision of May 17, 1954, ordering an end to the segregation of whites and blacks in the public schools of the land. The argument, with its reference to the relationship of education to citizenship, culture, special skills, social adjustment and success in life itself, is an echo of hundreds of earlier arguments which were first made over three centuries ago in the 1642 and 1647 school laws of the Massachusetts Bay Colony, and have echoed without interruption ever since.

There are few American institutions more difficult for outsiders to understand than education. This is in part because American education *seems* so much like European—which, in one form or another has influenced education in every other part of the world—but is in fact very different. It is different not only in organization and administration, but until quite recently, in spirit, because of the magnitude and variety of the American educational enterprise.

From the beginning American education was rooted in old world experience; how could it be otherwise? The Puritan settlers in Massachusetts brought with them a belief that education was fundamental to religion and to service for the commonwealth and a familiarity with English schools and universities. Over one hundred of the early settlers of the Bay Colony were graduates of Cambridge and Oxford universities: Boston and Salem probably had the highest proportion of university graduates of any community in the world in the mid-seventeenth century. The Puritans set up schools as instinctively as they set up churches: the Boston Latin School in 1635, Harvard University in 1636, and, thereafter, all through the colonial era, schools, academies, and colleges by the hundreds. Within a few

135

"A Prospect of the Colledges (*sic*) in Cambridge in New England." Engraving by William Burgis, ca. 1739. Harvard University was founded in Cambridge, Massachusetts, in 1636, just 25 years after the first English settlers arrived.

years of their arrival in the American wilderness they enacted school laws which required every community of fifty households to maintain schools that taught reading and writing to boys and girls alike, and every community of one hundred households to provide an education that would fit young men for university. There was nothing quite like this elsewhere in the world. None of the other American colonists, neither the English in Virginia nor the Dutch in New York nor the Germans in Pennsylvania, showed anything like the zeal of the New Englanders for education. Yet everywhere the American colonists created schools and brought in school masters. By the time of the Revolution public schools, charity schools, church schools, academies, and, for the rich, tutors, were teaching children to read and write and do sums, and perhaps a bit of Latin, and scattered through the American wilderness were eight colleges. Illiteracy—certainly among men—was almost unknown. Higher education, to be sure, was nowhere as high as at Edinburgh or Leyden or Göttingen, but for all their simplicity American colleges produced, in the second half of the eighteenth century, one of the most remarkable groups of statesmen the world has ever known. And already something of an American pattern of education was emerging: if there were few scholars or erudites, there were correspondingly few who were uneducated. Most American men, and doubtless women, too, read their Bible, the current almanac, and the newspaper, and the standards of public discussion were as high as those to be found among the best educated classes anywhere, then or since.

All the early schools, from the elementary to the college, were modeled on those of the mother country, whether England, Scotland, or Germany. Teachers and clergymen were often imported, and so too the school books, and all the schools inculcated religion as well as learning. But more fruitful than the borrowing was the originality, more striking than imitation was independence. American schools, after all, not only flourished in an environment very different from that of the old world; they had very different functions imposed upon them, and different objectives.

Schools everywhere are barometers of social philosophy; nowhere did they respond more sensitively to the climate of social opinion than in America, and this for two elementary but decisive reasons. First, Americans were, from the beginning, both equalitarian and democratic. There were no aristocrats in America and, except for indentured servants whose status was temporary, no legal classes among the whites. No distinction was made between the children of the rich and the poor, or the children of different denominations. It was assumed that every child should be educated both for his spiritual and his social welfare. Schools therefore belonged not to a privileged elite, as so commonly in other nations, but to everybody, and they were expected to respond to the needs of everybody. Second, Americans lacked, from the beginning, such institutions as the monarchy, the church, the aristocracy, the learned professions, the academies, the guilds, which elsewhere carried on so much of the educational enterprise. Lacking these, Americans turned instinctively to their schools, and required them to take on the duties performed by these institutions abroad—required them, in short, to do whatever society wanted done.

This meant, at a very early stage, a shift in emphasis from the "academic" to the practical. In the mid-eighteenth century, educational leaders like Benjamin Franklin were challenging the value of the study of Latin and Greek, and urging instead that children be taught accounting and navigation and surveying and similar practical subjects. Franklin's friend, Dr. Benjamin Rush of Philadelphia, stated flatly, "The study of the Latin and Greek languages is improper in the present state of society and government in the United States" for, so long as "Greek and Latin are the only avenues to science, education will always be confined to a few people." Far better, he added, to concentrate on science, modern languages, and practical subjects.

Because American society was equalitarian and its needs immediate and practical, American schools were—and still are—required to do many things not expected of schools in Britain or on the Continent: indeed the student of American educational history is sometimes tempted to conclude that formal education was one of the least important functions of American schools. They were expected to train the young for self-government and citizenship. They were called upon to create out of heterogeneous elements a homogeneous community—a people who would speak the same language, respond to the same history, know the same body of literature, folklore, and legend, admire the same heroes and detest the same villains—and thus to help create a sense of nationalism and cement national unity. This involved teaching not only school children but their parents as well, and over the years it has been the school that, through the children who passed through its intellectual and moral and social training, has been the most effective of all agencies for creating a reasonably homogeneous society. It is not wholly fortuitous that it is the Negro, long denied any schooling, and then fobbed off with inferior schooling, who has the least sense of membership in the American community.

Finally, schools were supposed to practice, as well as preach, the principle of equality and, within the white community, they did this with considerable success. Almost all American schools are public: only within recent years have private schools achieved some popularity, and this chiefly in New England and large Eastern cities. This meant that all American children received pretty much the same kind of education in the same kind of schools and from the same kind of teachers. All were subjected to substantially the same educational processes and disciplines in the classroom. All mingled in the school playgrounds, while on the athletic fields rewards and popularity went to achievement regardless of race or faith or social standing. This was not planned, nor was it administered by any central bureau—for American education is very much a state and

138

local affair—but it grew out of common soil. This contribution to equality among the white children of the country has been one of the more important functions of the school and, correspondingly, the inequality which Negro children experienced because of segregation or discrimination has been the most egregious failure of the school.

Even in our own day when these historic functions have been largely fulfilled, and responsibility for their ultimate fulfillment is (or should be) lodged elsewhere, schools continue to be held responsible for a great many nonacademic services, and students continue to engage in numerous nonacademic activities. Imagine a French lycée teaching automobile driving; imagine a Kenyan secondary school teaching social dancing; imagine a Mexican high school providing instruction in cheerleading! For that matter imagine the children of these schools held responsible for "school government," or editing the school paper, or maintaining school bands and symphonies.

From the beginning, too, schools loomed larger on the social horizon in America than elsewhere—larger even than in Scotland, Holland, or Germany, countries long zealous for public education. As the school itself was expected to adjust to society, so society was called on to adjust to the school. As the school performed numerous nonacademic functions, so it was the object of interest and center of involvement for many diverse elements in society. In a curious sense education was, and remains, the American religion. Americans long built their high schools and colleges to look like churches: note the Gothic and classical architecture of many a city high school, the Gothic towers of Yale and Duke and Chicago universities and scores of others. Schools are used not only as educational but as community centers, and much of the ceremony and ritual elsewhere associated with religion (or even with the military) is, in the United States, associated with public schools and colleges: thus the ritual of graduation with "academic robes," the ritual of school bands with gorgeous uniforms, the elaborate ritual at football and basketball games of school songs and cheering under the guidance of "cheerleaders" with only the dress differing from acolytes of the temple. Adults involve themselves in the affairs of their schools through the extensive network of Parent-Teacher Associations, with a membership of some fifteen million, and many other community organizations, such as the Dad's Clubs, dedicated, most of them, to encouraging school athletics. Where else does education play so large a role in politics—witness the California elections of 1969 which turned largely on attitudes toward the schools and the universities of the state? How striking that the man who has some claim to be considered the greatest figure ever to occupy the White House—Thomas Jefferson— was also the leading American educator of his time, and that the leading American philosopher—John Dewey—made education the basis and substance of his philosophy. Controversy over education is, in our time, what controversy over religion was in the seventeenth century. It is pretty safe to say that there is more talk about education and a more voluminous literature dealing with education in the United States than in the rest of the world combined.

Doubtless the most impressive evidence of the role of education in American life is the sheer magnitude of the enterprise. All American states require attendance in school until the age of sixteen, and some until eighteen. Altogether over fifty-six million Americans are in school—more than the entire population of Britain or France. Of these some thirty-five million children are in elementary schools, fourteen million in the secondary, or high, schools, and a staggering seven million in "higher" education, a phrase which embraces everything after high school. A vast army of over two million teachers (not counting half a million university teachers) ministers to these millions of students. Total expenditures for all these educational enterprises are hard to come by, what with the mixture of public and private school systems, but they are not far from sixty billion dollars a year. Expenditure per pupil, which was thirteen dollars in 1870, has increased to almost five hundred dollars a century later: even allowing for the decline in the value of the dollar, that is a pretty spectacular increase.

I n the almost two centuries since Independence we can distinguish three major eras of educational progress and reform, but during all of this period the principles which guided the progress and animated the reform remained substantially the same.

With the achievement of independence education came into its own: the Founding Fathers who laid down the principles and created the institutions of government which still flourish, laid down, at the same time, the principles and institutions of education which still flourish. They were, after all, themselves educators, persuaded, all of them, that the new experiment in self-government could not flourish except with an enlightened citizenry. Franklin, the oldest of them, and at once the most authentically native and the most cosmopolitan, led the way: he established an academy which grew into a university; started a circulating library; founded what became the American Philosophical Society and presided over its deliberations; helped establish academies for the Pennsylvania Germans and for frontiersmen, and, through his newspapers and famous almanacs, conducted a kind of adult education program throughout the colonies. Dr. Rush, the leading medical man of his time, and a statesman, too, busied himself incessantly with the founding of academies and colleges, the development of practical vocational education, and the encouragement of education for girls. Noah Webster, remembered chiefly for his dictionary,

Noah Webster, 1753-1843, "The Schoolmaster of the Republic." Lithograph
printed by Milton Bradley Co. ca. 1891. His dictionary, revised many times,
is still the standard for American English.

devoted his whole life to education and justly earned the title "schoolmaster to America"; not only dictionaries but schoolbooks of all kinds—spellers, readers, histories—poured from his study and spread over the land. George Washington—like Franklin innocent of any formal education—was a man of learning and interested himself in the creation of a national university; in his will he left endowments to two academies, one of which became Washington and Lee University.

Of all the Founding Fathers it was Thomas Jefferson who contributed most to American educational philosophy and practice. He pushed through important reforms provided in the common schools of Virginia; presided over governmental decision to support education in the west by grants of public land; started the Library of Congress; and, in his old age built almost single-handed, the first great state university in America—the University of Virginia. More than any other academic institution in the modern world it was, and is, the lengthened shadow of one man: Jefferson wrote the charter and pushed it through the legislature, designed all the buildings, laid out the grounds, collected the books for the library, drafted the curriculum, chose the professors and the students, and based the institution, as he wrote, "on the illimitable freedom of the human mind."

We can distinguish five basic principles governing the relation of American education to the commonwealth. First was the most elementary of all: that universal education was the only sound foundation for a republic. Heretofore the rulers of nations had been the rich, the well born, the powerful. They were usually, though not always, educated, but their views were limited by their own class interests. Americans had launched themselves upon an experiment where the common people would be the rulers. That experiment could not succeed unless the people were as well educated as their rulers had been. "No other sure foundation can be devised for the preservation of freedom and happiness" wrote Jefferson, and it was a principle which all Americans accepted. More, they wrote it into their constitutions, and into the Northwest Ordinance of 1787 which became a kind of constitution for all the new territories that were to be added to the original thirteen states: "Religion, morality, and knowledge, being necessary to good government and the happiness of mankind, schools and the means of education shall forever be encouraged." And that this admonition might be translated into practice, they provided that one section of public land in each township be set aside for the support of education, and two townships in each state for the support of a University. This pattern was followed in all the states of the old Northwest and, in 1862, was written into the Morrill Act which provided for the creation of "land-grant" colleges in every state of the Union.

Closely connected with this basic rationale for education—that without it democracy could not succeed—was the second principle, that education alone could ensure equality. "Education," Samuel Adams wrote to his cousin John, "will draw together the sons of rich and the poor, among whom it makes no distinction; it will cultivate the natural genius, and reward its patrons and benefactors by shedding its benign influence on the public mind." For education, as American understood it, not only contributed to equality; it was, itself, equality. By making schooling from the elementary school to the university available to all boys (advanced education for girls was still to come) it placed all of them at once on the same level, gave to all of them an equal chance.

A third principle, peculiarly Jeffersonian, was that popular education was essential to progress. The idea of progress was very much in the air of the eighteenth century, but the American concept of progress differed in important respects from that held in Europe where progress (as well as education) was thought of in aristocratic terms: to Europeans progress was the advance of arts, letters, philosophy, and science, a prospect ravishing to the upper classes but of little interest to the great mass of mankind. In America progress was a far more practical matter. It meant draining the swamps, clearing the forests, getting rid of the insects and reptiles that threatened man, and winning the land for cultivation. It meant establishing a government that would rule justly—"a wise and frugal government," as Jefferson put it, "that shall restrain men from injuring one another, shall leave them otherwise free to regulate their own pursuits of industry and improvement, and shall not take from the mouth of labor the bread it has earned." And it meant freeing man from the tyrannies and superstitions that had always heretofore weighed him down and making it possible for him to develop to the very limit of his natural capacities. None of this, Jefferson knew, could be achieved without education; most of it, he hoped, might be achieved with education.

A fourth principle that we associate particularly with Jefferson was the separation of education and religion—a natural consequence, this, of the separation of church and state which Jefferson had carried through in Virginia and which was to be one of the basic principles of the new nation. Yet the notion that education could be divorced from religion was new and seemed dangerous: How, after all, inculcate morality in the young without teaching religion?—and by religion was meant, of course, Protestant Christianity. The divorce of religion from education did not come all at once: indeed some vestiges of that ancient association still linger on to plague constitutional lawyers in our own day. But the basic decision was made, and accepted, from the beginning: that schools are erected, financed, administered, and taught, by the state, not by the church.

Noah Webster of Connecticut, rather than Jefferson, was chiefly responsible for a fifth principle or practice—education as a foundation for a *national* culture. The new nation lacked, after all, many of the common denominators which older nations possessed as a matter of course, and—what is more—it was confronted by a threat of racial and linguistic heterogeneity which seriously threatened social and cultural unity. How provide the far-flung, scattered, and miscellaneous peoples of the new

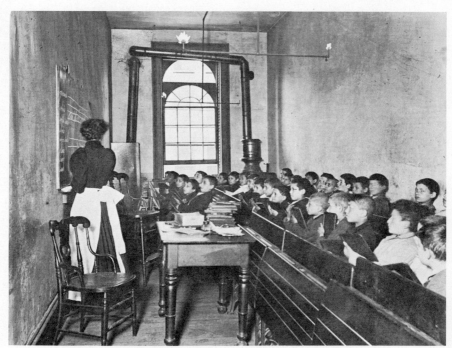

A Class in the Condemned Essex Market School. Photograph by Jacob A. Riis. Public schools assumed the responsibility for assimilating and "Americanizing" the children of immigrants.

nation with a common language, accent, and idiom, with a common literature and a common history, a common body of stories and legends, a common past? How, indeed, but through the schools. "The author," wrote Webster in the preface to his most famous book, the *Blue-backed Speller* (1783):

> wishes to promote the honor and prosperity of the confederated republics of America. This country must in some future time be as distinguished by the superiority of her literary improvements as she already is by her constitutions.

To provide for the "prosperity," to advance the "literary improvements" Webster flooded the country with a seemingly inexhaustible stream of readers, spellers, histories, and dictionaries, all of them preaching the gospel of Americanism. Generation after generation of American school children, from Maine to Georgia, from Maryland to Ohio and Iowa and beyond, went to school to Webster and through him and his disciples came to speak with a common accent, and to absorb a common body of literature and stories and legends. And what Webster began in the late eighteenth century, the McGuffey brothers, whose *Readers* sold, eventually, over a hundred million copies, completed in the next century.

Jefferson himself—he lived until 1826—linked up with a new generation of educational reformers emerging in every section of the nation but chiefly in New England. Most of them were transcendentalists, deeply influenced by the new educational practices and theories of Germany and France, though intensely American and determined to create mechanisms which would make Jefferson's ideals real in a new and different America. They did not modify the Jeffersonian inheritance, but extended it and rationalized it. They were confronted not with a pastoral America, but with one rapidly becoming urbanized and industrialized and with ever larger ingredients of foreign immigrants. Their problem was essentially a practical one. They were responsible for persuading state legislatures to improve public education in practical ways like building better school houses, providing for longer school years, paying something like a living wage to schoolteachers, and encouraging equal provisions for the education of girls and boys. They were responsible for establishing the first women's colleges in the world, for creating teachers training colleges (modeled on the "normal" schools of Germany and France), and for launching educational journals. Thus they began that professionalization of education which has been carried somewhat further in the United States than elsewhere. Along with this practical program went idealism—an extension, into advanced and even higher education, of the principle that every child was entitled to as much education as he could absorb. As Horace Mann—who put his imprint on this generation as Jefferson had on the earlier—wrote in one of his magisterial reports:

> The will of God . . . places the *right* of every child that is born into the world to such a degree of education as will enable him, and predispose him, to

145

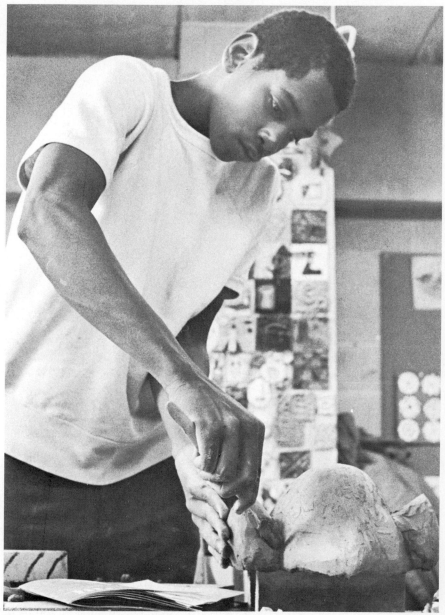

Hull House Association, Chicago, Illinois

Classes in sculpture, Parkway Community Center, Hull House, Chicago. The pioneer American social worker Jane Addams founded Hull House in Chicago in 1889, one of the first of many "settlement houses" in the United States designed to serve the neglected children of the slums.

146

perform all domestic, civil, social, and moral duties upon the same clear ground of natural law and equity as it places a child's *right,* upon his first coming into the world, to receive that shelter, protection, and nourishment which are necessary to his bodily existence. And so far it is from being a wrong or a hardship to demand of the possessors of property their respective shares for the prosecution of their divinely-ordained work, that they themselves are guilty of the most far-reaching injustice who seek to evade the contribution.

The third great era of educational reform and reconstruction was dominated by three remarkable social philosophers: the sociologist Lester Ward, the welfare worker Jane Addams, and the philosopher John Dewey. What this trio did was to provide scientific and sociological underpinning for the idealistic and transcendental principles of the past, and to adapt earlier educational principles and practices to the harsh realities of an urban, industrial America.

With Lester Ward we associate three ideas of far-reaching significance. First is the scientific principle that education is, in a broad way, the method by which mankind takes control of the evolutionary process and, by controlling it, bring about progress. Second, the democratic principle that talent, even genius, is evenly distributed in all classes of children; that in every hundred thousand boys and girls of whatever sex, color, race, social or economic condition, there are an equal number of potential scholars, scientists, musicians, artists, jurists, and so forth; and that it is the business of the state to discover these potentials and to educate the children so that they can be realized. And third—born out of these two— the conviction that education is the great panacea which will, in the end, make it possible to solve the problems that afflict mankind and to organize society and government on rational and scientific lines. To these primarily educational ideas should be added a fourth practical argument designed to strengthen the public school and university system: that government can do better than private enterprise anything that it puts its mind and resources to—a conclusion which has not yet won universal agreement among the American people.

Jane Addams, in many ways the greatest woman in American public life, was not only the leading practitioner of social welfare work of her generation, but an original and profound social philosopher. She created in the slums of Chicago in 1889 the famous Hull House and made it not only the very model of a social settlement house, but a great experimental laboratory for education. She was the first social philosopher to confront squarely the problem that now troubles Americans so deeply— that of dealing with the poor and neglected children of the slums whose backwardness reflects no lack of native ability, but an almost complete lack of background and denial of nourishment and training of any kind. Like Lester Ward, Jane Addams was confident that these children of the slums had potentially the same talents as the children of the rich, and, earlier than any other educator, she devised practical means of

147

discovering these talents and quickening them into life. To discover and encourage the social capacities of these children, she provided at Hull House facilities where they could act, play the piano and the violin, model and paint and draw, do carpentry or weave textiles, and find other outlets for their creative urge. She provided, too, one of the first school gymnasia in the country and the first "fresh air" vacations for city children. No wonder the leaders of American social and educational reform beat a path to the door of Hull House where they might find Jane Addams writing a letter to the President of the United States or to the mother of some immigrant who could not himself write, planning a campaign to persuade the state legislature to set up juvenile courts, or changing a baby's diapers. Among those who came to pay tribute and to learn were the economist John R. Commons, the sociologist E. A. Ross, and the philosopher John Dewey.

In her wise and practical fashion Jane Addams had anticipated much that John Dewey was to preach—Dewey who, with the publication of *School and Society* in 1899, was launched on his long career as the greatest and most influential of modern educational philosophers. Dewey had been rigorously trained in professional philosophy but came early to the conclusion that education was not a subordinate branch of philosophy, rather philosophy was a branch of education. It was as an educator that he made his greatest impact, not only in the United States but in China, Japan, Russia, and Turkey, for his fame and his influence were more nearly world-wide than that of any other modern philosopher.

Dewey's special contribution to American education was, in a sense, to modernize Jean-Jacques Rousseau. Like Rousseau he insisted that education was central to all other activities of society, a process of living in which the child and the young man and woman played a leading part. He saw education not as a preparation for life, but as life itself; the school not as a preparation for society but as an integral part of society. Like the good pragmatist that he was, he knew that truth was not a property of some discipline to be imposed on man, but that it emerged out of experience, and that education, from the elementary to the most advanced, created its own truths as it went along, and different truths for every student. It was characteristic of his way of thinking that when he came to the University of Chicago in the mid-nineties, he promptly set up a school which he called simply "The Laboratory," for he thought of the school as a laboratory as he thought of life itself as a laboratory which tested and discovered new ways of thought and conduct.

Rousseau had educated his Emile by exposing him to nature. Pestalozzi had made physical exercise central to the training of the young, and Froebel had taught children to take care of a garden—hence Kindergarten—as a method of learning about nature and life. Dewey translated these functional approaches to education into modern idiom, adapting them to the needs of children in an industrial society. He too made the

148

child the center of the teaching and learning process, introduced him to simple tasks like cooking and woodwork and to the discipline of the playground, making "the child's own instincts and powers furnish the material and give the starting point for all education." All this came to be called "progressive" education, but it might better have been called "romantic" or "democratic" (what is more romantic than the concept of democracy?), for it was rooted in the notion of the equal potentialities of all children and insisted upon the equal obligation of society to all its young. "What the best and wisest parent wants for his own child," said Dewey, in one of his most memorable axioms, "that the community must want for all its children."

In the half century since the First World War, Americans have transferred the experiment in mass education from the elementary arena to the arena of "higher" education—as observed earlier, a term which means education beyond the high school. In the nineteenth century, Americans had endorsed the principle that every child had a right to an education, and that it was the duty of the state to provide this, but the concept of an "education" was limited and the standard of "duty" not very high. As late as 1900 there were only seven hundred thousand children in the public high schools of the entire United States (plus several hundred thousand in private academies and parochial schools), and illiteracy stood at a sobering 11 per cent of the population; the college population for that year was about a quarter of a million. In the twentieth century the concept of public obligation was expanded to include the young of both sexes and all races and the notion of education to embrace education and professional training at the highest level. Most Americans now take for granted that they have a right to as much education as they can use. It must be added, however, that the "right" is circumscribed by economic considerations. State universities rarely charge tuition, but do charge "fees" which are often substantial. Private institutions—and one-third of American university students attend these—collect heavy tuition charges. Some of these are met by liberal "scholarship" funds, others by various state and federal aid programs but the burden of private education remains heavy and is growing heavier every year. It is a curious commentary on the American passion for education that it is, after all, tempered by this practical and serious limitation, while in countries like France, Germany, and Denmark, which do not express a similar enthusiasm, university education is completely free.

The sheer magnitude of the university enterprise in the United States is even more astonishing than the magnitude of elementary and secondary schooling. Proportionately there are far more students in universities today than there were in high schools at the turn of the century: a grand total, in 1969, of not far from seven million attending something over two thousand institutions that range from junior colleges to research institutes. Suggestive of the future is the fact that while the total number of students enrolled in colleges and universities doubled every twenty years between 1900 and 1960, the number has now doubled in the ten years 1960 to 1969. Almost half of all young people between the ages of eighteen and twenty-one now attend college or university; in the more prosperous states like Connecticut and California the proportion is substantially higher.

The explanation of the American readiness to support this immense educational enterprise can be found in much the same set of considerations that explains earlier support of elementary and secondary education: not only the principle that education is a right to which all young people are entitled, but the more practical consideration that in many respects the college is today what the high school was half a century ago. In much of the nineteenth century a high school education was sufficient for most of the tasks which society and the economy required. That is no longer the case. Almost everything, now, requires expertise—an expertise greater than can be obtained in secondary education, an expertise greater even than can be obtained in four years of college: hence the immense growth of graduate and professional education beyond the college. And just as, at an earlier stage, Americans turned to the academies and colleges to do whatever had to be done, so now they turn to the universities and require them to produce the experts to run their complex society and economy.

These considerations have been decisive for the character of the American university. Where in the old world the university developed its own character and functions over a long span of centuries into modern times, in the United States society and government impressed their stamp on the university.

Universities everywhere reflect something of their society, but nowhere so elaborately or so faithfully as in the United States.

Out of this special situation Americans created, quite unconsciously, a new and distinctive kind of university—what Clark Kerr, former president of the University of California, has called the "multiversity." Over a period of six or seven centuries the university had taken three characteristic forms—overlapping, to be sure, but distinct. The original university which emerged in Italy and France in the twelfth and thirteenth centuries, was what we would now call a professional school, designed to train theologians, doctors, lawyers, and philosophers who were usually teachers. This was the university that spread so swiftly throughout Europe from the thirteenth to the nineteenth centuries and to the new world as well. At Oxford and Cambridge there developed within this original pattern, a second pattern. These universities were rural rather than urban, and therefore residential; they took a collegiate form. Their function was

150

Schoolroom. Artist unknown. 1894.

not only to train the young for the professions, but to preserve the heritage of the past and transmit it to succeeding generations and to prepare them morally as well as intellectually for the larger duties of government and society. With the opening of Göttingen University in 1737 there emerged a third—and since then dominant—pattern of the university: an institution designed chiefly for carrying on research in order to expand the boundaries of knowledge.

To these three familiar kinds of university Americans have added the multiversity—an institution expected to perform not only all the old familiar functions but, in addition, to cater to all the interests and needs of society and to train in all the skills which society thinks it needs. This very American concept of the federal university was launched by the Act of 1862 creating so-called "land-grant colleges" in every state, designed to stress agriculture and the industrial arts. Where the traditional university had only four faculties, the American university might have (and often does have) a score or more. It was expected to teach all subjects, to prepare for all professions and all careers. It was required to instruct undergraduates in everything from remedial reading to classical archeology, and to train graduate and research students who could in turn go out and staff other universities. It was expected to prepare not only doctors, lawyers, and theologians, but engineers, architects, librarians, nurses, foresters, farmers, bankers, businessmen, school teachers, football coaches, and—for those who had no clear aim—"to prepare for life." It was also expected to carry on research in all conceivable and some inconceivable fields, scholarly and practical, and to serve government and society at every level—the local community, the state, and the nation. And for good measure it was assumed that it would provide moral and social guidance to the young, act as a matrimonial agency and a psychiatric clinic, and supply culture and entertainment to the public.

What this meant—among other things—was that the universities, especially the public institutions like California, Michigan, Wisconsin, Texas and Pennsylvania State, came to be enormous enterprises less like the traditional university of the old world than like governmental departments, such as Interior, or Health, Education, and Welfare: almost formless, bulging in all directions, spreading resources thin, trying to serve a dozen constituencies. Consider, for example, President Kerr's description of the University of California—he is speaking of the entire state system with its nine constitutent universities: It had, he writes,

> operating expenditures . . . of nearly half a billion dollars, with almost another 100 million for construction; a total employment of over 40,000 people . . . ; operations in over a hundred locations, counting campuses, experiment stations, agricultural and urban extension centers, and projects abroad involving more than fifty countries; nearly 10,000 courses in its catalogues, some form of contact with nearly every industry, nearly every level of government, nearly every person in its region. Vast amounts of expensive equipment were serviced and maintained. Over 4,000 babies were born in its hospitals. It is the world's

largest purveyor of white mice. It will soon have the world's largest primate colony. It will soon also have 100,000 students—30,000 of them at the graduate level; yet much less than one-third of its expenditures are directly related to teaching. It . . . has nearly 200,000 students in extension courses—including one out of every three lawyers and one out of every six doctors in the state. (*The Uses of the University* [New York: Harper Torch Book, 1966], pp. 7-8)

It is the effort to respond to these myriad pressures and demands that explains much of the miscellaneous and incoherent character of higher education in the United States—miscellaneous in external variety, incoherent in internal organization. Here two thousand institutions of "higher learning" reveal almost as many and diverse characteristics as would any two thousand business or governmental enterprises. Some are, by any standards, affluent and distinguished centers of learning; some are liberal arts colleges (an American invention, this, for the liberal arts college as such is unknown in European education) all of whose students are preparing for professional careers or for research. Hundreds are "junior" colleges and community colleges which provide an education equivalent to that of the French lycée, the German gymnasium, or the Swedish high school, though with less rigorous standards than these. Hundreds of vocational schools train farmers and teachers and accountants and nurses for their chosen careers—institutions which, abroad, are rarely attached to a university. The variety is both qualitative and quantitative. There are institutions, like Harvard, with a library of eight million volumes, or California with a glittering galaxy of Nobel Prize winners on its faculty, or the Institute for Advanced Study at Princeton devoted exclusively to research. There are struggling colleges with pitiful libraries of ten or twenty thousand volumes, laboratories inferior to those of a good high school, and students admitted without reference to academic qualifications. There are public universities, and private, and a mixture of the two; while the majority are secular, there are Protestant, Catholic, and Jewish universities. There are great urban universities like Columbia, Chicago, or the University of California at Los Angeles, and small colleges that retain something of their pastoral character, like Amherst, Carleton, or Grinnell.

All this is entirely natural, perhaps inevitable, and it is interesting to note that it is this American type of university that is spreading in the newly emerging nations of Asia and Africa. After all, a nation with two hundred million people needs the most miscellaneous institutions to provide it with the myriad services that it requires, and if it wishes to call these institutions universities, high schools, technical colleges, or normal schools, that is merely one reflection of a classless society. More, there is something to be said for the American practice of mixing various functions in the same institutional container. Europeans will argue that nursing or library training or business are not "university" subjects, and should therefore be banished from the precincts of Minerva to the workaday world. Americans respond, somewhat inconsistently, with three

153

arguments. First, they cheerfully challenge the traditional hierarchy of subjects, arguing that anything is a proper area of study if properly studied. Second, they submit that if you have to train nurses and librarians and businessmen anyway, how much better to train them at a university, where they will be exposed to the atmosphere of learning, where they will have a chance to pick up at least a smattering of "culture," and where they might catch a glimpse of the scientific potentialities of the subjects they are studying. And third, they ask the very hard-headed question why society should not use the institutions that it already has—the campus, the buildings, the libraries and laboratories and playing fields—for whatever it wants done, instead of going to the trouble and expense of building separate institutions for every separate discipline or professional career.

An educational system like a political system, must be judged, in large part, by results. At very considerable expense and with a good deal of waste, American universities seem to get both quantitative and qualitative results. They do provide, somehow, the teachers and accountants, the nurses and librarians, that a fast-growing society needs. They do provide, too, the scientists, the scholars, the jurists and theologians, the poets and musicians (if any institution can be said to provide these). The average of American "higher" education is not nearly as high as the average of English or French, but the peaks are just as high. American jurists can hold their own with the jurists of other nations; American medicine is not inferior to that of Britain or Germany or Sweden; American contributions to the study of classical philology and archaeology are as distinguished as those of any other nation; perhaps 80 per cent of all scientific research in the world is now carried on in the United States. Even the multiversity, for all its bigness and incoherence, seems to get results. As Clark Kerr puts it:

> . . . it has few peers in the preservation and dissemination and examination of the eternal truths; no living peers in the search for new knowledge; and no peers in all history among institutions of higher learning in serving so many of the segments of an advancing civilization. Inconsistent internally as an institution, it is consistently productive. Torn by change, it has the stability of freedom. (*Op. cit.,* p. 45)

Needless to say the intimate relationship of the American university to the community, and to government, is fraught with danger, as is the principle that the university exists to serve the community. One manifestation of that danger is the pressure from government during wartime to force universities to devote their resources to what is always euphemistically called "defense" work. Another is the demand from students that the university be "relevant" to their own interests, to the concerns of their society. For the university is not a servant of its own immediate society; it is the servant of the larger community of learning—the community of the past and the community of the future; it is not a servant merely of its own city or state or nation, but of mankind. Aristocratic societies, ever conscious of their debt to tradition and conscious, too, of their obligation to posterity, are better able to appreciate this than are equalitarian societies. Spectacular violations of this principle of the obligation of the university to the larger community of learning have occurred in countries like Germany, Italy, and Austria when the old, intellectual elite gave way to new rulers with no sense of the past.

There is no doubt that American universities have suffered, and continue to suffer, from the shortsightedness of the society which created them, finances them, and expects service from them. They have been required to accept students who are ill-prepared, sometimes totally unprepared, for the university, and tempted to adapt their standards to these incompetents. They have been asked to teach subjects that not only have little relation to the advancement of learning but often constitute a positive distraction from that advancement. They have been tempted to engage in activities designed to profit interested elements in the community rather than the cause of learning, wasting their substance on gladitorial athletic combats whose only purpose is to entertain or to profit the local community or the alumni. These and other distractions from the central business of teaching and research have been deplorable but not fatal. Far more serious are the demands which government makes upon the university to engage in the wrong kind of research for the wrong reasons. The obvious and dramatic example of this is the pressure from government on the universities to accept State Department or Defense Department contracts for research in areas that are relevant to fighting a war but irrelevant to the proper objectives of a university dedicated to the welfare of mankind. Such pressure is both overt and covert: overt through the demands by regents or trustees that universities accept contracts with the Air Force or the Navy or the State Department; covert in the mixture of pressure and temptation and seduction which Washington is always able to exercise, especially on the smaller and weaker institutions. Much of the current wave of student discontent—and of faculty discontent too— has been directed against government and university policies which prostitute the resources of the university to ends that the best elements in the academic community think either wholly irrelevant or positively unworthy.

One explanation of the special vulnerability of the American university lies in its legal character. Old world universities, though ultimately controlled by the state are for all practical purposes administered by their faculties. In the United States public (or state) universities are legally controlled by boards of regents, often politically appointed or elected, while private institutions are controlled by nonacademic boards of trustees, usually self-perpetuating. The potential for error here is great. But in fact most regents and trustees are men and women who are devoted to their universities and who serve them loyally and disinterestedly, according to their lights. After all, the trustee-regent system, for all its seeming faults, has served American higher education well over the years. The University

White marble garden designed by Japanese-American sculptor and designer
Isamu Noguchi, at the Beinecke Rare Book and Manuscript Library, Yale University.
The library was completed in 1964; Skidmore, Owings & Merrill were the architects.

of Texas, for example, the University of Illinois, the University of California, all run by boards of regents, spend more money on the libraries of their universities than is granted to the libraries of all the universities of Britain combined. And a trusteeship system which has guided the affairs of institutions like Harvard, Yale, and Chicago to their present eminence must be pronounced successful. Yet all this is itself no assurance that regents and trustees will always understand the nature and the functions of the university, or that they will be strong enough to resist pressures from those who do not. In the United States, as elsewhere, there are lamentable instances where boards of regents seem to have betrayed the institutions they were created to protect.

Yet over the years American universities have won a degree of independence and American professors an academic freedom that compare favorably with the situation even in Britain, Holland, or the Scandinavian countries. There are, from time to time, threats to the freedom of the university, but there has never been anything comparable to the seizure and destruction of the university by totalitarian regimes like the Fascist and the Nazi, nor is there as yet anything comparable to the control of the university by student groups so common in the countries of Latin America. If here and there—usually out of ignorance or folly rather than ill will—trustees, or the public, have threatened the freedom of teaching and of research, it can be said that on the whole academic freedom flourishes as prosperously in the United States as anywhere else on the globe. If, in theory, universities are controlled by outside boards and by top-heavy "administrations," in fact, all the best institutions are run by their faculties. Professors everywhere enjoy "tenure"; what is more, they have won freedom to teach what they will as they will, to engage in such research as seems to them valuable, and to publish their findings, and to act in public affairs like any other citizen. And though academic freedom as "student freedom" (lernfreiheit) came late to the United States, students now enjoy a degree of freedom from interference in their private lives by those who act in loco parentis almost as great as that enjoyed by students on the European continent, and they play a substantial, though not a decisive, role in arranging for the education which they pursue. They enjoy, too, as every foreign visitor notes with interest and envy, facilities, services, luxuries all but unknown to students at universities elsewhere in the world. Libraries are always open and available to them; housing is usually adequate and sometimes luxurious; medical, nursing, and psychiatric care is generously provided; and their universities provide them with facilities for theatre, music, art, sports and games, to a degree found almost nowhere else.

recommended reading

Barzun, Jacques. *The American University: How It Runs and Where It Is Going.* New York: Harper & Row (Colophon Books).

*Bestor, Arthur. *Educational Wastelands: The Retreat from Learning in Our Public Schools.* Urbana, Ill.: University of Illinois Press, 1953.

*Commager, Henry S. *The Commonwealth of Learning.* New York: Harper & Row, 1968.

Conant, James B. *The American High School Today.* New York: McGraw-Hill Book Company, 1959.

———. *The Education of American Teachers.* New York: McGraw-Hill Book Company, 1963.

———. *Slums and Suburbs: [A Commentary on Schools in the Metropolitan Area].* New York: New American Library (Signet Books).

Cremin, Lawrence A. *The Transformation of the School: Progressivism in American Education, 1876-1957.* New York: Random House (Vintage Books).

*Cubberley, Ellwood P. *Public Education in the United States.* Boston: Houghton Mifflin Company, 1934.

Curti, Merle. *Social Ideas of American Educators.* Totowa, N.J.: Littlefield, Adams & Company, 1959.

Dewey, John. *Democracy and Education.* New York: Free Press.

———. *Experience and Education.* New York: Macmillan Company (Collier Books), 1963.

*———. *The School and Society.* 2nd edition. Chicago: University of Chicago Press, 1915.

Eliot, Charles W. *Charles W. Eliot and Popular Education.* Edited by Edward A. Krug. New York: Teachers College Press.

*Flexner, Abraham. *The American College: A Criticism.* New York: Arno Press.

*Hansen, Allen O. *Liberalism and American Education in the 18th Century.* New York: Octagon Books, 1965.

Herndon, James. *Way It Spozed to Be.* New York: Bantam Books.

*Hofstadter, Richard, and Metzger, Walter P. *Development of Academic Freedom in the United States.* New York: Columbia University Press, 1955.

Hofstadter, Richard, and Smith, Wilson. *American Higher Education: A Documentary History.* 2 volumes. Chicago: University of Chicago Press (Phoenix Books), 1968.

*Hutchins, Robert M. *The Conflict in Education in a Democratic Society.* New York: Harper & Row, 1953. OP

James, Henry. *Charles W. Eliot, President of Harvard University, 1869-1909.* 2 volumes. Boston: Houghton Mifflin Company, 1930. OP

Jencks, Christopher, and Riesman, David. *The Academic Revolution.* New York: Doubleday & Company (Anchor Books).

Johnson, Alvin. *Pioneer's Progress: An Autobiography.* Lincoln, Neb.: University of Nebraska Press (Bison Books), 1960.

Kerr, Clark. *The Uses of the University.* New York: Harper & Row (Harper Torchbooks).

Kozol, Jonathan. *Death at an Early Age: [The Destruction of the Hearts and Minds of Negro Children in the Boston Public Schools].* New York: Bantam Books.

*MacIver, Robert M. *Academic Freedom in Our Time.* Staten Island, N.Y.: Gordion Press, 1955.

Mann, Horace. *The Republic and the School: Horace Mann on the Education of Free Men.* Edited by Lawrence A. Cremin. New York: Teachers College Press, 1957.

*McCuskey, Dorothy. *Bronson Alcott, Teacher.* New York: Arno Press.

McGuffey, Alexander. *McGuffey's Fifth Eclectic Reader.* Foreword by Henry Steele Commager. New York: New American Library (Signet Classics), 1962.

*Morison, Samuel E. *Three Centuries of Harvard, 1636-1936.* Cambridge, Mass.: Harvard University Press (Belknap Press), 1936.

*Nevins, Allan. *The State Universities and Democracy.* Urbana, Ill.: University of Illinois Press, 1962.

Riesman, David. *Constraint and Variety in American Education.* Lincoln, Neb.: University of Nebraska Press (Bison Books), 1965.

Shepard, Odell. *Pedlar's Progress: The Life of Bronson Alcott.* Westport, Conn.: Greenwood Press, 1968.

Shoemaker, Ervin C. *Noah Webster: Pioneer of Learning.* New York: AMS Press, 1936.

Taylor, Harold. *On Education and Freedom.* Carbondale, Ill.: Southern Illinois University Press (Arcturus Books), 1967.

*————. *Students Without Teachers: The Crisis in the University.* New York: McGraw-Hill Book Company, 1969.

*————. *The World as Teacher.* New York: Doubleday & Company, 1969.

Thayer, V. T. *Formative Ideas in American Education: From the Colonial Period to the Present.* New York: Dodd, Mead & Company, 1965.

Veysey, Laurence R. *Emergence of the American University.* Chicago: University of Chicago Press.

10. social and cultural traits

There are two familiar concepts of culture, which might be called the "traditional" and the "scientific." The first defines culture as what is best in thought, taste, manners, and refinement—a definition clearly formulated by a class society and designed to sustain aristocratic values. Needless to say it begs the central question of what is "best" and who is to decide. The second conception of culture is as a bundle of patterns of behavior, habits of conduct, customs, laws, beliefs, and instinctive responses that are displayed by a society—a definition which derives from ethnology and sociology. The two are not mutually exclusive, for a society tells a good deal about itself by distinguishing the things it thinks elegant and refined, while familiar social activities—like engaging in religious ceremonies or building shelters—have an almost irresistible tendency to develop into philosophy and art.

It would be folly to try to interpret the whole range of the best in American thought—art, letters, science, and philosophy—in a few random paragraphs. American intellectual history can no more be sketched in a few broad strokes of the brush than can the French or Chinese; it must be traced, touch by touch, with an art that brings out everything that is original or characteristic. A few words on the novels of Henry James or William Faulkner, the poetry of Ezra Pound or Robert Frost, the painting of Winslow Homer or Thomas Eakins—these are not only useless but misleading because inescapably superficial.

Let us rather consider American culture in its second, and more generally accepted meaning—culture not as the manifestation of genius but as an expression of attitudes, habits, and beliefs. The first thing that strikes an observer here is that even in its most elementary and common-place form, as in its most sophisticated, American culture is derivative. This is, after all, what we should expect. America was, down to just the other day, a land of immigrants, mostly European, who brought their culture with them and kept it as long as they could—or as long as their children would let them. If it must be confessed that the melting pot did not truly fuse the racial admixture, it cannot be denied that it did fuse the cultural. What emerged from the fusion was an amalgam of European culture, and by virtue of the miscellaneous ingredients that it absorbed, the United States has some claim to be considered the most European of nations, while by virtue of susceptibility to environment and geographical isolation, it is also the most American.

Thus, for example, American religion is an inheritance from Judea, Greece, Rome, and the Middle Ages, modified by innumerable contributions from many Christian theologians including Huss and Luther, Calvin and Knox, Loyola and Newman, Kierkegaard and Barth. Even American-born religions like the Mormon and the Christian Scientist owe a major part of their theology to traditional Christianity. Americans made some contributions to architecture, but their overwhelming debt, again, is to the old world, from Periclean Greece to the Bauhaus school in Germany after the First World War and, in the realm of the decorative arts, to China and Japan as well. Thus gardening, which reveals so much of culture, was never cultivated in America as assiduously as in the old world or Japan, probably because the vast extent of available nature made the creation of formal gardens seem superfluous, but where it was cultivated it was either in the Italian or English tradition. Thus science is by its very nature cosmopolitan: there is no such thing as English chemistry or Japanese physics or Mexican mathematics, though there are of course national styles in the approach to these sciences—the amateur spirit in England, the elitist approach in France, the emphasis on organization and teamwork in America. In this area dependence on the science and scientists of the old world, on their academies and universities, has been continuous from the days of Newton to those of the nuclear physicist Nils Bohr; only since the Second World War has the center of scientific gravity moved to this side of the Atlantic.

The most obvious and universal cultural inheritance was of course language, and it was the one perhaps least modified. Americans brought their languages with them from their mother countries and still call their speech the "mother tongue," but this term now encompasses only one speech—English. There are millions of Germans, Italians, and Russians in America, but their language is rarely called the mother tongue. The immigrants of non-British stock and their descendants have neither retained their own native speech nor contributed anything important from it to the stock of American speech. It is of course possible to find German, Yiddish, Spanish, or even Indian words in the American language, but these are relatively few, and are not unique to the United States: after all the English, too, have incorporated such words as moccasin, rodeo, and kindergarten into their vocabulary. Even more astonishing than the near-monopoly of the English on the American language is the fact that over the years the American language has departed so little from that spoken in England. This is not to be taken for granted: most languages, transferred to distant parts of the globe, undergo far-reaching modifications. The eighteenth-century lexicographer, Noah Webster, and others of his generation were confident that in time the best English would be spoken not in old but in New England. No Englishmen today would admit this

162

soft impeachment, but even they recognize that in the United States the English language somehow escaped both the regional and the class dialects that long plagued it at home, and even today it is possible that an educated Londoner might understand the speech of Boston, Massachusetts, better than the speech of Boston, Lincolnshire.

Consider two of the so-called fine arts—a term which Americans have taken over uncritically, just as they have taken over the terms *belles lettres* and *haute cuisine,* which distinguish the elegant from the mechanical arts—music and architecture. Like science, music is by its nature cosmopolitan, more susceptible to inheritance and less to environment than any other major art; it is, at the same time, perhaps the easiest of the arts to transmit from country to country. As the great inheritance of music was readily available to Americans, it would be unrealistic to expect them to make many original contributions to this art, and they did not. For two hundred years most Americans were content to sing the familiar hymns and folk songs: to this day most of the church songs are English or German and most babies are rocked to sleep to the tune of old English or German lullabies. In the nineteenth century a genuine American music emerged, but it was black American, not white—the spirituals, taken over, many of them, by composers like Stephen Foster and woven into folk songs like "My Old Kentucky Home," or "Nelly Was a Lady," or "Massa's in the Cold, Cold Ground," that have become an enduring part of the American musical heritage. Later American contributions—the blues and jazz—came likewise from the Negroes. But except for religious music, cultivated chiefly by the Moravians of Pennsylvania and North Carolina, the *lieder* preserved by the German singing clubs, and the Negro spirituals, music was simply not part of American culture. At times it seemed almost alien to it.

For a long time music, like other forms of "culture," was considered a proper concern for women but not for men. It was quite all right for girls to take music lessons, but woe betide the boy who was caught with a violin or a flute! Men could disport themselves in barbershop quartets or in college glee clubs, for this was not so much music as good-fellowship, but to make a career of music was a confession of failure, perhaps even of failure of masculinity. An exception was made for Germans and Italians and, for a long time, they pretty much monopolized the musical scene in America. America itself produced few composers

Zubin Mehta, Indian-born conductor of the Los Angeles Philharmonic Orchestra, conducts a rehearsal.

—and none who commanded attention outside her borders; until only a few decades ago most of her performers and conductors were imported. President Jefferson could confess that music was "the favorite passion of my soul," but probably not one of his successors in the White House could say the same thing.

Beginning with the Federal Works Project subsidy of music and musicians during the depression years of the 1930s—a program which altogether put on over two hundred thousand musical performances— music took on a new and resounding popularity. The United States does not yet support many operas, but maintains over one thousand symphony orchestras, while school orchestras, and amateur chamber music and choral groups are now found in every community. The production of recorded music became overnight a major industry, and if the Beatles outsell Bach, it says something of changing tastes that the American public snapped up twenty thousand albums of the Bach "Goldberg Variations" in a period of three months. Music festivals sprang up, from the mountains of Vermont (Marlboro) to the mountains of Colorado (Aspen), and every college and university supported a composer-in-residence or a chamber music group. Throughout the country local radio stations dedicated themselves exclusively to the performance of music, and world-famous artists found receptive audiences not only in New York and Chicago but in provincial towns that had long been innocent of musical ambitions.

All of this revealed enthusiasm but did not demonstrate creativity. Is there, in all this, evidence of the emergence of an American music? Certainly there is a rich pool of folk music in America—the ballads of the Appalachian mountain people, the chanteys of the New England sailors, the songs of the riverboatmen, and of the cowboys, the marching songs of the Civil War. These constitute, perhaps, the authentic American music, these and the Negro spirituals. There are, in addition, distinctly American "light operas" or more simply, "musicals," as Americans call them: Jerome Kern's *Show Boat,* Rodgers and Hammerstein's *Oklahoma!,* George Gershwin's *Porgy and Bess,* Leonard Bernstein's *West Side Story,* Douglas Moore's *Ballad of Baby Doe,* and the triumphant *My Fair Lady,* whose entrancing melodies can be heard on the streets of Vienna and Milan, Tel Aviv and Hong Kong.

Meantime the cosmopolitan character of music, and the role of America as a cultural beneficiary, was dramatized by the flight of many of Europe's leading conductors and composers from totalitarianism in the thirties and forties. Conductors like Bruno Walter, Otto Klemperer, Erich Leinsdorf, George Szell, and Pablo Casals, and composers like Igor Stravinsky, Paul Hindemith, Darius Milhaud, Arnold Schönberg, Kurt Weill, and Ernst Toch, enriched American culture with their talents.

The Seagram Building, New York City. The skyscraper is America's unique contribution to architecture.

Architecture—a term which ideally embraces all building, land-scaping, and town planning—is perhaps the most democratic of the arts. Yet traditionally the history of architecture is the record of palaces, cathedrals, public buildings and monuments, not of shops and houses, schools and factories. As the United States has no palaces, few magnificent churches or public monuments—compare the White House with Versailles, for example, or Grant's Tomb with the Taj Mahal—the traditional concept of architecture has little relevance to the history of American building, and we turn of necessity to a history of houses, flats, office buildings, banks, bridges, roads, factories, and mills. Certainly in the arena of public buildings—universities are perhaps an exception—the United States has little original to offer to distract the eye of the artist from the riches of the Orient and the old world. It is perhaps in this arena that the United States has been most derivative or imitative: our national capital built to look like ancient Rome, our universities built to look like Oxford, our theatres built to look like La Scala, our churches built to look like Notre Dame or St. Peter's, or—in New England—like London's St. Martin's in the Fields. Almost all of the most distinguished American architects were trained abroad—in Rome or in Paris—or where disciples of those who had been. Jefferson sat and gazed at the Maison Carrée in Nîmes "like a lover gazing at his mistress," and designed the state capital in Richmond as an exact copy of this Roman building. When he came to build his own house, it was as a diminutive edition of two magnificent Palladian villas, Malcontenta and a Rotonda; he even gave it an Italian name, Monticello. Bulfinch of Boston—architect of the Boston State House—designed in the style of his eighteenth-century contemporaries, the Adam brothers; Benjamin Latrobe, chief architect of the national capital, was a protagonist of the Greek and Roman revival. Of the great mid-nineteenth-century architects, Henry Hobson Richardson favored the Romanesque; Richard Morris Hunt, the most resourceful imitator of them all, thought French Renaissance equally appropriate for stately homes on New York's Fifth Avenue and in the mountains of North Carolina. Imitation flourished in the arena of cheap housing and "developments" long after it had been repudiated by the major architects, and the suburbs of every major city in the country are littered with "Elizabethan," "Queen Anne," "Norman," "Swiss chalet," and "colonial" imitations—colonial meaning almost anything that is built of wood and painted white.

It was only with the coming of functionalism in the early years of this century, with architects like Louis Sullivan and Frank Lloyd Wright, that America achieved some measure of architectural independence.

Functionalism, to be sure, had long antecedents. The first settlers in America had to make do with such building materials as were at hand,

167

and to adapt their houses to weather both colder and warmer than any that they had known in their old world homes. The houses they built were functional: small rooms and low ceilings to preserve the heat, with steep slanting roofs to take care of heavy snow in New England, large rooms and high ceilings and open halls to mitigate the heat of the South; the kitchen, with its vast fireplace, the center of the New England home, but in the South separate from the main house altogether. The tools that the early settlers fashioned were functional too: new axes, ploughs, and guns. Birch bark canoes copied from the Indians and clipper ships of their own design were beautiful because functional; so, too, as part of the landscape, were the walls built from the rocks in the soil that served as fences. As the pioneer sculptor Horatio Greenough observed in 1852, "the mechanics of the United States have already outstripped the artists and have, by their bold and unflinching adaptation, entered the true track, and hold up the light for all who operate for American wants. . . . By beauty I mean the promise of function. By character I mean the record of function."

Even in laying out a town, the New Englanders departed from established English models of houses cheek by jowl along a High Street, and created instead that greatest triumph of American town planning, the New England town, with church, parsonage, school, town hall, and the houses of the townspeople—all in native wood and painted white or pumpkin yellow—built around a village common. You can see examples of this seventeenth- and eighteenth-century town today in Litchfield or Suffield, Connecticut, Hadley or Petersham, Massachusetts, Newfane or Dorset, Vermont.

American architecture—as Greenough saw—has been at its best in practical things like ships, bridges, factories, grain elevators, and—more recently—hospitals, schools, and libraries. The great architect Henry Hobson Richardson once said that what he wanted most to design was a grain elevator and the interior of a Mississippi steamboat; he did neither, but what he did wonderfully well were small town churches, railroad stations, and warehouses. Louis Sullivan, the greatest of American decorators, made a specialty of bank buildings, and one of Frank Lloyd Wright's major triumphs was the Johnson Wax building in Racine, Wisconsin. In our day it is not cathedrals, state capitols, or the palaces of millionaires that interest students of architecture but Edward Stone's American embassy in New Delhi; Skidmore, Owings & Merrill's Connecticut Life Insurance building in West Hartford, Mies van der Rohe's Seagram building in New York City, and Minoru Yamasaki's Reynolds Aluminum building in Detroit.

It is the skyscraper, however, that is, in the eyes of Europeans, the most characteristic expression of American architectural genius. It had its origin not—as might be expected—in the crowded cities of the old world or of the eastern seaboard, but in the Chicago and St. Louis of the 1880s, where there was in fact no problem of crowding; it was a product not so much of traditional architecture as of modern engineering, made possible by the development of structural steel and the elevator. Its popularity was a response not so much to high land values, as to its symbolic potentialities. A dozen skyscrapers, thrusting into the sky, proved that a city had "arrived," or that a rural university was in the same league as an urban. However irresistible its appeal to the sense of power or vanity, the skyscraper created more problems than it solved, if indeed it solved any. It accentuated urban congestion, aggravated traffic jams, and engulfed whole areas in perpetual shadow. Louis Sullivan called it "the eloquent peroration of the most bald, most sinister, most forbidding conditions of American life," and the greatest of city planners, Lewis Mumford, described it as an "architecture for angels and aviators." Civilized cities like London, Paris, and Florence have hitherto resisted its inroads, but it is slowly conquering in Europe and even in Asia, and city planners may yet agree that its invention was the greatest catastrophe in the history of architecture.

It is perhaps domestic architecture that most clearly reveals national traits. America is no exception to this general rule, for here all the familiar pressures of equalitarianism have operated from the beginning. Though there is more great wealth in the United States than elsewhere, the differences between the housing of the very rich and that of the middle classes are less than one might expect, just as are the differences between the automobiles of the rich and of the rest of society. The American rich no longer build palaces or even châteaux; they rarely maintain extensive pleasure gardens; they prefer to travel, or to keep a "summer" house. Circumstances have denied them one symbol of conspicuous wealth: a large retinue of servants. Footmen, coachmen, gardeners, chefs, butlers, nurses, and so forth are almost the last thing the rich elsewhere give up, while Americans, except perhaps in the South, have never faced the problem of giving them up because they never had them. To this day an American with the income of a prince will drive his own car and even work his own garden, while his wife will busy herself happily enough in her all-mechanized and air-conditioned kitchen. Americans, in any event, do not have "servants"; they have "help," and it is an important distinction.

For all the conveniences of the upper-class suburban home (Americans always live in "homes," not "houses") its most arresting feature is perhaps the extent to which it leads out rather than draws in. It boasts a two- or even a three- or four-car garage, a swimming pool, and a television room; the first to make it possible for every member of the family to get away as easily as possible, the second to make it possible to escape from the house during play hours, and the third to substitute darkness and vicarious noise for light and conversation. These houses have many baths, but the large library is a thing of the past, and so, too, the music room with its grand piano. Even the most luxurious American houses do not boast the elaborate decorations, the sumptuous furnishings of their foreign counterparts—the galleries stocked with ancestral portraits, libraries of morocco-bound books, crystal chandeliers, and marble floors, the splendor of brocade and silk and velvet on the walls, the elaborate silver services and the gold plate. American gardens, too, reflect equalitarianism. They are rarely extensive, for gardeners are hard to come by; and they are made for play rather than for display. Not acres of flowers but a well-kept lawn on which children can disport themselves, not greenhouses but a swimming pool, not summer pavilions and tea houses, but a bar by the pool or the tennis court—this is the familiar pattern. The houses themselves are rarely palatial: almost all the grand houses have been torn down or converted to school or other institutional uses.

Much of the decline of the City could be ascribed to the American failure to control technology and particularly the automobile. Here again Americans have no monopoly on failure. Those familiar with what technology is doing to the cities of Europe, parts of South America, and Japan, will readily admit that the problem is world wide, and so, too, the failure: certainly neither London nor Paris, Hamburg nor Rome, Tokyo nor Buenos Aires has solved its traffic problems. But it can be said of technology, as of so many things, that it has been more uncritically applied in America than elsewhere, and that the American experience is perhaps both a prophecy and a warning.

The most obvious symbol of technology is the automobile, but it is a symbol of far more than technology, it is a symbol of civilization itself. Certainly it conditions the lives of all Americans today, and the ramifications of its influence are everywhere. The car is everybody's necessity and almost everybody's pride. Without it a man cannot hold a job; without it a wife cannot run a household. It controls both work and play. It was responsible—on a superficial level anyway—for the shift from the city to the suburbs, for it enables the worker to live pretty much where he will, rather than being bound to his place of work. It has broken up the pattern of neighborhoods: it transports children to distant consolidated schools; it broadens the circle of friends and acquaintances and thus makes them independent of their neighbors. It has changed the architecture of houses, the design of cities, and the pattern of the landscape, for houses must have garages and driveways, cities must have roads and highways, parking lots and garages and filling stations, (two-thirds of inner Los Angeles is now given over to roads, filling stations

Colonial Studio

Monticello, President Thomas Jefferson's home in Virginia. One of the most distinguished historic homes in America, and one of the most nearly palatial, Monticello is simple compared to the residences of the mighty in Europe and Asia.

and garages, and parking lots), and the countryside must have highways and throughways, and room somewhere for the debris of the several million cars that are junked every year.

The automobile has introduced new patterns of social life as well. Ownership of a car is not only an economic necessity but a social one; indeed ownership of two cars is rapidly coming to be, in middle-class families, a necessity. The car is the symbol of being somebody; for the young it is the symbol of arriving at manhood. It is one of the vehicles of courtship; without it the institution of matrimony itself might collapse! It is a stimulus for bad temper and a school for bad manners. It is also a school for lawlessness and for crime: six hundred thousand automobile thefts are reported every year, while the number of minor offenses—

Manhattan Bridge Loop. Edward Hopper.

172

speeding, illegal parking, and so forth, are too numerous even for computer statistics. It is one of the major killers, more lethal than war itself: it takes a toll of fifty-five thousand lives every year, and has claimed altogether, since its invention, over two million lives—more than three times the total of all battle casualties in all wars in which the United States has been engaged.

Perhaps the most pervasive impact of the automobile is on the economy. It is the barometer of prosperity or depression. A hundred industries depend upon it—steel, rubber, glass, oil, gas, garages, highway construction, insurance, finance, advertising, and television, among others. Taken together, these account for a large part of American business and employment. Of the ten leading corporations in the United States, three are directly engaged in the manufacture of automobiles, three in the production of oil. Every state budget depends on car, license, and gasoline taxes; every family budget is geared to the insatiable demands of the family car.

Never before in history has man been so much the servant of a machine as he is today of the automobile. And there are already ominous signs that the airplane will play, in the next generation, a role analogous to that which the automobile has played in the last. The landing on the moon was undoubtedly the greatest technological and scientific triumph in the history of man, and showed what could be achieved when the resources of government, technology, science, industry, and the human spirit were enlisted for the task, but there is no assurance, indeed no evidence, that these same affluent ingredients will be combined to solve the problems of our cities.

Most of the basic forces that determine the latitude and longitude for society and culture in the modern world are much the same from country to country, particularly in the Western world—technology, urbanization, the welfare state, the growth of leisure, and new media of communication among them. Yet these forces do not operate everywhere the same way or produce civilizations of a single pattern. The differences in cities in, let us say, the United States, Latin America, and Europe may not be profound, but they are ostentatious and significant. So, too, with the impact of the automobile, or the uses of leisure, or the functioning of television. What interests the student of American culture is the special American response to these general forces.

Consider the city. American society has changed more rapidly from rural to urban than most others, and has made the adjustment less gracefully than most. At its birth, the new United States was overwhelmingly rural, and in its rural character, so its leaders thought, lay its republican safety. That tyranny, poverty, misery, and vice flourished in the crowded cities of the old world—London, Paris, Naples—was clear to every observer, and it was equally clear that the new world, where everyone lived on the farm or in villages, was the scene of happiness and virtue. Jefferson thought all cities "pestilential to the morals, the health and the liberties of men," and warned that "when we get piled upon one another in great cities as in Europe, we shall become as corrupt as in Europe." American writers, too, celebrated the pastoral virtues and deprecated the urban, and so did the artists. Ralph Waldo Emerson's first important essay was called "Nature" and Henry Thoreau's *Walden* has remained an American classic; the best loved American poets, from Henry Wadsworth Longfellow to Robert Frost, have sung the beauties of the countryside. The reverse side of this attitude was no less prominent: the American writers and artists have been at war with the city until just the other day. Some Americans, to be sure—William Dean Howells and O. Henry for example—came to terms with the city, but the one great novelist who embraced the city and made it a part of his stories was Henry James, who rejected American life—and American cities—for Florence, Venice, Paris, and London.

In 1888, Lord Bryce wrote, in *The American Commonwealth,* that the city was the one conspicuous failure of American democracy. He was thinking in political terms, to be sure, but the observation was equally appropriate in social and artistic terms. Certainly the city is the most conspicuous failure in American life today, and it is a failure which embraces and symbolizes many other failures: poverty, public health, crime, pollution, and racial tensions. All of these are subsumed in the term "urban blight."

What explains the failure and the blight? The explanation is rooted in history, but it is found in current malpractices too. First, ancient cities— Prague, Kyoto, Lima—grew slowly over many centuries and developed a distinct character long before they were exposed to the pressure of nineteenth-century expansion; when they did grow, the last century or two, it was within the ancient pattern, and growth left most of the ancient city intact. But American cities were all new; most of them are creatures of the railroad and industry, and can boast only a hundred years or so of history. The growth of cities such as Pittsburgh, Chicago, Houston, and Los Angeles was so sudden and so rapid that they did not have time to develop either a character or a pattern before they were overwhelmed by tidal waves of newcomers, and it may be said that the typical American city plunged into decay before it reached its full growth. Second, most foreign cities began as centers of government and of the church: that meant palaces, cathedrals, the mansions of officials and merchants, royal

174

gardens and parks and parade grounds—the nucleus of even the smallest state. But American cities, with few exceptions, lacked all this—lacked official or ecclesiastical splendor, or the wealth of the aristocracy; they were born of industry and throve on industry. This meant, third, that by bad luck American cities emerged and took on a permanent character during the era of the industrial revolution, with all its grime and soot and ugliness. That era was also the nadir of taste in architecture and the peak of speculative private greed. Fourth, American cities grew under the impact of heavy immigration. Most of those who came to the United States came not from cities but from farms: the move to America was their move to the city. They came empty-handed, and had to take such housing, and such jobs, as they could find. Tenements and slums and sweatshops were the American response, a response dictated partly by greed, but partly, too, by an almost complete unfamiliarity with the demands of urban life, and by a recognition that mobility made any building temporary.

In the twentieth century the cities were battered by new invasions of the very poor from abroad, and of Negroes and the Appalachian poor from the American South; these put further strains on the already over-burdened resources of the city. At the same time rapid transit and the automobile made it possible for the rich to escape the city into suburbs, and thus began that process of draining the city of its wealth, talent, and leadership which is still going on.

Yet many European and some Asian cities, confronted by the same problem of rapid growth and shifting population and industrial patterns, somehow managed to escape the worst ravages that afflicted the American city, to survive and to flourish. Why is it that American cities were not able to triumph over threats to their survival?

One explanation is deeply embedded in the American character: the romantic preference for the countryside, the distrust of the city, the fear of aliens, of whatever color, and—perhaps most important of all psychologically—the habit of impermanence and mobility. Most old world cities at least were governed by a patriciate—old families, some of them aristocrats, others merchants, bankers, lawyers, scholars, government officials, who identified with their cities and put their roots down deep into the soil of the city. They protected their cities against the onslaughts of the barbarians who would destroy them. They clung to their houses and gardens, often in the very heart of their city (favorable tax policies—which they dictated—made this possible), they kept up their style of life, they supported the opera and the theatre, the local university and the botanical garden, the academies and the churches. They were the governing class, socially and economically as well as politically, and even when they lost political control they retained social and economic influence. Except for Boston, Philadelphia, and Charleston, America had no patriciates, and even in Boston and Philadelphia the "first families" were prepared to give up what they thought a hopeless struggle against the new forces engulfing their cities, and move out—to the suburbs or, perhaps, Cleveland or San Francisco. Once under way the flight of the upper middle classes fed on itself; as each year the city became more expensive, less attractive, and more dangerous, the flight became a rout. Business, industry, shopping, even cultural centers, followed population to the suburbs, and beyond.

By the decade of the 1960s the decay of the inner city was in full swing. For the first time city population began to decline. Schools deteriorated and—as in Washington, Philadelphia, and New York—were given over largely to poor Negro children; the slums spread into what had been middle-class residential areas; lawlessness and violence increased. With some cities, as with the pollution of some stretches of water, like Lake Erie, there seemed to be a "point of no return." City and federal governments poured hundreds of millions into city rehabilitation, but the slums spread faster than the rehabilitation.

Past civilizations—those of Athens, Rome, Renaissance Italy, the Low Countries in the seventeenth century, and the Empire in the eighteenth —have been judged by their cities. If American civilization were to be judged by its cities, the verdict would be harsh.

Americans, in a sense, invented time; now they have time on their hands. Most modern societies have achieved some degree of leisure for their working people, but only in the United States has leisure risen to the dignity of a major social "problem," the subject of hundreds of sociological investigations and conferences.

Throughout the nineteenth century workingmen toiled from sixty to eighty hours a week in factory and mine, and women almost as long hours in shops and in domestic service, while farmers worked from sun-up to sundown. In the course of the twentieth century all this changed. By the 1960s the average American was working only seven or eight hours a day, five days a week. It was one of the swiftest and most unsettling revolutions in social and economic history.

Nor is leisure now something for the working man alone. Thanks to smaller families, to such inventions as the electric washing machine, dryer, dishwasher, refrigerator, and stove, and to the family car and the supermarket, there was at last leisure for women—for those anyway who did not take jobs on the side. Children, too, were beneficiaries of the new ethos. Not much more than a century ago boys and girls of eight and nine years worked long hours in mines and mills; now child labor is a thing of the past. Around the world, youth who do not go to university—and only a small number do—customarily go to work at fifteen or sixteen and in some countries much earlier; Americans, white Americans at least, rarely take jobs before they are eighteen, and perhaps one-third of them stay on in college until they are twenty-one or twenty-two.

There is leisure at the other end of life as well, but enforced leisure. With the growth of life expectancy, ever more men and women are living on into their sixties and seventies, and ever fewer of these are working, for modern industry and business has little use for the old. Nor has modern society, for that matter, much use for the old. Almost nowhere else are old people objects of more verbal flattery and less human consideration than in the United States. With characteristic unwillingness to face unpleasant facts, Americans have coined a new vocabulary designed to conceal the reality of age: "senior citizens," "golden agers," and so forth, and they tend to shunt the elderly off in what are called "leisure villages" where they can live out their declining years in physical comfort without bothering anybody. This is no doubt more humane than the habit of primitive tribes of simply leaving their aged behind to die, but it deprives the young of the inestimable advantage of living with and knowing about old age and death—something all previous generations have known and taken for granted. Among civilized nations the United States is perhaps the least pleasant country in which to grow old.

The coming of leisure was accompanied by one paradox that throws some light on the class structure of American society. In the past it was the masses of the people who worked long hours every day from childhood to old age, while a privileged aristocracy enjoyed perpetual leisure, or at least exemption from work except of their own making and choosing. That had never been true in America, except among some of the slave-owners of the Old South, and most of them worked with their slaves in the fields. As for the much-romanticized Southern Lady,

She was at work by candlelight,
She was at work in the dead of night, . . .
Guiding the cooking and watching the baking,
The sewing, the soap-and-candle-making,
The brewing, the darning, the lady-daughters,
The births and the deaths in the negro-quarters.

Stephen Vincent Benét, *John Brown's Body*
(New York: Holt, Rinehart and Winston, Inc., 1960)

But now the situation is reversed: it is the working classes who have leisure; it is the elite—statesmen, lawyers, doctors, scholars, business executives—who, for the most part, work longer hours and longer years than any others. True to the compulsions of equalitarianism, leisure has shifted dramatically from a prerogative of the rich to a privilege of the middle and working segments of society.

What do Americans do with their leisure? Some garden, some travel, or go "camping" or fishing, some read—newspapers and magazines rather than books. Some twenty-five million, no less, submit themselves to "adult education," a term which covers a multitude of activities, intellectual and otherwise. Some are deeply involved in politics, or in the affairs of their churches or fraternal orders. Some pursue hobbies such as photography or stamp collecting, and a vast magazine literature caters to them. The huge majority engage in, watch, read, and talk about sports; most of the time they look at television.

Sports, for long the indulgence and preoccupation of the privileged classes who alone could afford them, have spread in our time to every part of society. One test of the growth of democracy is the extent to which sport reflects class lines, or functions as a common denominator, just as one test of nationalism is the ability of a new state to field an Olympic team. In England, where games and sports were for so long most assiduously cultivated, there were marked differences between those enjoyed by the upper and by the lower classes—differences dramatized by the distinction between the amateur and the professional. Very little of this carried over to America—perhaps only the amateur tradition, and by the mid-twentieth century even this was pretty much a thing of the past. The amateur tradition lingers on, now, in colleges and universities, but more honored in the breach than in the observance, and some "universities" seem to exist primarily to train players for professional football or basketball. With the exceptions of polo and yachting all the sports once reserved for the rich have been taken over by ordinary folk. Now every clerk or school teacher can take off for Vermont or the Sierras for a weekend of skiing, and every high school boy can acquire or rent a set of golf clubs and go on to the municipal links which, for his purposes, are quite as good as those at St. Andrews. Once it was clearly established that the whole populace was interested in sports, town governments cooperated by building golf courses, laying out tennis courts in parks, installing swimming pools in high schools, and creating artificial lakes for ice skating, while business cooperated by bringing winter sports within the budget of the middle classes. The yeast of equalitarianism has worked more effectively here than in any other area of American life.

The interest in sports and games probably reached its peak in the 1960s, but more and more Americans indulged that interest vicariously. Where, in earlier days (when there was more space), parents and children played mild domestic games like croquet and quoits and girls skipped rope while their brothers played baseball in some corner lot, now most people, of all ages, are content to sit in front of a television box and watch it grind out games hour after hour. Not only is the exercise vicarious —with what consequences to the physical well-being of the American male we do not yet know—but so, too, is the psychological and emotional experience. After all, competition is one thing when you are pitting your

Baseball mania disrupts whole cities in October, when the World Series is played.
Above, a New York Mets fan races through streets littered by paper thrown down
from the headquarters of such corporate giants as Standard Oil Co., Radio
Corporation of America, and Sperry Rand after the underdog team won the
1969 World Series, playing against the Baltimore Orioles.

strength and skills against an opponent, but a very different thing when you have merely identified (usually for the moment) with some "team" that you know only on a television screen. Television speeded up that decline in sportsmanship which was already under way, because with so much at stake for players and sponsors no one could really afford to lose.

Like so many other things, sports quickly became a Big Business, vitally important to the economy of the television networks, the newspapers and journals that battened on them, and, of course, to the industries that provided sporting goods or that exploited famous players for the delight, and at the expense, of their infatuated fans. Inevitably sports became an instrument of these business interests, so that instead of sportswriters and journals existing to celebrate the games they reported, sport itself came to exist in order to support television, newspapers, and magazines. The interdependence of these interests and activities was by no means confined to the United States; British and Italian newspapers give proportionately more space to sports than do American.

The growth of sports had two unforeseen sociological consequences of some interest. The growing depersonalization of American life—the impersonality of the great city and of the great corporation—created a need for something to which men could attach themselves and which would command their interest and inspire their loyalties. In America, and not in America alone, teams provided just this: a sense of belonging for those who did not feel that they belonged to anything else, a sense of excitement for those whose lives were drab, an object of loyalty for those who had no other concrete objects of loyalty. And at its most elementary, teams provided something to talk about to those whose conversational range was otherwise meager. If, as the philosopher Josiah Royce asserted, loyalty is its own reward, and loyalty even to a bad cause better than none at all, then loyalty to the New York Mets (baseball), the Baltimore Colts (football) or the Boston Celtics (basketball) served some moral purpose. Whether conversation about the relative merits of professional football players like O. J. Simpson and Joe Namath is better than silence is a more awkward question.

A second sociological function of professional sports is to provide a refuge for males in a society where the division between the sexes has otherwise all but disappeared. Women have invaded almost every arena once the special province of men—politics, business, the professions—but still retain their own special provinces where men cannot enter. Aside from war, almost the only province left to men is sports, though even in these two fields the monopoly has broken down. It is, characteristically, the man who sits in his shirtsleeves in the baseball stadium (romantically, with his son), mopping his brow and munching his hot dog; it is the man who lolls in front of his television screen, creating, for purposes of advertisers and the comic strip, a new category of "football widows"; and the supporters of the Little Leagues of baseball players and of the high school football teams are members of Dads' Clubs. There is as yet no sign that professional sports will appeal to women as strongly as to men; whether this is an indication of higher mentality or higher morality in women, or whether it is merely a response to the elementary fact that women have more to do in the home than men, is not wholly clear.

Doubtless more leisure time goes into watching television in the United States than anywhere else, but nothing is more difficult than to interpret the significance of this new instrument which is almost a culture in itself. There are not far from one hundred million television sets in the United States—more than one for each household—and statisticians tell us that the average American spends some three hours a day looking at television programs. If this is indeed true, then television is quantitatively the most important interest of the American people.

The situation could doubtless be matched elsewhere: Other people are almost as infatuated with television as are Americans, but they have far fewer hours in which to look at it than Americans have. This is merely one of many differences between television in the United States and elsewhere on the globe. From the beginning, and quite deliberately, Americans adopted their own pattern of radio and television, and have clung to it with growing stubbornness over the years. Whereas elsewhere in the world radio and television are run by government, in the United States they are controlled and run by private industry. This broad generalization requires some, but not much, qualification. Britain, for example, and Canada, license private corporations to produce television, but regulate them very carefully and effectively. The United States government exercises a broad supervision over all private television broadcasting, but it is theoretical rather than real; private television sets its own standards and regulates itself. The principle that the air waves belong to the people, not to the companies, is given lip service but otherwise ignored.

Not the government, or representatives of the public, but private interests determine what the American people are to see and to hear. These private interests are not, as might be supposed, the television companies themselves—the three great networks that command the national scene—but the advertisers who finance and "sponsor" programs. Sponsors not only fill the air waves with their advertisements (called "messages") but determine what is to be shown on the programs themselves. They determine this in a broad way—the choice of one rather than another broadcast, of a comedy rather than a documentary, let us say, or a Western

181

over a mystery film; and they determine it in detail, as well, through censorship of any word or idea they think unsuitable.

It is precisely here that television differs so sharply from all other comparable enterprises—newspapers, publishing houses, films, museums, libraries, universities. Some of these are business enterprises—newspapers and films, for example—but only television permits the "sponsors" or advertisers to dictate the substance of the product. Advertisers have little directly to say about the content or the editorial policy of a newspaper or magazine, and donors have little directly to say about the way a symphony orchestra, a hospital, or a university is run, but advertisers have everything to say about what the public is allowed to see and hear on television.

It is from this original misconception of the nature and function of television that almost all of its failings flow. It is this that accounts for the generally low standard of the fare that is dished up to the people: sponsors are interested in the largest possible audience which, to them, means the highest common denominator of audience toleration. This means, in turn, that cultural, musical, or educational programs are generally shunted off into hours which are not considered "prime" time, that is to the early hours of the morning or the late hours of night. It is this that accounts for the timidity of the television networks, their fear of controversy or of controversial characters, their readiness to yield to forces of reaction like McCarthyism in the early 1950s, or to organizations like the House Un-American Activities Committees, their willingness to resort to blacklisting of writers or actors thought to be overly liberal. It is this that accounts, too, for the failure of television to develop professional standards, its failure to develop its own leadership, and its failure to develop, or create, its own materials. Yet insofar as television presents news and current events, either directly or through documentaries, it cannot really avoid impartiality or be wholly subservient to its business sponsors. Thus, merely by showing the McCarthy Senate hearings, television helped topple Senator Joseph McCarthy and end McCarthyism. And if television has not abandoned censorship it has pretty well abandoned the malpractices of blacklisting that disgraced it in the fifties.

What American television does best is reporting. This may take the form of continuous and intense concentration on world events: probably no other war in history has been reported in such detail as the Vietnam conflict, and there can be little doubt that daily familiarity with the brutality of that war provided by television played a role in bringing about popular revulsion against it. It may take the form of documentaries—elaborate reports on some national problem such as race relations, race riots, student discontent, water pollution, or the exploration of outer space. It may take the form of massive portrayal of some historic event such as the funeral of Winston Churchill or of President Kennedy or the Apollo landing on the moon. Or it may take the form of the news commentary, impartial,

182

succinct, ranging over a wide field of domestic and foreign affairs. Just as Walter Lippmann had no peer among journalists, so it is probable that an Edward R. Murrow in radio, a Walter Cronkite and a David Brinkley in television exercise greater influence than the editors of papers like the *New York Times,* the London *Times,* or *Le Monde.*

It is, however, not at all certain that continuous exposure to miscellaneous news has made Americans more cosmopolitan than other people, or better informed and more judicious about world problems than their grandparents were. Perhaps too much news and too much commentary is worse than too little, for it is not apparent that superficial and unadorned reports of complex political or social issues—which is all that most Americans get or will take—add much to popular understanding.

It is in any event sobering to reflect that the generation that is presumably better informed about all other countries and peoples on the globe than any previous generation has been the generation that appears to make more and more calamitous mistakes in foreign policy than any of its predecessors. Surely not even the most infatuated champions of television would argue that the current television-trained generation is politically as mature or as creative as the generation of the Founding Fathers—which was innocent of television, radio, and, for that matter, newspapers.

What kind of world is it that the American sees flickering before his fascinated gaze as he sits in front of his television screen? It is a world in which almost everything is experienced vicariously: it is not only sports that are "spectator," after all, but travel, adventure, even love. It is a world of action, often of violence where there is no time for contemplation and no advantage in taking thought. It is a world where all problems have simple solutions, usually physical and material—the solution of knocking down your opponent or killing him, the solution of money. It is, above all, a world filled with *things*—this is, of course, the pervasive theme of all advertisements—things without which there can be no happiness, without which life itself is empty and vain. The charge of materialism which has so often been leveled against America has not heretofore been a just one, but it is being justified by television. It is doubtful if in all history there has ever been a religion, an education, or a propaganda as purely materialistic as that to which television exposes the American people.

183

recommended reading

Allen, Frederick L. *The Big Change: America Transforms Itself, 1900-1950*. New York: Harper & Row (Perennial Library), 1969.

————. *Only Yesterday*. New York: Harper & Row (Perennial Library).

Andrews, Wayne. *Architecture, Ambition and Americans: A Social History of American Architecture*. New York: Free Press, 1964.

*Barnouw, Erik. *A History of Broadcasting in the United States*. 2 volumes. New York: Oxford University Press, 1966-68.

Dulles, Foster R. *History of Recreation: America Learns to Play*. 2nd edition. New York: Appleton-Century-Crofts.

Giedion, Siegfried. *Mechanization Takes Command*. New York: W. W. Norton & Company, 1969.

Hart, James D. *The Popular Book: A History of America's Literary Taste*. Berkeley, Calif.: University of California Press, 1950.

Holland, Laurence B., editor. *Who Designs America: A Comprehensive Survey of the Challenge to Good Design*. New York: Doubleday & Company (Anchor Books).

Jacobs, Jane. *The Death and Life of Great American Cities*. New York: Random House (Vintage Books), 1961.

Kouwenhoven, John A. *Arts in Modern American Civilization*. (Original title: *Made in America*.) New York: W. W. Norton & Company, 1967.

Lynd, Robert S. and Helen M. *Middletown*. New York: Harcourt, Brace & World (Harvest Books).

*Lynes, Russell. *The Domesticated Americans*. New York: Harper & Row, 1963.

*————. *A Surfeit of Honey*. New York: Harper & Row, 1957.

————. *The Tastemakers*. New York: Grosset & Dunlap (Universal Library).

Mills, C. Wright. *The Power Elite*. New York: Oxford University Press (Galaxy Books), 1959.

————. *White Collar: American Middle Classes*. New York: Oxford University Press (Galaxy Books), 1956.

*Mott, Frank L. *Golden Multitudes*. New York: R. R. Bowker Company, 1960.

Mowry, George E. *The Urban Nation: 1920-1960*. New York: Hill & Wang (American Century Series), 1968.

Mumford, Lewis. *Art and Technics*. New York: Columbia University Press, 1952.

————. *The Brown Decades: A Study of the Arts in America, 1865-1895*. 2nd edition. New York: Dover Publications, 1955.

————. *The City in History: Its Origins, Its Transformations, and Its Prospects*. New York: Harcourt, Brace & World (Harbinger Books), 1968.

*————. *The Culture of Cities*. New York: Harcourt, Brace & World, 1938.

————. *Sticks and Stones*. Revised edition. New York: Dover Publications, 1955.

Packard, Vance. *The Hidden Persuaders*. New York: Pocket Books.

Rosenberg, Bernard, and White, David M., editors. *Mass Culture: The Popular Arts in America*. New York: Free Press.

Seldes, Gilbert. *The Seven Lively Arts*. Cranbury, N.J.: A. S. Barnes & Company (Perpetua Books), 1962.

————. *The Public Arts*. New York: Simon & Schuster, 1957.

*Tunis, John R. *The American Way in Sport*. New York: Duell, Sloan & Pearce, 1958. OP

*Wertham, Fredric. *Seduction of the Innocents*. New York: Holt, Rinehart and Winston, 1954. OP

Whyte, William H., Jr. *The Organization Man*. New York: Doubleday & Company (Anchor Books).

---

* Hard-cover edition. Titles not so marked are paperback editions.

OP indicates the book is out of print.

11. America and world power

The whole of American history is in one sense a struggle between forces of integration and of exclusion—on the one hand participation and membership in the community of western civilization, on the other isolation and uniqueness. Even now it cannot be said that the dilemma has been wholly resolved, for if isolation is no longer an issue, uniqueness —one of the forms of isolation—is.

Those who made America, not in the seventeenth and eighteenth centuries alone but down to the First World War, were for one reason or another, refugees from the old world. They had turned their backs on Europe and embraced America, and to many of them the essence of America was precisely that it was not Europe. Yet it was, of course, Europe—a Europe transplanted, a Europe transformed, a Europe perhaps translated into something different. America was the child of the whole of Europe and—in a curious fashion—of Africa, too. Her language, religion, social organization, culture, science, technology, were all inherited, and however different the child was from its mother, Europe, the inheritance was plain; we have only to imagine how very different American civilization would have been had America been settled from the west instead of from the east, from China or Japan rather from Europe and Africa.

The problem that arose from this conflict of inheritance and independence is of course a familiar one, recapitulated in the history of every young man who acknowledges that he is part of a family but is determined, nevertheless, to be independent. Just as with the individual the very gesture toward independence is an unconscious tribute to the tenacity of the family attachment, so the very intensity of the American search for identity is a tribute to the tenacity and persistence of the old world relationship.

Independence could be equally well assured in either one of two ways: by an isolation so complete that it cut the new nation off from the old world and allowed her to develop in her own way, to form her own character and follow her own policies, or by power so great that it enabled the nation to fix the terms on which she chose to be part of the larger community of western civilization. Clearly at the beginning only the first of these alternatives was open to Americans; in our own day it is the second alternative that many Americans embrace, consciously and unconsciously, and in vain.

A View of the Bombardment of Fort McHenry. One of the decisive battles in the
War of 1812 with Britain, a second "War of Independence" which consolidated
the United States's position as an independent nation. The battle was the inspiration
for the national anthem, "The Star-Spangled Banner"; it includes the lines,
"the rockets' red glare, the bombs bursting in air/ Gave proof through the night
that our flag was still there."

Isolation was favored by geography—a very powerful factor whose
power was steadily weakened as the industrial revolution overcame the
barrier of the Atlantic, and one which now exercises little influence. It was
ratified by two wars of independence, which gave it a political character.
It was strengthened by economic self-sufficiency—by the ability of the
new nation to get along without help and to avoid outside interference.
It was confirmed by an emigration from the old to the new world unprecedented in volume and unprecedented, too, in its voluntarily deracinated
character—terms that do not apply to the Africans brought to the American
continent.

186

In addition to these material factors were almost equally impressive intellectual, psychological, and moral considerations. Even in colonial days Americans began to think of themselves as a people apart, and during the Revolutionary and nation-making era the concept of cultural and moral independence was as prominent as that of political independence. The American was a new man in that he did not pull his forelock to his betters. He was new in that he owned land and could pass it on to his children. He was new in that to him children were not a curse, as elsewhere in so much of the world, but a blessing, for he knew that here would always be meat and drink for them, clothing and shelter. He was new in that he was free of the tyranny of the church, of the state, of the military. He was new in that he was not condemned forever to the class to which he had been born, the work or trade which he had inherited, but could raise himself by his boot-straps. These considerations were material, but all had moral implications.

What they meant, quite simply, to the average man was that life in the new world was far better than life in the old. It is that conviction, more perhaps than any other, that explains the deep loyalty of newcomers to their adopted land, and their reluctance—until well into the twentieth century—to return to their native country. What it meant to the intellectuals, native-born most of them, was something more romantic: new world innocence and old world depravity. Let us build a wall between the old world and the new, said the poets and idealists. No one was more insistent on the principle of moral superiority of America to Europe than that ardent cosmopolitan, Thomas Jefferson. To his old mentor, George Wythe of Virginia, he wrote in 1786:

> If all the sovereigns of Europe were to set themselves to work, to emancipate the minds of their subjects from their present ignorance and prejudices . . . a thousand years would not place them on that high ground, on which our common people are now setting out. Ours could not have been so fairly placed under the control of the common sense of the people, had they not been separated from their parent stock, and kept from contamination, either from them, or the other people of the old world, by the intervention of so wide an ocean.

A half century later the poet James Russell Lowell admonished his countrymen to

Forget Europe wholly, your veins throb with blood,
To which the dull current in hers is but mud; . . .
O my friends, thank your God, if you have one, that he
'Twixt the Old World and you set the gulf of a sea . . .
　　　　　　　"A Fable for Critics"

What it all meant was clear enough: what God had put asunder let no man join together! Nature, Providence, History—call it what you will—had decreed that America was to go her own way, and who, looking at the two continents, the two societies, could doubt for a moment that it was a better way!

Inevitably all the forces making for isolation crystallized into a policy; inevitably that policy found expression in a document which was to take on ever larger symbolic meaning: the Monroe Doctrine. Just what President Monroe meant when he declared that any attempt on the part of the European powers "to extend their system to any portion of this hemisphere" would not be tolerated, was not to be clear for another half century, but what Americans eventually read into it is clear enough: that Europe and America had different interests, character, and civilization, and that they should leave each other alone. Implicit in it—and in the modifications, additions, and corollaries that clustered about it—are two great myths about America and about her relations with the rest of the world: the myth of uniqueness and the myth of superiority.

Not until she had fought a Second War of Independence—usually called the War of 1812—did the new nation really win freedom from involvement in the wars of the old world. The conclusion of that war, in 1815, ushered in a new era of independence and of isolation. Britain was still in Canada, Spain in most of South America and much of North America, too, but there had been a symbolic withdrawal, and for a century the United States was to be free from interference in her internal affairs, and free to expand into the territory she thought hers by natural right. Just as isolation found its justification in the doctrine of uniqueness and its symbol in the Monroe Doctrine, so westward expansion, which in a single generation carried America to the shores of the Pacific, found its justification in the principle of superiority and its symbol in Manifest Destiny.

Westward expansion across the continent was not without its paradoxical qualities. To be independent from Europe the Americans plunged into a series of broils with European nations. They expelled in one way or another the Spaniards from Florida and eventually from the Caribbean, Mexicans from Texas and California, the British from Oregon, the Russians from the northwest coast and Alaska. In the end their desire for independence from Europe landed them in Hawaii and the Philippine Islands. All this meant, of course, that Americans had to create a military, wage wars of aggression and of conquest, rule over alien peoples, and engage in power politics—just the things they had wanted to escape from. Thus to vindicate their divorce from the old world they embraced the policies and instruments of the old world. Did they embrace their principles as well?

American immunity from Europe was not seriously challenged in the nineteenth century, nor was American isolation. It was, in the end, the United States that abandoned isolation, not Europe that invaded it. That abandonment came in the 1890s, and was dramatized by the Spanish-American War. But the United States did not have to intervene in Cuba in 1898 to oust the Spaniards. No American interest was seriously at stake, and it was a sardonic commentary on the whole enterprise that in the end Cuba became a Communist state feared and condemned by the United States, and the United States found herself sustaining a regime of a military dictator in Spain far more repressive than that of the liberal Alfonso XIII who ruled in 1898! Nor did the United States have to annex the Philippines, or Hawaii, or get involved in the affairs of China. She did all this on her own. Thus while she continued to proclaim isolation, repudiate power politics, and reject colonialism, imperialism, and militarism, she launched herself upon all these courses. However Americans might envision themselves, in the eyes of the rest of the world there was little perceptible difference between their conduct and that of other peoples. And while responsibility for these new ventures into world politics can be put down, with reassuring vagueness, as the price of power and of wealth, the achievement was in fact neither unconscious nor uncalculated. It was not (as is sometimes assumed) a vague force called "destiny" that made the United States a world power; it was a combination of circumstances and deliberate will.

Yet isolation persisted, tenaciously, long after these first ventures into world power, and even after the crisis of two world wars it died a lingering and reluctant death. The first serious breach of isolation had come in the eighteen-nineties. The First World War brought a major challenge. This chapter of American history provides an illuminating microcosm of the forces pressing on the United States and competing for American support.

President Woodrow Wilson had not mentioned foreign affairs in his eloquent first inaugural address (March 1913). The outbreak of war in Europe took him by surprise, as it took most Americans by surprise, and his response was for "neutrality in thought and in action." For two years the President succeeded in keeping the nation out of war, and he went into the 1916 Presidential campaign with that slogan. When, the next year, he did carry the United States into war it was not merely a response to unrestricted submarine warfare against American shipping, or even to the mortal danger in which Britain and France found themselves. No, it was nothing less than a moral crusade "to make the world safe for democracy."

The history of American participation in the First World War, peace-making, and eventual withdrawal into sullen isolation recreates a familiar pattern of immunity, uniqueness, and superiority. Both the war and peace-making demonstrated (to the satisfaction of Americans) that it was the rest of the world that was abandoned to militarism, colonialism, secret diplomacy, and so forth, and not the United States, and that it was therefore the unavoidable duty of the United States to stand for morality and law. And it was typical of the American character at this time that the failure to achieve the unattainable goal of *making* (note the word) the world safe for democracy and creating a new international order to preserve peace led to swift and deep disillusionment. Not with themselves—for most Americans were sure that their policies were statesmanlike and their conduct irreproachable. No, it was the intransigence and the selfishness of the old world that accounted for the failure of the war and its aftermath to bring about the hoped-for reign of peace! Clearly the new isolation into which the United States now withdrew was one more flattering to American vanity than to American intelligence. It was based on the assumption that Europe simply could not come up to American moral standards. President Wilson, to be sure, saw through the hypocrisy of this, but Wilson was discredited, along with his Versailles Treaty and his League of Nations, by Americans at the polls.

Yet the new isolation was more formal than real; actually the United States was by this time so inextricably involved in Europe and Asia that it was impossible for her to follow a policy of disinvolvement. All through the twenties the United States did in fact participate in international organizations, send representatives to international conferences, and even "meddle" in the affairs of other continents and nations. Yet she never joined the League of Nations nor—despite repeated urgings by successive Presidents—become a member of the World Court.

Failure to make even these gestures can be ascribed to a public opinion which was increasingly isolationist and to an inept leadership which was unprepared either to educate or to challenge that opinion. Isolation was fed first by the depression of the 1930s which concentrated attention on domestic needs, and then by revulsion against totalitarianism and the outbreak of war in China, Ethiopia, and Spain. All of this confirmed Americans in their conviction that the other nations were ineradicably corrupt. Even Franklin Roosevelt, more of a genuine internationalist than Wilson, did not—perhaps could not—make American influence effective in world affairs in the thirties. American isolation reached some kind of a climax when, in the mid- and late thirties, Congress enacted a series of "Neutrality Acts" which, in the words of the poet Edna St. Vincent Millay, "sketched her a fortress on a paper pad." These acts tried to preserve American neutrality by requiring that Americans close their eyes and ears to the reality of the wars which were rapidly spreading over the globe. Though American sympathies were clearly with Britain, France, and China, her policies were more helpful to Germany and Japan than to these beleaguered nations.

After his triumph in the 1940 elections, President Roosevelt moved more confidently towards a policy of "aid to the Allies"—aid which he tried to reconcile with formal neutrality. The effort proved as vain as Wilson's effort to follow much the same policies in the early years of the First World War. All through 1941 the United States moved steadily toward support of the Western Allies, covering its conduct with a patina of moralism—a moralism unquestionably justified by facts. Once again, as in

190

1916, the United States found herself more deeply involved than the public had anticipated. Then she was unexpectedly plunged into the war by the Japanese attack on Pearl Harbor.

The modern era of America as a world power dates from Pearl Harbor. At earlier times—in the 1890s and again in the 1920s—it had been possible for the United States to retreat from commitments which went beyond those that public opinion was prepared to support. After Pearl Harbor there was no retreat nor, for that matter, did public opinion demand one. The United States emerged from the war indubitably the strongest of nations, and the only one in a position to exercise power in every continent and almost in every nation on the globe. She emerged with obligations that were unavoidable, responsibilities that were inescapable, and opportunities that were inexhaustible. The great overarching question for the future concerned the nature of those obligations and responsibilities and the policies the United States should follow to fulfill them.

The Second World War brought out, and confirmed, familiar traits of the American character. When the United States entered the war the totalitarian powers were victorious almost everywhere, and it was uncertain whether American power could turn the tide of defeat into one of victory. The special American contribution was in the production of everything needed to fight a war, and it was in the factories and shipyards that the war was won. President Roosevelt had called upon the nation to become the "arsenal of democracy," and she did. To the astonishment of the Germans and the Japanese the United States rallied her resources with unprecedented speed and efficiency. By almost a miracle of organization she raised over fifteen million men and women for the armed forces, armed and equipped them with everything that they needed—and more—and transported over four million of them abroad. At home American productive capacity seemed limitless: before the end of the war American factories and shipyards produced enough of almost everything; tanks, jeeps, trucks, airplanes, submarines, radar sets—and food—to supply not only their own needs throughout the globe, but the needs of Britain and, to a large extent, those of Russia. In the arena of science, too, the American talent for organization and production was decisive. The government and universities quickly rounded up almost all the vast scientific talent of the country and channeled it into military production. Drawing on discoveries of British, German, and Danish scientists, and on the skills of scores of scientists who had fled from

The Spanish-American War: Cuba, 1898. The United States's fight to oust Spain from Cuba marked the beginning of the end of the isolationism to which the country clung throughout the nineteenth century.

totalitarian countries to the United States, the government carried through what it called the Manhattan Project—the creation of the first atomic bomb. This weapon proved decisive in the war against Japan, but in the end it too created more problems than it had solved.

Something of the same talent for organization and cooperation marked America's relations with her allies and associates throughout the globe. Roosevelt and Churchill—himself half-American (and later an honorary citizen of the United States)—created a military and political coalition that worked better than had any previous coalition of this kind in the history of war. They created, in fact, a single military enterprise whose command was drawn in almost equal proportions from both countries. It was characteristic that the commander in chief of the Allied forces in the west should have been a soldier whose chief qualification was his ability to organize, reconcile and administer: General Eisenhower.

On the domestic scene, too, American institutions and the American character stood up well under the strain of total war—a strain, to be sure, far less severe in the United States than in the other warring nations. The nation achieved a greater unity than it had displayed before—or than it has displayed since: political partisanship was in abeyance and progress towards racial equality in the armed forces together with booming prosperity did much to quiet racial antagonisms and tensions at home. The constitutional and political processes remained intact: there was no dictatorship, no suspension of legislative authority, no attempt by the military to take over from the civilian (that came later, in the Korean War, when General MacArthur challenged President Truman and lost). Except for the shameful episode of gathering up Japanese residents in the western United States and "relocating" them in military camps in the wilderness, constitutional guarantees of civil liberty stood up better than in the First World War.

The United States emerged from the war with her vast resources unscathed, her resources of men and materials, industry and finance, science and intelligence. By American standards losses had been heavy—some three hundred thousand battle deaths—but by the standards of Russia, Germany, Japan, and other combatants, they were light. Certainly the United States grew in numbers, in wealth, and in strength all through the war, and at the close of that conflict she bestrode the globe like a colossus, the most powerful nation in the world, probably the most powerful in history.

At this juncture of her history, the United States conducted herself with magnanimity and wisdom. She did not impose a punitive peace on the stricken enemy, but helped the defeated countries to rebuild economically and politically: it was American aid that provided the stimulus for the immense prosperity of present-day West Germany and Japan. Second, the United States extended aid to her allies and associates—a continuation of the enlightened lend-lease program, with the emphasis, of course, on economic aid. Initially through the Marshall Plan, then through a succession of foreign aid programs, some economic, some military, the United States contributed in the post-war years a total of one hundred billion dollars to other nations around the world. Third, the United States was chiefly responsible for setting up a new international organization designed to preserve peace: the United Nations. This time the United States (as contrasted to 1919) not only joined, but persuaded other nations to establish the U.N. headquarters in New York City.

All of this augured well for the peace of the world and for the prospects of American leadership.

Alas, within a few years the clouds drew over the bright horizon. Instead of solving the herculean tasks that confronted them, the two major powers, the United States and the Soviet Union, launched themselves upon a "Cold War" which threatened, again and again, to break out into a real war, which divided rather than united the globe, and which wasted material, political, and moral resources on the burdens of conflict instead of using them to further international cooperation. The tasks were there, a challenge which in principle all recognized—to rebuild the stricken world, limit a population explosion which threatened disaster, explore together the potentialities of science, and to cooperate in the greatest revolution of all history: the upsurge of two-thirds of the peoples of the globe seeking to catch up in one convulsive leap with the nations of the west. But the will to perform them was gone.

The story of the next few years is too familiar to rehearse: the growth of misunderstanding and suspicion that evolved swiftly into open antagonism and hostility; the transformation of the temporary division of Germany into a permanent one; the lowering of the Iron Curtain all along the boundaries from the Baltic to the Adriatic and the military buildup along both sides of that curtain; the outbreak of ideological hostilities in the Middle East and President Truman's response with a doctrine that appeared to promise American aid against communism everywhere; the communist takeover of hapless Czechoslovakia; the Soviet blockade of Berlin and the Anglo-American penetration of that blockade; the upsurge of nationalism and racism in Africa, Asia, and South America; the nuclear race between the United States and the Soviet Union which neither could possibly win; the victory of the communists in China and the extension of the Cold War to Asia; and finally, in 1950, the first of the great postwar climacterics, the Korean War.

Thus within five years the great coalition which had destroyed Axis totalitarianism fell apart and its two leaders glared ceaselessly at each other and armed ceaselessly to defend themselves against each other. Once again the world was racked by hostilities which might at any moment take form in a third world war. Happily the prospect of a nuclear war which would have been suicidal for all deterred even the extremists in the contending countries. But it did not discourage their belligerency.

Instead, as the problems of the world grew every day more intractable, the revolution of the underprivileged peoples every day more dangerous, and the chances of a little explosion growing into a gigantic conflagration every day more ominous, the United States, the Soviet Union, and China settled down to the Cold War in earnest.

How explain the American readiness to engage in the Cold War and to wage it with a dedication and a fervor that matched the fighting of the Second World War itself? The explanation—insofar as there ever are explanations in history—is rooted in the American character; and the Cold War, as Americans conducted it, was an expression of familiar elements in that character.

First, since Americans had long thought of themselves as the champions of freedom and democracy (which indeed they were in the early decades of their history), it was easy for them to persuade themselves that now once again, as in the era of the Revolution, the fate of freedom in the world depended on them. Jefferson had called the United States "the world's best hope" and Lincoln, "the last best hope of earth." President Wilson had called upon his countrymen to "vindicate the principles of peace and justice in the world as against selfish and autocratic power." The tradition of a special mission was old and respectable.

Second, as Americans had long thought of themselves as standing up against the great powers of the old world, the role of opposing communist power was an old one in new form. Old world powers were, by definition, militaristic, expansionist, and aggressive, and eager to "extend their system" to every part of the globe. That had been the history of Britain, of Napoleon, of the Holy Alliance, and of Spain in the Americas, and of almost all powers—both European and Asian—in the nineteenth and twentieth centuries in Africa and Asia. It was easy to believe that communism fitted into this familiar pattern, for clearly the communists were dedicated to spreading their power and their ideology everywhere on the face of the globe—even to the United States. It was this fear which took paranoiac form in Senator Joseph McCarthy's campaign against "subversives" in the government and universities, and in the crusade for "loyalty" and "conformity." Just as the United States had to resist subversion at home—so the argument ran—it was called on to resist subversion elsewhere: in the Caribbean, Latin America, the Near East, Southeast Asia, and so forth. Thus American moral commitments became global.

Third, while Americans recognized readily enough the dynamic and complex nature of their own institutions, they had long thought of the culture and institutions of the old world in simple and unsophisticated terms. Thus monarchy was, per se, bad—see Mark Twain's *The Prince and the Pauper*—and so, too, were empire, colonialism, militarism, aristocracy, the class system and the established Church. To these it was natural —indeed inevitable—to add communism, especially as it was associated in the minds of most Americans with atheism. In the traditionalist view all of these institutions were not only politically misguided and socially unsound, but morally wrong. How easy, then, for Americans to conclude that they were called upon to resist the spread of communism on *moral* grounds, that they had to resist it everywhere because it was everywhere equally immoral, and that they would have to gird themselves to resist it into the indefinite future, or until it was finally defeated, because it would always be the same. Thus Americans almost instinctively embraced three convictions that were to condition the conduct of their foreign policy for twenty years: that communism was primarily a moral (or immoral) system; that it was monolithic; and that it was unchanging and permanent. The first of these convictions was not susceptible to evidence, but it was so powerful that it provided a kind of immunity for the second and third against contrary evidence that would have been conclusive to any unprejudiced mind.

Fourth, Americans had customarily assumed that the ideas and principles which they themselves espoused—freedom, republicanism, democracy, equality, and in the twentieth century, free enterprise—were so unequivocal and irrefutable that they did not need to be spread by force but could be counted on to make their own way throughout the globe. Not so, however, with the pernicious ideas of the old world. As in the past we had assumed that no one would voluntarily embrace a monarch or a class system or an established church and that these institutions could be spread only by force—the principle behind the Holy Alliance of infamous memory—so now Americans assumed that no people would voluntarily embrace communism and that it could be spread only by subversion or by force. Events in Czechoslovakia in 1948, China in 1949, Vietnam in 1954, and Hungary in 1956 all seemed to confirm this diagnosis. These events strengthened the American conclusion that communism was not so much an ideology as an "international conspiracy," and that as it relied on subversion and force it would have to be contained by subversion and force. Thus the reliance on nuclear superiority; thus the desperate armaments race which promised to bankrupt all those caught up in it; thus the promises of the Truman Doctrine and the Eisenhower Doctrine, the Kennedy, the Johnson and the Nixon promises of intervention against subversion. And thus, most important, the armed intervention of the United States in Taiwan, Guatemala, Lebanon, Cuba, Santo Domingo, Laos, and Vietnam. The last of these was to burgeon into one of the major wars of American history.

In the quarter century after the end of the Second World War, American policies and philosophies involved her in two major wars: the Korean and the Vietnam. Superficially the two were much alike. Both were fought along the periphery of Asia but both profoundly affected China, and with China the whole of the vast Asian continent. Both were precipitated by civil war and both sucked in the United States through the whirlpool of the Cold War. Each involved roughly the same armed forces by the United States and exacted roughly the same casualties.

But the two wars were, nevertheless, very different—different in the response which they drew forth, different in their implications for the future of American and world history. The Korean War presented an example of unmistakable communist aggression—an aggression formally recognized by the United Nations—but it was never quite clear who was the aggressor in the Vietnam war; in the eyes of most of the world it was probably the United States. American participation in the Korean War was a response to a United Nations resolution, and she fought, in Korea, under the flag of the United Nations and alongside some nineteen other nations. The Vietnamese crisis was never submitted to the United Nations or to any other international tribunal, and the United States fought there alone, with merely token help from Australia and New Zealand and Korea. An overwhelming majority of the American people supported American military action in Korea: there were no anti-war demonstrations, no wholesale draft evasions, no revolt of the young, no dissension within the party that had made the war, no widespread political or moral revulsion against the war. United States intervention in the Vietnam War, on the contrary, seemed to ever increasing numbers of Americans and foreigners a clear violation of international law, of the charter of the United Nations, of morality, of sound military strategy, and of common sense. The administrations that fought the war never succeeded in making clear to the American people (to say nothing of the rest of the globe) what were American interests in Southeast Asia, or how the war would serve any interests at all. Nor did they formulate a convincing legal or moral defense of their conduct. Clearly behind all the rhetoric about "solemn commitments" or "vital interests" was fear of Communist China; yet China had not entered or taken an active part in the war, and during the whole long period of American intervention, China refrained from sending in any soldiers to match the half million that the United States sent to South Vietnam. The conduct of the war, too, contrasted sharply with the conduct of the Korean War: the large scale and indiscriminate bombings of towns and villages, the defoliation of forests, the use of chemical warfare, the systematic laying waste of an entire country.

As what was originally planned as small-scale intervention—really a kind of glorified police action—grew into a major war; as American casualties mounted to over forty thousand dead, and casualties inflicted on the all-but-helpless Vietnamese into the hundred thousands; as the demands of the war drained the material, the financial, and the intellectual resources of the nation; and as the moral nature of the war increasingly outraged larger elements of the American people, dissatisfaction grew into revolt. By the summer of 1968—after four years of fighting—that revolt threatened to split the Democratic party asunder and to inspire wholesale civil disobedience in almost all classes of the people—whites and blacks, old and young. Bowing to what seemed the inevitable, President Johnson removed himself from the political scene and promised to initiate negotiations looking to peace. Mr. Nixon, who had been a strong supporter of intervention in Asia, promised in his campaign for the Presidency to bring about peace. For the first time in American history public opinion had toppled a President; for the first time it had brought about a readiness to admit that a war in which the nation was engaged was misguided and should cease. As so often in the past quarter-century the philosophical conclusion was allowed to dangle in a vacuum; the war went on.

If the war itself had been misguided in inception and ignoble in conduct, the public reaction to it offered some reassurance that the mass of the people still believed in morality in international relations, even if they did not know how to realize their beliefs.

I n the four or five years after the close of the Second World War many peoples throughout the globe looked to the United States for protection against aggression and for massive economic aid. As the danger of aggression and subversion diminished and prosperity and stability revived, they no longer needed the United States and sought, instead, independence; as the cost and the danger of the cold war mounted they looked with growing apprehension on American commitments, and sought neutrality. But Americans found it as difficult to concede that they were not needed as to imagine that they were not wanted. Instead, therefore, of withdrawing gracefully from Europe, disengaging itself from its commitments, and funneling much of its foreign aid through the United Nations, the United States turned in the other direction: it expanded its responsibilities and its commitments to embrace Asia as well as Europe and Latin America. This enlargement of ambition was matched by a corresponding enlargement of power. By treaty, by executive agreements (sometimes secret), by congressional resolution even, the United States extended her commitments to almost every part of the globe and extended her military presence

Lloyd George, Clemenceau, and Woodrow Wilson in Paris during World War I peace negotiations, 1919. The United States rejected Wilson's proposals for international cooperation and withdrew into isolationism in the 1920s.

to match the new commitments. Thus by the end of the sixties the United States had guaranteed scores of nations against communist "subversion," maintained over four hundred major and over twelve hundred minor military posts scattered across the globe, operated the Central Intelligence Agency (C.I.A.) in sixty countries, boasted the largest nuclear armaments of any nation, and was spending each year some eighty billion dollars on war. Most Americans assumed that this display of arms made for peace, but other nations saw in it rather a continuous risk of war, a war of which they might well be the victims. Nor were their fears without foundation. The United States did come to the very brink of war many times: with Russia over Berlin, with China over Taiwan and the Pescadores, and with Russia again at the time of the Cuban missile crisis. All of these crises might well have become global wars, but in no instance was the rest of the globe consulted about them.

Wide World Photos

Bombers for Britain, 1940. American industrial might was the decisive factor in the Allies' victory in World War II. Before the United States entered the war, she supplied bombers for Britain's Royal Air Force.

It was high tide for American power but ebb tide for American prestige; as the United States engaged in more and more adventures the rest of the world disengaged itself more and more from the United States. No wonder NATO grew steadily weaker and was eventually reduced to searching for some new role that would justify its continuation, while General De Gaulle set himself up as the champion of Europe against American power and influence. Elsewhere, too, around the globe American influence declined and, soberly enough, declined most precipitously in those nations which had been allies and associates during the great crisis of the World War. Britain was restless under what seemed to many a case of economic imperialism; Scandinavians were outraged by the Vietnamese war; the Arab world thought American policies were pro-Israel; India and Pakistan both resented the American policy of selling arms to the other nation; China was understandably outraged at what it considered American aggression in Vietnam and smarted under her exclusion from the United Nations. Even Germany and Japan, whose prosperity owed so much to American help, showed restlessness at the danger of war, and at the continuation of American military presence. Nor did the United States find compensation for all this unpopularity in the Western Hemisphere. Here American military intervention in Guatemala, Cuba, and Santo Domingo, and support to military dictators in Brazil and Haiti, and what Latin Americans regarded—with some injustice—as American economic imperialism, aroused widespread antagonism.

Thus by the end of the decade the United States found herself pretty much abandoned by her former associates and distrusted by much of mankind. It was a dusty answer to the bright promises of the 1940s.

It is a mistake to think of world power exclusively in military or political terms. Athens of the fifth century B.C. was a world power, and so, too, were Renaissance Florence and seventeenth-century Holland. Elizabethan England conquered the world in a sense that twentieth-century England cannot. Certainly in the eighteenth and nineteenth centuries, American power was to be recorded not in terms of military might or empire, but in those of the influence of the ideas and institutions identified with America in the eyes of the rest of the world: self-government, equality, religious freedom, and a second chance for the common man.

In the realm of ideas American influence and power is probably less today than it was a hundred years ago. The United States no longer inspires revolution, as she inspired revolution in Latin America and in

Europe in the nineteenth century; she no longer spreads the ideas of equality, for most Western nations have caught up with and surpassed her in this arena. She no longer attracts "the teeming masses yearning to breathe free," and if she did, would not let them in. But in other realms, the social, the economic, the technological, her influence is profound and pervasive.

These three modes of influence—social, economic and technological—are inextricably blended both in their manifestations and their impact. What has happened in the last quarter century is something comparable to the expansion of England through the eighteenth- and nineteenth-century industrial revolutions: the spread of an American culture that is not primarily intellectual or artistic but predominantly social and technological.

This is what European critics have in mind when they complain of the "Americanization" of Europe or warn against the "American Challenge"—not a political takeover, for politically the American model has lost its attraction (of some sixty new nations, not one has adopted the American constitutional model), and certainly not an old-fashioned empire, for though the rest of the world distrusts American power it does not believe that the United States yearns to be an imperialist power. No, what disturbs Europe, and other continents as well, is the spread and penetration of American economic interests and techniques, the infiltration of American cultural habits and standards, and the fascination of American social practices and institutions.

The economic impact is the most ostentatious—not merely the fact that American investment abroad is not far from one hundred billion dollars (much of it to be sure in Canada and Latin America), or that some seven hundred of the one thousand largest American corporations have moved into Europe, or that the European operations of Ford and General Motors and Esso and Bank of America overshadow those of all but the largest European corporations and banks, but that American business habits and practices are rapidly coming to be a kind of norm that businessmen in other countries must accommodate to and, if possible, imitate. This they are often reluctant to do, not merely because American notions of efficiency go against the grain, but because they are *American.*

Far more serious, in the eyes of the intellectuals, is what they regard —with jaundiced eye—as the "Americanization" of the masses. What Tocqueville predicted a hundred and thirty years ago has now come to pass: that social and economic equality operates in Europe pretty much as it operates in the United States. The farmers and the workingmen of Western Europe (and of Eastern, too, no doubt) have made greater progress in economic well-being, social position, and education during the past quarter century than in any comparable time in the past and, except along the edges of the Mediterranean world, the class structure of society is disintegrating. What the people of Britain, France, Germany, Austria, Scandinavia, Holland, even Italy and Spain, want with their newly

The attack on Pearl Harbor, December 7, 1941. The U.S.S. California, above, was one of the ships that sank in Pearl Harbor, Hawaii, after being hit by Japanese aerial bombs and torpedoes in a surprise attack. The attack precipitated the United States's entry into World War II.

The first atomic bomb explosion, Alamogordo, New Mexico, 1945. The United States dropped atomic bombs on Hiroshima and Nagasaki in the summer of 1945, hastening the end of the war but unleashing a power that could destroy mankind.

won freedom and prosperity are material things. These are now within their reach: automobiles, washing machines, refrigerators, television, central heating, and a hundred other "improvements" and labor-saving devices. In order to buy these they demand more money; in order to enjoy them they demand shorter working hours. What they want, in short, is that higher standard of living which they have heretofore associated with the United States. And with many, though not all, go other expectations: education for their children, even university education, playing fields and swimming pools, ready-made clothes, supermarkets, the pleasures of travel and vacations, and so forth.

Now the United States is not responsible for all this, but rather for the universal conviction that happiness depends on material possessions and that the quickest way to happiness is a higher standard of living for everybody. Doubtless the American example, familiar over the years in films and in television and demonstrated by millions of American soldiers scattered around the globe during and after the Second World War, had a powerful influence in creating the ideal of a material utopia. But what critics—mostly intellectuals who profess to despise materialism, and the rich who saw themselves paying for it all—called "Americanization" was in fact the almost inevitable operation of the new prosperity and the new technology. And because the United States had so long made something of a religion of prosperity, and because it had embraced technology more fervently than had any other nation, it was fatally easy to blame the whole thing on the United States.

"Blame" expressed the attitude of the intellectuals and the elite, not that of the masses of the population. European intellectuals had long despised "Americanization" because they considered it a calculated rejection of the past, tradition, beauty, and culture, and a surrender to crass materialism. The ruling classes—the rich, well-born, and powerful— rejected Americanism because it threatened to level all ranks, at their expense. So just as in the United States during the fifties the term "communism" was a kind of code word for everything that conservatives disliked or feared, so abroad "Americanism" became an analogous code word for what the social and intellectual elite hated and feared.

This was an old story, but in a new setting. From the beginning European governments and ruling classes had looked upon the upstart American republic as dangerous, and quite rightly, too, for to them she was dangerous. Over the years the United States had lured millions of their people away from their native soil—men and women whom they had nourished and supported, and whose services they thought they had a right to command. The United States had threatened the stability of monarchical and aristocratic government by the example of its own self-government; threatened the stability of the class system by its own classless society; threatened religion and the church by its success in separating church and state. It had threatened their prosperity by the competition

National Aeronautics and Space Administration

A man—and an American flag—on the moon. On July 20, 1969, Neil A. Armstrong took man's first step on another body in the galaxy.

of its own limitless resources and by its rival economic system.

By the twentieth century, to be sure, even the ruling classes of the old world had reconciled themselves to American political practices and American economic standards. What they found difficult to accept was the new culture that America appeared to represent: the mass culture that one famous American expatriate, Henry Miller, called an "air-conditioned nightmare," but that was in fact merely a natural extension of the culture of equalitarianism.

But throughout all these years, the hostility of the European ruling classes had been counterbalanced by the admiration of the masses. Whatever their "betters" said, these knew that America was the promised land, and they gave it, over the years, the greatest vote of confidence that any nation in history has ever received: forty million Europeans chose to leave the old world for the new. In this fateful transplanting they gave up the advantages of social stability, of an established church, and of an ancient culture for a new chance in a new world. When, during the American Civil War, the ruling classes of Europe supported the Confederacy and rejoiced in the prospect of the breakup of the Union, the European masses championed the Union cause. They were not put off by the newness and rawness of it all, by frontier violence, by the exploitation of blacks and of immigrants, by jerry-built cities, by the vulgarity of manners, by the absence of an ancient culture; or if they were, they found compensations. They were, to be sure, put off by slavery, but they met this problem quite simply by avoiding the South. Clearly it was not only those who migrated to the new world who wanted to assimilate themselves to the American culture: so too, on the whole, did those who stayed home.

Now by mid-twentieth century the common people of the world found themselves reacting to social equality and prosperity and the technological revolution pretty much as Americans had reacted to these things in the past. As they adopted American ideas, institutions, and machines, so they embraced the cultural patterns and practices that went by the name American. They watched Hollywood films and, later, American television programs; they read American comic strips and knew Charlie Brown and Snoopy as well as they had known Laurel and Hardy and the Marx brothers; they bought American magazines—*Reader's Digest* for the masses, *Playboy* for the young, and *The New Yorker* for the sophisticates; they listened to American jazz and American blues and swung to American rock music; they shopped in American supermarkets for frozen food, Coca-Cola, and TV dinners, clamored for American superhighways, and built American skyscrapers. Even the intellectuals made some gestures across the Atlantic: they read American novels, accepted American literary critics, acknowledged the superiority of American scientific laboratories, even Americanized their ancient universities.

Yet in the fifties and the sixties the United States, for the first time in its history, forfeited much of the affection and the confidence of the common people. The explanation can be found in developments already familiar: the Cold War, and the war in Vietnam; the image of the United States as a great military power; the spectacle of a nation committed to equality but denying equality to its large minority populations, of a nation incomparably rich but unable to take care of its poor, of a nation dedicated to self-government but unable to enforce its laws, support its cities, or preserve its environment from the ravages of corporate greed.

These are, let us hope, temporary rather than permanent features of American life. Already there are signs that the United States is prepared to abandon its pretentions to be the policeman of the globe, and to adopt a role more consistent with reality and her own traditions. The temper of the people is clearly against "globalism" and, in a somewhat timorous fashion, the new Nixon administration has recognized and accommodated to the change in the public mood. If, and when, the United States extricates herself from the Vietnam quagmire, moderates the Cold War, gives up her global ambitions, turns her energies from the military to the civilian arena, and resolutely tackles the prodigious problems which glare upon her from every quarter of the horizon, she will surely regain the confidence and admiration of the peoples of the world which she enjoyed for so many years. If not, we may see a dramatic reversal of the ancient relationship of old world and new. In the nineteenth century the best of European civilization found a new life in the United States. What we think of as American civilization may, in the twentieth and twenty-first centuries, find refuge and rebirth in Europe.

recommended reading

Adler, Selig. *The Isolationist Impulse: Its Twentieth-Century Reaction.* New York: Free Press, 1966.

Bemis, Samuel F. *Latin American Policy of the U.S.* New York: W. W. Norton & Company, 1967.

Blum, John M. *Woodrow Wilson and the Politics of Morality.* Library of American Biography. Boston: Little, Brown & Company, 1956.

Carleton, William. *The Revolution in American Foreign Policy: Its Global Range.* Revised edition. New York: Random House, 1967.

Commager, Henry S. *Freedom and Order: A Commentary on the American Political Scene.* New York: World Publishing Company (Meridian Books), 1968.

———, editor. *America in Perspective.* New York: New American Library (Mentor Books).

*Cunliffe, Marcus. *Soldiers and Civilians: The Martial Spirit in America, 1775-1865.* Boston: Little, Brown & Company, 1968.

Dulles, Foster R. *America's Rise to World Power: 1898-1954.* New York: Harper & Row (Harper Torchbooks).

*Ekirch, Arthur A., Jr. *The Civilian and the Military.* New York: Oxford University Press, 1956. OP

Fairbank, John K. *The United States and China.* Revised edition. New York: Viking Press (Compass Books).

Fulbright, J. William. *The Arrogance of Power*. New York: Random House (Vintage Books), 1967.

Griswold, A. Whitney. *Far Eastern Policy of the United States*. New Haven: Yale University Press, 1962.

Hersey, John. *Hiroshima*. New York: Bantam Books (Pathfinder Books).

Hilsman, Roger. *To Move a Nation*. New York: Dell Publishing Company (Delta Books), 1968.

Huntington, Samuel P. *The Soldier and the State: The Theory and Politics of Civil-Military Relations*. New York: Random House (Vintage Books).

*Joseph, Franz. *As Others See Us*. Princeton, N.J.: Princeton University Press, 1959. OP

Kennan, George F. *The Realities of American Foreign Policy*. New York: W. W. Norton & Company, 1966.

*Lippmann, Walter. *The Cold War*. New York: Harper & Row, 1947. OP

*————. *U.S. Foreign Policy: Shield of the Republic*. Boston: Little, Brown & Company, 1943. OP

Mead, Margaret. *And Keep Your Powder Dry*. Revised edition. New York: Apollo Editions.

Mills, Walter. *Arms and Men*. New York: New American Library (Mentor Books).

*————. *The Martial Spirit*. Boston: Houghton Mifflin Company.

————, editor. *American Military Thought*. Indianapolis, Ind.: Bobbs-Merrill Company (Liberal Arts Press), 1966.

Perkins, Dexter. *A History of the Monroe Doctrine*. Revised edition. Boston: Little, Brown & Company, 1955.

Rahv, Philip. *The Discovery of Europe*. New York: Doubleday & Company (Anchor Books), 1960. OP

Raskin, Marcus G., and Barnet, Richard J. *After Twenty Years*. New York: Random House (Vintage Books).

*Reischauer, Edwin O. *The United States and Japan*. 3rd edition. Cambridge, Mass.: Harvard University Press, 1965.

Servan-Schreiber, Jean-Jacques. *The American Challenge*. New York: Avon Books.

Spanier, John W. *American Foreign Policy Since World War II*. 3rd edition. New York: Frederick A. Praeger, 1968.

Steel, Ronald. *Pax Americana*. New York: Viking Press (Compass Books), 1968.

*Strout, Cushing. *The American Image of the Old World*. New York: Harper & Row, 1963. OP

---

* Hard-cover edition. Titles not so marked are paperback editions.
  OP indicates the book is out of print.

Part 2

a practical guide for foreign students in the United States

The following digest of practical information for foreign visitors coming to the United States was prepared by IIE staff to supplement Dr. Commager's analysis of American life and the American character. It is directed particularly to the foreign student.

In 1969-70, there were nearly 135,000 foreign students in the United States, representing 110 countries. The material in this section, therefore, is intended to inform an extremely varied audience.

higher education in the United States

Higher education is the term used in the United States for formal education beyond the twelve years of elementary and secondary school. As Dr. Commager has pointed out, American education is decentralized and diversified. Some educational institutions are supported by states, some by private organizations, some by religious denominations. Each U.S. institution of higher education is headed by a president or chancellor and usually controlled by a governing board of *trustees* or *regents*.

In everyday speech, the terms *college* and *university* are used interchangeably. However, there is a distinction. The American college has no exact counterpart in the educational system of any other country. Although most colleges offer courses in many fields, including the sciences, they are called *liberal arts colleges*. A college may be an independent institution or a part of a university.

A university is made up of a group of schools which include an undergraduate liberal arts college, graduate schools, and professional schools. Some universities also have schools which offer undergraduate professional programs in such fields as business administration and agriculture.

The liberal arts college offers a four-year program leading to a bachelor's degree in arts or sciences. The student working for a bachelor's degree is called an undergraduate. Undergraduates usually attend college between the ages of eighteen and twenty-two. The academic year lasts between thirty-two and thirty-six weeks, beginning in September or October and lasting through May or June. Most colleges and universities divide the school year into two equal parts called *semesters* or *terms*. Some divide the year into a system of three equal *trimesters*. Others have four *quarters,* of twelve weeks each, and require their students to attend classes during the three quarters which fall between September and June.

Many schools have summer sessions which last from six to twelve weeks; tuition fees charged are additional to those paid for the academic year. Students from colleges and universities may take summer courses at schools other than their own, but credits are often not transferable from one school to another.

UNDERGRADUATE STUDY

Undergraduate students are classified according to their year of study. First-year students are called *freshmen;* second-year students, *sophomores;* third-year students, *juniors;* and fourth-year students, *seniors*. Students from abroad do not necessarily enter American colleges and universities as freshmen. The institution determines the level of entry for each foreign student. Some students who have had extensive experience in a field may be admitted as juniors or seniors. Many schools admit foreign students as special students and do not determine their level or class until they have completed one semester and demonstrated the quality of their work.

In general, undergraduate courses at American colleges and universities are less specialized than most courses at European universities.

The first two years of a four-year college program are devoted to general learning. Study programs include many subjects, and the scope of each course is usually broad. Courses which treat a vast area of subject matter, such as the history of art from prehistoric cave painting to pop art, are known as *survey courses*. Since they survey an entire field of study, they are usually taken as introductory courses or as prerequisites for more specialized courses. If a student is particularly interested in a certain course but is unable to take it because he lacks the prerequisite courses, it is often possible to *audit* the course—to attend classes without taking examinations or receiving credit.

During the third and fourth years of college, students specialize in one subject by concentrating most of their courses in it. The field of concentration is called a *major*.

The courses offered at each college or university and the regulations and requirements are listed in the college catalogue, published by each institution. Some courses are required for certain degrees; some may be chosen as *electives*. Faculty advisers can offer the student guidance and help in choosing electives.

Some schools offer special courses in reading and study techniques. Generally, no credit is given for these courses, but they can be useful in helping to improve reading speed and effectiveness in taking notes and making outlines.

Colleges and universities are organized into different departments for each field of study: an English department, a French department, a history department, and so on. There is, however, a trend toward interdepartmental courses which usually cover the relationships between various fields.

Often a professor from the department of your major will be assigned to help you select your courses. He is your *academic adviser*.

The attitude of the American professor toward his students is usually characterized by informality and genuine friendliness. Professors are interested in their students and often devote a good part of their time to answering individual questions after class hours.

methods of instruction

The method of teaching in most colleges and universities consists of lectures supplemented by reading assignments and class discussions between the professor and students. Science courses include lectures and laboratory periods. Art courses (except history of art courses) generally include lectures and studio classes in which the students work with artistic media. Education courses sometimes offer opportunities to observe class sessions and to practice teaching in elementary and secondary schools.

Assignments usually call for the student to read a number of books and/or articles and to write essays, reports, and/or term papers. They may

214

also include individual research, laboratory experiments, field trips, etc. In most undergraduate and some graduate courses, *reading lists* are distributed to the students at the beginning of the semester. These list books, pamphlets, articles and chapters which the students are required or advised to read by a given date.

examinations

Most examinations are written, not oral. *Quizzes* or *tests* are short examinations. They may be given regularly each week, or they may be unscheduled and even unannounced. Quizzes may consist of short questions requiring short responses. Some quizzes have one or two questions requiring essay-type answers. Multiple-choice tests consist of sentences with a word or phrase omitted; the student chooses among two or more words or phrases to complete the sentences. Some quizzes require answers of "true" or "false" to a series of statements.

Midsemester examinations are usually longer than quizzes and are given in the middle of the school term. *Midyear* exams are given at the end of a term when a course carries over to the next semester. *Finals* are examinations which cover the subject matter of an entire course.

hours, credits, points

Every course is worth a certain number of *hours, credits* or *points,* depending upon how many hours of lectures, class meetings, laboratory work, etc., are offered each week. A course which lasts for one term and consists of three one-hour class periods a week is valued at three hours, points or credits. Most colleges and universities require each student to complete successfully a minimum of 120 credits in order to receive an undergraduate degree. Students generally take from 15 to 17 credits each semester.

grades

Grading systems vary among institutions. Many employ the first five letters of the alphabet to denote levels of achievement. To receive full credit for their courses, students must maintain an average of grade C, considered a satisfactory level of academic work. B denotes above-average or superior work and A indicates excellent achievement. D is a passing grade, but denotes lower-than-average work, and E or F symbolizes completely unsatisfactory work. Some colleges allow students who receive an E to take a second final examination, but a student who receives an E or an F as a final mark fails to receive credit for the course. The course therefore does not contribute toward his degree requirements. When a student receives an unsatisfactory grade for an examination or a course he is said to have *failed* or, colloquially, *flunked*. In most graduate schools, B is the lowest satisfactory grade. Some institutions mark on a numerical basis, with decimals to show intermediate grading. Often an elective course may be marked only Pass or Fail.

Some schools use the symbol I to denote incomplete work and allow the student to make up the work for a course after the end of a semester. If a student's work is incomplete or unsatisfactory, the college may put him on *probation* — that is, allow him a period of time, usually one school term, in which to make up incomplete work and/or raise his grades to a satisfactory standard.

GRADUATE STUDY

Graduate work leading to a master of arts (M.A.) or master of science (M.S.) degree requires at least one year's study beyond the bachelor's degree. In fields such as engineering and business administration, a two-year program of study is usually required to obtain a master's degree. The typical requirements for the master's degree include successfully completing 30 to 32 credits of graduate courses, including 20 credits in the major field of study; maintaining a minimum average of grade B; writing a thesis; and passing examinations in all required courses. Study for the master's degree is sometimes undertaken as preparation for further graduate work or as an extension of the general education of the bachelor's degree program. In general, advanced studies leading to a master's degree and those leading to a doctor's degree emphasize preparation for research or for professional practice.

Degrees for doctor of philosophy (Ph.D.), doctor of education (Ed.D.) and doctor of science (Sc.D.) require a minimum of two years' full-time study beyond the master's degree, but in most fields more is necessary. For example, completion of the requirements for a doctorate in the field of science usually takes four to five years of study beyond the master's degree. Requirements for the doctor's degree often include demonstrating a reading knowledge of one or more foreign languages. These languages are usually French, German or Spanish, but some institutions may accept the foreign student's own language to meet the requirement.

Graduate students attend lecture courses and seminars and carry out research under professional guidance. Graduate study leading to a doctorate emphasizes original research.

Research has become one of the chief functions of the graduate school. Universities carry on research in all fields and are extending their services to business organizations, government agencies and other non-academic and academic organizations.

Many graduate schools make *assistantships* available to candidates for graduate degrees. Assistantships are in a sense paying jobs. Sometimes the assistant is paid in cash; sometimes he receives free tuition for his services. An assistant's duties may limit the time he has to pursue his own studies and prolong the period necessary to earn a degree. Assistantship duties range from grading papers or serving as a laboratory technician to teaching freshman courses or doing specialized research. Some very advanced research assistants may be permitted to pursue independent research projects of their own choosing, but in general research assistants will work on the projects of the particular school or department in which they are employed. Hours of service generally range from ten to fifteen per week, but some research assistants may be expected to devote up to twenty hours.

216

PROFESSIONAL AND TECHNICAL SCHOOLS

Graduate study which prepares the student for professional practice is largely a function of the university, but there are also many individual tax-supported teachers' colleges and private schools of music, art, law, engineering, medicine, nursing and other professions. The standards of professional schools are usually established by the professional associations and societies in each field.

The *teachers' college* is a form of professional school which prepares its students for elementary and secondary school teaching. There has been a recent trend among teachers' colleges to broaden their programs so that they resemble those of liberal arts colleges, and many liberal arts colleges offer teacher-training programs. Courses in this field are usually called education courses.

Institutes of technology specialize in science and technology. Many of these schools have graduate programs. All institutes of technology grant degrees. *Technical institutes,* on the other hand, offer shorter courses and do not grant degrees equivalent to four-year college degrees.

TWO-YEAR COLLEGES

The *junior* or *two-year college* provides a two-year program corresponding to the first two years of undergraduate study. These programs lead to an associate in arts (A.A.) or science (A.S.) degree. Junior colleges offer several kinds of programs. A liberal arts program is offered to students who wish to complete their formal education at a two-year college or who plan to continue their studies at a four-year institution. Other programs offer training for positions requiring specialized education, such as dental hygienists, legal secretaries, and laboratory technicians.

All schools expect the students to learn the regulations of the college and to comply with them. Many colleges require their students (especially freshmen) to attend all classes, allowing a given number of *cuts* — absences from class. Schools which have rules for compulsory class attendance do so because they believe the majority of students are not aware of the gap which irregular class attendance may leave in the knowledge of the subject of the courses. If a student does not follow the rules of the college, he may be subject to an academic or social penalty.

travel to the United States

BEFORE YOU LEAVE

After you have fulfilled the legal requirements for your visit to the United States (see pages 239-241), you should arrange for your transportation at least a month before you plan to leave.

Unless you have been awarded a grant with special travel arrangements, it is best for you to purchase tickets in your own country for travel from the U.S. port of entry to your destination. Foreign students coming from outside the Western Hemisphere by air are entitled to a 50 per cent discount on air transportation within the U.S., providing the domestic tickets are bought in conjunction with transatlantic or transpacific air transportation.

You can also save money by buying a round-trip ticket, if you are sure the return portion will still be valid when you are ready to leave.

If you are flying, you should arrange with a shipping and forwarding agent to send your heavy baggage to the U.S. port of entry by ship. These arrangements should be made well in advance of your departure so that you may call for your baggage at the shipping customs office when you arrive.

If possible, reserve in advance a room in a hotel or in a YMCA or YWCA (Young Men's or Young Women's Christian Association) in the city where you will arrive in the United States. This will assure you of a temporary place to stay before you reach your destination. The YMCA and YWCA have branches throughout the country. Their rooms are much less expensive than hotel rooms. When writing for a room, ask for a letter confirming your reservation. If you will notify the International Student Service at 291 Broadway, New York, New York 10007, of the time and city of your arrival, a representative of that organization will meet you at your port of entry and will help you, free of charge, with problems of immigration, lodging, and transportation.

If you are going to attend an American college or university, arrange to reach the United States about two or three weeks before classes begin. This will allow you time to visit places of interest en route, if you have the funds to do so. It will also give you the opportunity to become settled in your new surroundings. However, be sure that you will have a place to stay, especially if you plan to live in a dormitory. Dormitories are not always open before the term begins.

Be certain not to arrive late at your destination. If you are a student, late arrival will be detrimental to your academic work. Some schools charge a fee for late registration, and some do not accept students who wish to enroll after registration has closed. Your school may notify you to arrive on a specific date to attend a special orientation course prior to the regular registration period.

If you plan to spend the summer in the United States before beginning your studies, you may want to participate in one of the many summer study or work programs which are open to newly arrived foreign students. These include study programs, seminars, tours, work camps, service and intern projects, English-language classes, and orientation programs. Some of these programs offer financial aid and scholarships to foreign students. A list of programs appears in the *Handbook on International Study: For Foreign Nationals*, published by the Institute of International Education.

what to bring with you

It is not necessary for you to wear American-style clothing either on the college campus or in cities. However, for the sake of comfort, you may want to own certain garments. Although there are sharp variations of climate throughout the United States, all regions have a winter season. Even though you may be living in the South, where the winter season is much warmer and shorter than it is in northern states, you will need a warm coat for cool evenings and for traveling. You will also need a raincoat.

Before deciding what clothes to bring with you, inquire about the climate of the area where you will be living. You will not need very heavy clothes for indoors, since American homes and buildings are well heated.

In general, casual clothes are worn at colleges and universities, except for formal or semi-formal dances and parties. It is not advisable to bring many dresses or suits which require frequent cleaning and pressing.

During the fall and winter months, women usually wear wool dresses or skirts or pants with blouses and sweaters. In the spring and summer, dresses or skirts with blouses of cotton, linen, or synthetic fibers are generally used for daytime wear. Clothes suitable for campus wear may often be purchased less expensively in the United States than abroad. Women students wear low-heeled, casual shoes most of the time. Less casual shoes, sometimes with higher heels, are worn to more formal social engagements, such as parties and dances. Women visitors will probably need one evening dress or formal national dress and at least one hat. Wool hats or scarves are worn on campus during cold weather.

Men at colleges and universities usually wear slacks and sport shirts or regular shirts with sweaters and/or wool jackets. Neckties and jackets should always be worn in places of business, in church, usually to parties and dances, and when dining at someone's home or in a restaurant. In general, a dark suit is appropriate for most parties and special occasions.

Many college dormitories and boarding houses provide bed sheets, blankets and pillows. Schools which do not supply them have facilities where they may be rented. In general, hotels and rooming houses supply bedding and towels. If you should have to provide your own sheets and pillowcases, blankets, or towels, you can buy them fairly cheaply in the United States. Many college dormitories have facilities where students may wash their clothes, and in most American towns and cities there are public automatic laundry and dry-cleaning facilities which one may use for a small fee.

Many people are interested in seeing pictures, national costumes and other items which depict the culture and life of your country. Such material is particularly useful for illustrating talks which you may be asked to give before student groups and other organizations. You may also wish to bring with you some small souvenirs, typical of your country, to give to American friends and hosts.

ARRIVAL IN THE UNITED STATES

You should have approximately $50 in American currency when you arrive in the United States. You will need this for gratuities (tips) and immediate expenses before your trip to or arrival at the institution where you will be staying. Some of this currency should be in one-dollar and five-dollar bills and a small amount of change: 25-cent pieces (quarters), 10-cent pieces (dimes) and 5-cent pieces (nickels). (For further information on the American monetary system, see page 228.)

Before landing, most steamship companies and airlines distribute instructions to their passengers explaining the complicated procedure of entering the United States as a foreign visitor. When you arrive, you must have all your papers *with you and in order*. Do not pack them away; they must be easily available.

The Public Health officials are the first to meet you. They will examine your chest X-ray, vaccination certificate and other health certificates. A person who does not have all the necessary medical documents or whose state of health is questioned may be sent to a U.S. government hospital for tests or treatment. If everything is in order, you will then go to immigration inspection.

Immigration officials will inspect your passport, visa, letter of acceptance from a college or university and the appropriate government forms (see pp. 239-241), and documents indicating how you will finance your stay in the United States. You may also be asked to show some indication of your plans for your return home. If the immigration inspector does not find all of the papers satisfactory, there will be a delay for further questioning. In rare cases, this delay might last several days or a week. If this should happen to you, *immediately* notify your sponsor at the institution where you are enrolled. When everything is in order, the immigration inspector will stamp the date on your Landing Card and passport and thus permit entry into the United States. As a student you will also be given Form I-94, known as the Arrival-Departure Record. Keep this card with you always; you must surrender it when you leave the country.

Next you must go through customs inspection. While on the ship or plane you will have filled out a Customs Declaration. If you are bringing with you only personal belongings, you may simply write "personal effects" on the declaration sheet. Articles brought into the country as gifts must be declared, since there is a duty on gift items. Microscopes and medical, dental and other scientific instruments manufactured outside the United States, if essential to your study or work, may be brought in under bond for one year. Arrangements for such a bond can be made with U.S. customs officials.

If you arrive by plane, your baggage will be brought to the terminal which you enter immediately after immigration inspection. If you arrive by ship, your baggage will be placed under a sign bearing the first letter of your last name. After you have found your baggage, you should line up for a customs inspector who will open your baggage and inspect the contents. After he has placed a stamp on each piece of luggage and any necessary duty has been paid, you may leave the airport or pier. If you sent heavy baggage by boat, arrange to call at the shipping customs office to collect it before you travel to your college or university.

temporary lodging, local transportation

After you have gone through customs and gained official permission to enter the United States, temporary lodging and local travel will probably be your first concern.

If you need information or help with lodging, transportation, or other matters on your arrival, ask the Travelers Aid Society. The Society has representatives at ports, railway stations and bus terminals. There is no charge for this service. If you have contacted the International Student Service (see page 218) they will have a representative at the dock. You can recognize the representative by his or her blue armband with white lettering "Foreign Student Adviser."

If you have come to the United States by airplane, it will probably be best for you to use the airline's bus service when you leave the airport. The bus service, which may cost from $1.50 to $2.50, will take you to the center of town. As airports are usually located some distance from the center of town, a taxi is likely to be extremely expensive.

If you arrive by ship, however, the most convenient way for you to travel from a pier to a railroad or bus station or hotel is by taxi. In most parts of the country, taxi fare is registered on a meter. Fares are fixed according to distance traveled, with an additional charge for heavy luggage, such as trunks. There is no charge for suitcases. Taxi drivers should always be tipped, usually 15 per cent of the fare.

Most hotels operate on the "European Plan." This means that the hotel rate includes only your room and not your meals. Rates for the "American Plan" do include meals. (Most American-Plan hotels are at vacation resorts and will not concern you at this stage of your visit.) Most hotels have restaurants and coffee shops where meals may be purchased. Coffee shops are less expensive and less formal than the restaurants. The desk clerk will be able to suggest nearby eating places.

Upon arriving at a hotel, register at the reservation desk. If you do not have a reservation, ask the room clerk for one. In your hotel room will be a sign giving the time for checking out. *You will be charged a full day's rate if you do not leave your room by this time.*

Once you have deposited your luggage and are ready to do some sightseeing, you will probably not want to spend money on taxis. Transportation within a city is usually provided by bus, subway, and street (tram) cars. Fares can often be paid in cash, but some transit lines, such as the New York subways, use tokens. They may be purchased at subway stations. When it is necessary for you to use more than one method of public transportation to reach a certain location, inquire about transfers. A transfer will enable you to change from one vehicle to another, either by paying only part of the second fare or without paying any additional fare.

If you need information on how to reach your college or university, you can telephone or go in person to the Information Desk at a railroad or bus station or an airline office. Local travel agencies will not only plan your trip but will purchase tickets for you if you have not done so in your own country.

travel within the United States

Although trains are usually faster and more comfortable than buses, a bus trip is less expensive and affords you an opportunity to see more of the country. Bus routes go through cities and towns, enabling you to see the landscape and residential and commercial areas. The airplane, of course, is the fastest method of travel and for long distances is often the cheapest, with student discounts.

Train accommodations are coach, sleeping car, or parlor car. Coach accommodations are the least expensive. Coach seats are not reserved, except on special trains. Many of the coaches are air-conditioned and have seats which may be put into a reclining position. On overnight trips a pillow may be rented.

Sleeping car and parlor car (both are first class) and special coach reservations must be made in advance. First class fare is 50 per cent more than coach fare.

Sleeping-car passengers may use the lounge car, which has comfortable chairs and reading matter and where refreshments may be bought.

On long trips there are dining cars where meals are served three times a day. Dining-car prices are expensive. Some trains also have grill cars which have counter service and are less expensive. In coach cars there are vendors who walk through the train selling sandwiches, coffee, milk, juice, candy, fruit, and magazines.

On both train and bus trips, if you have time for sightseeing, you can arrange to stop off at different places en route and then continue your trip on another train or bus, at no extra cost.

Bus tickets should be purchased before the time of departure. Buses travel at night as well as during the daytime and make rest stops from time to time, usually at places where meals may be purchased.

Plane connections may be made from port cities to all larger cities throughout the United States. Your flight reservations should be made as far in advance as possible. Following the particular regulations of each airline company, tickets must be paid for, picked up and reconfirmed in advance of the flight. You must call the airline office if you change or cancel your flight. If you fail to cancel, there is a service charge.

There are two classes of domestic plane travel — first class and tourist. The price of regular daytime flights is the same for all airline companies, but a number of airlines offer domestic night coach service. The departure and arrival times of the night coach flights are not as convenient as are those of regular flights, but night coach flights are cheaper.

On the standard flights, meals are served at no extra charge, but night coach service does not include meals.

Persons between the ages of 12 and 21 may obtain a Youth Fare identification card from any domestic U.S. airline office. It entitles them to a 50 per cent discount on air travel within the U.S. on all domestic airlines until they reach their 22nd birthdays, provided they travel as "standby" passengers. "Standby" passengers may travel only when there would otherwise be vacant seats on the plane. Therefore, the holder of a Youth Fare card cannot plan with confidence to travel at peak periods, such as weekends and holiday eves. However, the young student who is able to travel at odd hours or in midweek can save considerably. It takes about two weeks or more to receive a Youth Fare card after you apply for it.

Bus companies have special rates for foreign visitors — $99 pays for 99 days of unlimited travel. Tickets for these special rates must be purchased abroad. Information may be obtained from a travel agency or the American Express office in your home city.

baggage

If you travel by train or bus, your ticket enables you to send 150 pounds of baggage to your destination without cost. This baggage is automatically insured for $25. Additional insurance may be purchased at the rate of 25 cents per $100. Life insurance is sold both at counters and by machine at most airports. The cost for insurance on any flight is 25 cents for every $1,500.

Baggage may not be left at a pier or airport. Heavy baggage, which you will not need while traveling to your destination, may be sent from your home via a transfer company to the railroad or bus station in the city where you will first arrive in the United States. You can then "check it through"—send it at no extra cost to your final destination — by showing your railroad or bus ticket. When checking baggage through on your ticket you will receive a baggage check which is your receipt. Be sure to keep this check in a safe place. You will need it for claiming your luggage once you arrive at your destination. It is best to send heavy baggage to your destination as soon as possible, since a passenger and his luggage are not always transported on the same train or bus. If your baggage arrives before you, it will be stored at the station and you will be charged a small fee for each day of storage. When you arrive at your destination you can arrange for a transfer company to deliver your luggage to your permanent lodgings. You can usually take small trunks and suitcases to your lodgings by taxi. It is best to carry only as much luggage as you can handle, for porter service is not always available.

Most stations have parcel check rooms where you may leave baggage for a time, at the rate of 35 cents a piece for twenty-four hours. You will receive a redemption ticket for each piece of baggage. Most railroad and bus stations and airports have lockers in which you can store luggage for twenty-four hours. Vacant lockers have a key in their locks. After inserting your baggage in the locker you put a coin (usually 25 cents) in a slot, then close the door and remove the key. Keep the key until you are ready to claim your luggage. The key will have a number on it corresponding to the number on the locker. If you leave your luggage in the locker beyond the allotted time, it may be removed to the parcel check room, and a storage charge of 35 cents a day will be made.

When traveling by plane from one city in the United States to another, you are allowed to carry one large and one medium bag plus a small bag that will fit under the seat at no additional charge. This baggage will be carried on the same plane you use. The additional charge for excess baggage is high.

All trunks and suitcases should bear tags giving your name and address in the United States, or the address of your college if you do not know where you will be living.

time zones

There are four time zones in the United States: Eastern, Central, Mountain and Pacific Standard. If you travel from east to west, you must set your watch *back* one hour when entering a new time zone. If you travel from west to east, you must set your watch *ahead* one hour at each time zone. During the summer many cities use Daylight Saving Time, which is one hour ahead of Standard Time.

telephone and telegraph service

If you wish to use a telephone, public telephones can be found both along streets and roads and in railroad and bus stations, airports, hotels, restaurants, drugstores, department stores and most government and office buildings. The price of a local call is usually ten cents for the first three minutes. In most places you can dial the number you want, but in some small towns it is necessary to dial "O" for Operator and then ask the operator to place your call. Instructions for placing calls are posted near every public telephone.

Out-of-town and overseas calls (long-distance calls) may be made in two ways. If you dial directly, you must pay for it no matter who answers the telephone at the number you wish to reach. However, if you place a person-to-person call, you tell the operator the name of the person to whom you wish to speak, and if you do not reach that person you will not be charged for the call. Person-to-person calls are more expensive than direct-dial calls. Long-distance rates, except for overseas calls to certain countries, are less expensive in the evening, on Sundays and holidays. It is possible to have a long-distance call charged to the person you are calling. If you wish to place such a call tell the operator that you want to "call collect" or "reverse the charges." The operator will then ask the person you call whether he will accept the charges.

Telephone directories are available in public places. The classified telephone directory, sometimes called the "Yellow Pages," lists organizations and names of people according to their business or profession. You can look up interpreters under "Interpreters" and "Translators," and transfer companies under "Transfer Companies," "Expressing and Baggage Transfer" and "Trucking." There are telephone information services which tell you the time of day and report the weather. In an emergency you dial the operator and ask for the Police Department, the Fire Department or an ambulance. In some cities there are special emergency numbers for the Police Department.

Telegrams sent within the United States are handled by the Western Union Telegraph Company. Telegrams may be dictated over the telephone, simply by asking the operator for Western Union. If this is done on a private telephone, the cost of the telegram will appear on the telephone bill. If a public telephone is used you pay for the telegram at once by inserting money into the coin slots in the telephone. Telegrams, like long-distance calls, may be sent collect. The usual rate for telegrams is based on a 15-word message. The names and addresses of the person to receive the telegram and person sending it are not included as part of the 15-word message. They are included, however, in messages sent overseas by cablegram or radiogram.

There are three types of telegrams. Straight telegrams, based on a minimum of 15 words, are delivered immediately. A day letter takes some hours to be transmitted and delivered. The minimum charge for day letters covers 50 words. A night letter is the least expensive way of sending a telegram. The night letter is held overnight and then delivered the following morning. The minimum charge is based on 50 words. There is no charge for the address in any form of telegram.

Charges for cablegrams or radiograms vary greatly since there are different rates per word, depending on the destination of the message. There are two types of cablegrams. A regular cablegram is delivered at once; a letter cablegram is delivered the day after it is sent. The charge for a letter cablegram is for a minimum of 22 words.

when you arrive at your college or university

WHO WILL HELP YOU

At almost all colleges and universities, certain members of the faculty and staff are assigned to offer professional and personal help and advice to students. Visit your Foreign Student Adviser as soon as possible after your arrival. When you see him for the first time, be sure to take your passport, visa, and any other documents which relate to your admission to the United States. He needs these documents, since he must report your arrival and enrollment to the U.S. Immigration and Naturalization Service. Always inform your Foreign Student Adviser of changes of address, passport expiration date, and other developments which may affect your immigration status or program of study.

In addition to your Foreign Student Adviser, your academic adviser (who will help arrange your course of study), and your professors, there are others to whom you may turn for professional advice and guidance. Many schools have guidance counselors who will be able to help you with social and emotional problems. You may also consult with clergymen who are affiliated with your college or with a nearby house of worship.

WHERE TO LIVE

The classroom buildings and residence halls of American colleges and universities are grouped together in one area called the *campus*. Some colleges require their students to live in campus dormitories. Others offer a choice of living in a dormitory, cooperative, fraternity or sorority house on the campus, or in an International House, a rented room, or an apartment away from the campus.

College dormitories are owned and operated by the school. Their facilities range from single rooms for one or two students to suites which may be shared by three, four or more students. Dormitories generally have smoking rooms and

225

other rooms for studying or socializing. Many have dining rooms where meals are served three times a day.

Cooperatives are dormitories in which the students do all or most of the maintenance work, such as cooking and cleaning. Residents of cooperatives therefore pay less for their board. Cooperative houses are often restricted to scholarship students.

International Houses have been established in some cities to provide housing for foreign as well as American students. They also sponsor many activities such as lectures, language classes, sports programs, Sunday suppers and teas and introductions to American families. There are many nonresident members who also participate in International House activities. Requests for information on International Houses may be sent to International House, 500 Riverside Drive, New York, New York 10027.

If advance arrangements for lodgings have not been made, go to the rooming or housing office at your college for information and help. Furnished rooms may be rented in hotels (where the rent is expensive), boardinghouses, or private homes. Rented rooms usually do not have cooking facilities.

Apartments may be rented furnished or unfurnished. Buying furniture for an unfurnished apartment is very costly, and the resale value is very low. A three-room apartment consists of a bedroom, living room, kitchen and bathroom. Apartments normally have a refrigerator and stove and toilet facilities. Rent usually includes the cost of water and heat. For some apartments it also includes the cost of gas or electricity, or both. When renting an apartment it is often necessary to sign a lease for a year or more and to give the landlord the rent for one or two months in advance. This "security" payment will be returned to the tenant when he moves out, unless the apartment has been damaged. Do not sign a lease if you do not intend to stay for the full term of the lease. A lease is a *binding legal agreement*. It should be carefully read and understood before it is signed. If you do not understand any part of a lease, discuss it with your Foreign Student Adviser or the housing official of your school.

If your living arrangements do not include meals or kitchen facilities, you will want to find out about eating places in your neighborhood. In addition to restaurants, there are coffee shops, drugstore counters, and lunch counters where one may order anything from a cup of tea or coffee to an entire meal. Service at these counters is speedy and prices are generally lower than those of restaurants. At self-service cafeterias you may dine even less expensively.

The person with whom you share a room is called a "roommate." You ought to consider rooming with an American student. Many students from abroad, especially when they first arrive in the United States, want to room with students from their own countries. However, you will usually find that opportunities to improve your English, to learn about the United States, and to participate in American life will be increased by living with Americans.

When living on campus you may have to obey certain rules for curfew and quiet hours. Most men's colleges do not have many social restrictions, but most women's colleges do. At coeducational institutions, the rules are usually more restrictive for women than for men. Quiet hours are imposed to provide undisturbed time for studying and sleeping. It is, of course, most inconsiderate to break any of these rules.

Students who live off campus, or in sections of the campus which are not close to classroom buildings, often buy or rent bicycles for going to and from classes. If you find you need a bicycle, it is possible to buy a used one at low cost.

REGISTRATION

Registration for classes takes place at the beginning of each semester. At most colleges and universities the Registrar's Office keeps a supply of instructions for registration or enrollment. Registration requirements are also listed in the college catalogue.

Your first step in registering will be to choose, with the help of your academic adviser, the courses you wish to take. You will have to complete enrollment forms which will be distributed to each of your professors. If, after classes begin, you wish to change from one course to another you should speak to your academic adviser. If the change is approved, you must fill out more forms and take them to the Registrar's Office. Most schools allow program changes to be made only during the first or the first and second weeks of the semester.

ORIENTATION

The time between the opening of school and the date when classes officially begin — which ranges from a few days to a week — is usually dedicated to the orientation of new students. You will probably be busy during this time. Aside from getting settled in your new lodgings, you will most likely take several examinations to establish the level of your work so that you will be placed in the proper classes. You will attend introductory lectures and visit various buildings and sections of the campus.

These orientation activities in several ways will help you to become familiar with your new surroundings and the American system of higher education and will help you become acquainted with your colleagues.

the costs of living and studying in the United States

The American monetary system follows the decimal system. The basic unit of the U.S. monetary system is the dollar, which can be divided into 100 cents. "$" is the dollar symbol. Bills in denominations of $1, $5, $10 and $20 are the most widely used.

The following list will give you an idea of the value of a dollar:

cup of coffee ....$.15 to $.25
reasonable meal ....$2.00 to $4.00
hotel room ....$10.00 to $20.00 minimum, per night
subway, streetcar or bus fare in city...$.20 to $.50
package of cigarettes ....$.25 to $.60
man's haircut ....$1.50 to $2.50
woman's haircut ....$2.00 to $4.00

Because of inflation, living costs in the U.S. were rising at the rate of five to six per cent a year at the beginning of the 1970's.

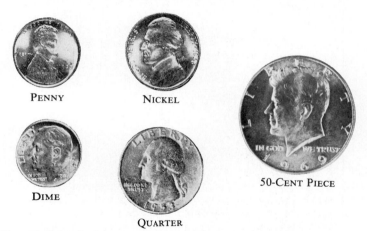

PENNY   NICKEL

DIME

QUARTER

50-CENT PIECE

The Chase Manhattan Bank Museum of Moneys of the World, New York

Coins are used for self-service machines. Soft drinks, milk, coffee, candy, cigarettes, postage stamps*, etc., may be purchased in many public buildings by dropping a coin into a vending machine. Coins are also used for telephones, lockers for checking baggage, some public lavatories, parking meters on city streets, and washing and drying machines in some dormitories and apartment houses.

In the United States, service charges are not included in a bill. Waiters and taxicab drivers should be tipped approximately 15 per cent to 20 per cent of the bill. Porters and bellboys should receive from 50 cents to $1.00 for carrying luggage. The usual tip for a man's haircut is 25 to 50 cents, for a woman's shampoo and hair set or haircut, 20 per cent of the bill. No tips are given to theater ushers, gas station attendants or airline employees.

*Stamps bought from a machine cost more than the same stamps bought at a post office.

228

currency restrictions and transfer of funds to the United States

Some governments restrict the amount of money that can be taken out of the country. Others may restrict funds until a letter from your college or university confirms your enrollment. You should know the regulations of your own government before leaving home.

United States banking connections should be established before you leave home. To transfer money to the United States, you should instruct your home bank to issue a foreign draft on a United States bank in a city close to where you will study.

traveler's checks

When traveling, it is best to carry any large sums of money in the form of traveler's checks. These are sold at banks and also at American Express offices. Individual checks may be purchased in denominations of $10, $20, $50 and $100. There is a $1.00 charge for each $100 worth of traveler's checks. At the time you buy traveler's checks, you sign your name on each one. You sign each one again when you cash it, in order to prove your identity.

using a bank

You may open a savings account, a checking account or both, at a bank. Money kept in a savings account draws interest at the rate of 4 per cent to 5 per cent a year, depending on the policy of the bank. You may deposit money in a savings account and withdraw from it as you wish.

There are two types of checking accounts. A regular checking account requires that you keep a minimum amount of money in the account at all times. In this type of account, there is no charge for checks. A special checking account requires you to keep no particular sum as a balance. Checks for special checking accounts cost 10 cents each, and there is a service charge of approximately 75 cents a month. Checking accounts do not provide interest. Keep a careful record of all checks drawn from your account, to avoid overdrawing. American banks do not temporarily cover checks drawn against insufficient funds.

Do not leave money in your living quarters.

EXPENSES AT COLLEGE

Before you plan your trip to the United States, try to estimate your expenses for the entire period of time you will spend in this country. A student's major expenses will be transportation, college tuition, board and lodging.

College catalogues publish information on tuition and living costs. Schools in the Northeastern and North Central parts of the United States are usually more expensive than those in the South and West. Tuition at private institutions is usually higher than at schools supported by public funds, and expenses at women's colleges are generally higher than at men's schools.

Students from outside the state, including those from other countries, pay an additional fee for tuition if enrolled at a state-supported school. Yearly tuition fees at state universities for nonresidents of the state range from $400 to $1,200 a year. Tuition fees at private institutions of higher education range from $750 to $1,500, and the fee for tuition plus room and board at private colleges ranges from $1,750 to more than $3,500. There are a few private colleges which charge more or less. For exact costs, check with your college or university.

To avoid miscalculations, note in the college catalogue what period of time the charges cover. Summer school, for instance, will normally not be included in the charges for the academic year, usually the nine-month period from approximately September to June.

There may also be admission or registration fees, laboratory fees, athletic fees or fees for use of musical instruments or practice rooms. The total amount of these may come to several hundred dollars.

In addition to your expenses for transportation, room and board, you will have vacation expenses; perhaps some expenses for furnishings; personal expenses for things such as clothing, laundry, stamps, entertainment, etc.; expenses for textbooks, a typewriter, and health and accident insurance.

Secondhand textbooks usually may be purchased for much less than the original cost. Used books may be bought from the college book store or from individual students. Do not purchase any books before you receive lists of required reading for your courses. Since these lists are generally changed each year, you should not buy textbooks from a student who has already taken a course you plan to take until you are sure you will need the same books. The cost of books may range from $100 to $200 per year.

medical expenses

It is, of course, hoped that you will enjoy good health, but you should protect yourself from financial stress in case you meet with an accident or illness during your stay in the United States. You may protect yourself by paying the infirmary fee at the college or by buying health and accident insurance. Since wives and children of foreign students are not usually allowed to use campus medical services, you should be sure they have adequate insurance policies.

Many colleges and universities provide insurance plans for students who want a policy. Some schools require students to obtain a minimum amount of health insurance. Information on college policies is usually in the college catalogue or it may be obtained from the dean of the school. Charges range from $22 to $65 a year for a single student and from $66 to $95 for married couples. If possible, you should try to obtain insurance for the entire year so that you will be covered during vacations as well as during the school year. Most insurance plans do not cover expenses for dental care or eyeglasses. Therefore, if possible, you should have all necessary dental work done in your home country, and have your eyes examined. If you wear eyeglasses, it is advisable to bring an extra pair of glasses and your prescription with you in case you should lose or break a pair.

Insurance policies usually do not cover all expenses, and as medical services in the U.S. are very high, you should plan to have additional personal funds to cover these.

If you become ill, go to your college infirmary or telephone the college physician. If you become ill while away from school, you can obtain the name of a medical doctor by calling a local hospital or looking under the heading "Physicians and Surgeons (M.D.)" in the classified telephone directory. You may also telephone the Visiting Nurse Association. If you are ill, this Association will send a nurse to call on you. The cost is usually $5.75 a visit.

Miscellaneous expenses covering laundry, haircutting, entertainment, etc., for one year average approximately $500. This amount does not include expenses for tuition, lodging, board, round-trip transportation or travel within the United States.

student employment

Many college students in America hold part-time jobs during the school year, and a great number of students work during summer vacations. Employed students perform many types of work while at college. Students work in restaurants, take care of children, work in libraries, sell, and type. If the language of your home country is not English, it may be possible for you to teach or tutor people interested in learning your native tongue. Many foreign students, however, find it difficult to hold a part-time job and still keep up academically, especially during the first year in the U.S. It is best not to count on such employment.

U.S. Government regulations for employment of students from abroad vary according to the type of visa the student holds. In most cases, work permits for foreign citizens are difficult to obtain. If your financial condition should change after you arrive in America and it becomes necessary for you to earn money, or if you find you need a job for practical experience in a field of study, you may apply to your sponsor for permission if you hold a J visa, or you may submit an application for a work permit to the local Immigration and Naturalization Service if you hold a F visa. Such applications should be obtained from the Foreign Student Adviser or the Dean of Admissions of the college. Summer employment requires special permission that may be obtained from the Foreign Student Adviser, who is authorized by the Immigration Office to grant such permission. Summer employment may be on a full-time basis. (See page 241 regarding government regulations.)

Information on available part-time and summer jobs may be obtained from the vocational (sometimes called placement) or scholarship offices of the college. For off-campus jobs — both part-time jobs during the school year and summer jobs — it is helpful to consult the classified advertisement or "Help Wanted" section of the local newspaper. In addition to the kinds of jobs already mentioned, many students work as summer camp counselors, assistants in offices and factories, and construction laborers.

If you earn more than $600 during one year it will be necessary for you to fill out and file a Federal Income Tax form. Income taxes are withheld from salary payments. If an employer has withheld more than you owe in taxes, the Internal Revenue Service will refund the overpayment. The proper tax forms may be obtained from any bank. They must be filed by April 15 for all income earned in the calendar year ending the preceding December 31, whether or not income tax has been withheld.

Students who hold university assistantships that pay regular salaries should consult the Foreign Student Adviser about the possibility of securing the same income tax status as American citizens. If a student expects to study for an indefinite period in the U.S. — at least two years — he may sign an Internal

Revenue form claiming residence for tax purposes. This does not affect your immigration status.

loans

Many of our colleges and universities have special funds for student loans. The usual loan consists of a sum of money which the college advances toward the student's tuition. After leaving the school, the student returns the money to the college. Students who borrow money from a college are usually given a year or more in which to pay it back. Sometimes a very low rate of interest is charged, often none at all. Students from other countries usually are required to have studied in the United States for a certain period of time before they may apply to their college for a loan.

If it is necessary for you to borrow money, it is always best to do so from your college or a bank. Only in an emergency should you borrow money from a friend.

Students are advised not to borrow money from private loan companies; the rates are often quite high. Speak to your adviser before making any decision about borrowing money.

manners and customs

In general, social customs which are considered courteous abroad will be respected in the United States. Visitors from other countries are never expected to conform to all patterns of American social behavior.

Casual friendliness is a characteristic of Americans and should not be mistaken for intimate friendship, which is usually developed over a period of time. Americans call each other by their first names much sooner and more often than do people of most other countries. It may take you a little time to learn the nuances of our manners and customs; the meanings implied by certain gestures, verbal expressions and tones of voice. College students have a certain vocabulary all their own, which changes somewhat with each group of students.

Americans are informal about shaking hands. Men usually shake hands when they meet, but a man does not shake a woman's hand unless she offers it to him.

Introductions are simple: "Mr. Smith, Mr. Jones"; or "Bob Smith, John Jones," or "Bob, John." For a more formal introduction, you may say, "Mr. Smith, may I present Mr. Jones." The wife of a man who holds a doctorate is not addressed by her husband's title as she might be in some other countries.

232

When you are introduced to someone you usually say "How do you do?" or "It's so nice to meet you." An informal introduction may even be responded to with a simple "Hello." When introducing a man to a woman, say the woman's name first.

In this country the main meal of the day, called dinner, is usually served in the evening, except on Sundays and some holidays when it is customary to serve dinner at midday. The typical American breakfast consists of fruit or juice, cereal or eggs, toast, and milk, tea or coffee. The midday meal is usually simple, often consisting of a bowl of soup, a sandwich, something sweet such as cake or pie, and coffee.

If you dine at someone's home and you are doubtful about American table manners, follow the example set by your hostess. If you cannot eat certain foods because they are prohibited by your religion, explain this to your hostess at the time you are invited.

You may smoke during a meal if others do so and if there are ash trays on the table. The first person who wishes to smoke at dinner requests the permission of his hostess.

Written invitations which ask for a response should be answered promptly. Formal, printed invitations do not require a response unless they say R.S.V.P. or "Please Reply." However, it is always courteous to let your host or hostess know whether to expect you, even if the handwritten invitation does not say R.S.V.P. If a written invitation has a telephone number, you may respond by telephone. It is usual to ask the permission of your host or hostess if you wish to bring an escort or friend to a party.

Punctuality is important, and people who are consistently late for appointments are thought to be inconsiderate. If you must be more than a few minutes late you should, if possible, telephone the person with whom you have an appointment. However, when you receive an invitation which does not request your presence at a specific time, such as 8:00 P.M., but extends over a period of time — 4:00 to 7:00 P.M., for example — you may arrive at any time during the time span of the invitation, except within the last half hour.

It is always considerate to send a thank-you note to your hostess. If you have been a guest in someone's home overnight, a note of appreciation should be sent. It is not necessary to take a gift to your host or hostess unless you have been invited to celebrate someone's birthday, a wedding anniversary, or Christmas. It is never necessary to give an expensive present. Flowers or candy are probably the most common hostess gifts. A book or a bottle of wine or liquor may also be welcome gifts but only for hosts whose tastes in books and beverages you know.

dating

When a man invites a woman to join him in a social activity such as dinner, a movie, concert, museum exhibit, etc., the man, the woman, and the event are each called a *date*. On occasion a woman may invite a man to a social function such as a dance or dinner party. This, too, is considered a date. However, the prevailing custom is for the man to do the inviting and pay all the expenses.

You do not need a formal introduction before inviting someone to go out on a date or accepting such an invitation. It is quite proper, under certain circumstances on campus, to speak to people to whom you have not been introduced. It is quite acceptable for classmates and other students to greet each other and to strike up conversations without having been introduced.

A special type of date, both on and off the college campus, is the *blind date*. A blind date is one in which the young man and woman have not seen each other prior to the actual date. Tom may wish to introduce Don to his neighbor Barbara. Don telephones Barbara, explains that he is Tom's friend and asks her for a date. They do not actually meet until Don calls for Barbara on the afternoon or evening of their appointment.

A form of dating at colleges and universities, especially at women's and men's colleges, is the *weekend date*. There are many types of weekend celebrations held at American schools throughout the year, when dates are invited. They may also be invited when no special celebrations are scheduled. If you invite someone to spend a weekend at your school, do so at least one week, and preferably two weeks, in advance. As soon as you know that a weekend date will be visiting you, reserve a room for him or her in a nearby hotel or rooming house. You should also inform your date of the plans for the weekend so that he or she knows what type of clothing to bring.

Women's college weekends are occasions when a woman may invite a man on a date. On such occasions the woman pays for the man's room, tickets for a dance or other types of planned entertainment and meals eaten at her dormitory or sorority house. If, however, the man invites her to dine in a restaurant, he pays for the meal.

The casual quality of most American dating enables one to date several people successively during the same period of time. If a man invites a woman out for several dates and she accepts his invitations it may mean simply that they enjoy each other's company. It does not necessarily imply sustained or serious interest.

clubs, sports, and recreation

ORGANIZATIONS

American students, like all Americans, form associations for practically every purpose. On campus, some student associations are organized and controlled completely by students; others are administered by faculty members.

Student government associations work with the college administrators to develop and control academic and social regulations. Each college government has a constitution, and different responsibilities are assigned to councils or committees. Each member of the student body is actually a member of the student government. Many student government associations are affiliated with the U.S. National Student Association.

Most schools have religious organizations which conduct services and celebrations and sponsor lectures, discussions and social activities such as teas and dances. There are many Protestant organizations, Hillel Foundations for Jewish students, and Newman Clubs for Roman Catholics.

Scholastic organizations cover a wide range of interests. There are foreign-language clubs, mathematics clubs, science clubs, psychology clubs, photography clubs, etc. Each college has several publications; usually a newspaper, a literary magazine and a yearbook which are published by students. There are several types of music clubs; many college singing groups make public appearances. Colleges and universities usually have an orchestra or a band. There are dramatic societies and dance groups, international relations clubs and political groups. Many schools have a student-operated radio broadcasting system.

When you are considering which academic organizations to join, it is not necessary to restrict yourself to a field with which you are familiar. One purpose of these clubs is to promote interest and understanding in new fields. If you are interested in the production of a newspaper, do not let lack of experience deter you from trying out for the newspaper staff. You will receive training from experienced students, and your new ideas may be welcomed.

fraternities and sororities

Fraternities and sororities are social clubs which assume an active role in student life. Membership is by invitation only. There is a period called *rushing*, during which prospective members are invited to open-house gatherings. After these gatherings the members meet to decide which students will be invited to join. At some schools, rushing takes place during the freshman year; at others, students may not attend an open house until they are sophomores. Once a student has accepted a fraternity or sorority invitation for membership, he enters a period of pledging or hazing. During this period the student is called a *pledge* and he or she must perform various tasks which may be constructive but are sometimes merely embarrassing. After the pledge period has been successfully completed, an initiation ceremony is held and the student becomes a member — a fraternity "brother" or sorority "sister."

Fraternities and sororities offer a form of security to their members. They sponsor social events, require their members to maintain an acceptable academic standard, and often provide residence and dining facilities. Many students and educators, however, disapprove of fraternities and sororities because they are exclusive and therefore, in a sense, undemocratic. However, this does not mean that all fraternities and sororities are snobbish or bigoted. Some are very hospitable to students from other countries and even offer guest memberships to one or two foreign students each year. If you are interested in joining a fraternity or sorority, judge it by its membership.

honor societies

There are several academic honor societies such as Phi Beta Kappa. You cannot apply for membership in an honor society but must be chosen on the basis of high scholastic achievement.

SPORTS

Participation in college athletics provides a fine opportunity to get to know other students in an atmosphere based on teamwork. Most colleges offer many team and individual sports. The principal team sports are football, basketball, baseball, hockey, soccer, lacrosse, and crew. The individual sports are track, tennis, swimming, golf, wrestling, boxing, squash, fencing, archery, skiing, horseback riding and rifle shooting. The *varsity* teams of various schools compete with each other. *Intramural* competitions are held between teams from the same school.

Even if you do not participate in sports activities, you will undoubtedly find yourself watching some American athletic events, live or on television. The traditional American national sport is baseball. Enthusiasm for baseball reaches its peak each year in October at the time of the World Series — a series of games between the leading teams in the two professional national leagues. The teams in these leagues represent the principal cities in the United States. There are also minor leagues, semi-professional leagues, and school and college leagues. Small boys learn to play in the "Little League," sponsored by voluntary organizations in most American towns. Baseball is the spring and summer sport.

Football is the fall sport. College football games attract many spectators, as do baseball games, basketball games, tennis matches and other sports competitions. In football the college teams, also organized into leagues, attract a great deal of attention, though professional football leagues have become extremely popular. The names of many "pro" football players are household words throughout the United States. With eleven players on each side, and with a ball which may be, under various circumstances, kicked, tossed or carried, football is an impressively scientific game. The colleges have professional coaching staffs who plan each play like a military maneuver. The champions in the different college leagues oppose each other in January in contests attended by much ceremony and excitement.

The winter team sports are basketball and ice hockey, played by both professional and college or school teams. Soccer is not played nearly so much as in Europe, though it is gaining popularity. In recent years skiing has aroused great enthusiasm, especially among college students. More and more ski lifts are being erected in the East and Far West. Golf is traditionally the businessman's game, but with the shorter work week it is becoming democratized. Younger people play a good deal of tennis. The long coast lines of the United States and the large number of lakes make water sports of all kinds extremely popular.

Sports contests are less often international in the United States than they are, for instance, among the soccer teams in Europe. The United States participates, however, in all the Olympic contests.

There is usually much shouting and cheering at sports events in this country, and many spectators accompany their applause with whistling. In some countries whistling denotes disapproval, but in the United States it is a sign of appreciation.

236

RECREATION BEYOND THE CAMPUS

Participation in college clubs and sports and dating can take up a great deal of time, but you should allow some time for other recreational activities. At most American colleges one finds a variety of entertainment and recreational activity such as special lectures, plays, movies, concerts, art exhibits and sports events. At colleges and universities which are not located in metropolitan areas, there are generally concert and lecture series by guest artists and speakers.

Many students have record players and radios in their rooms and many dormitories and fraternity and sorority houses have radios, record players and television sets in their living rooms. Daily listings of radio and television programs are published in newspapers.

Near many schools are woods and hills where students may go hiking and picnicking. There are also national forests and parks throughout the United States, which provide opportunities for hiking, picnicking, camping, motoring, fishing, boating, swimming, etc. Hunting is forbidden in national parks but not in national forests. Fishing is permitted in national forests and most national parks. Fishing and hunting, in both parks and forests, usually require a license and are governed by state game laws. Guns must be registered with the college or university as well as with local authorities; the regulations vary from place to place. National forests generally have long trails for skiing, riding and hiking; some also have ski lifts and shelters. The Appalachian Trail, for example, extends 2,050 miles, crossing eight national forests and two national parks.

The U.S. Government also maintains certain monuments, memorials and other historic sites. You probably will be able to reach the sites near your college by bus or train.

Forms of unorganized recreation which are part of the everyday scene at American colleges and universities are playing bridge, listening to the radio and record player and watching television. Contract bridge is very popular at colleges. It is usually played for a short time after dinner, before students resume their studies.

Most students enjoy attending dramatic and musical productions and visiting museums as part of their leisure-time activities. Popular Broadway plays are usually taken on tour to the large cities throughout the United States for two- or three-week engagements. The American professional theater is concentrated on New York City's "Broadway." The production of successful plays may last for a number of years. In New York City there are also "off-Broadway" and "off-off-Broadway" theaters, which have grown in number in the past few years. Off-Broadway theaters are generally small and are located outside of the commercial theater district. Their plays are performed by actors who work for lower salaries and whose goal is artistic achievement. Off-off-Broadway theaters are even smaller and their work is usually experimental and avant-garde. Non-commercial theaters are also maintained in many large cities throughout the United States.

Large museums and art galleries bring art to smaller cities and towns by sending special exhibits or parts of their collections on tours.

In your leisure-time activities you may wish to include the celebration and festivities of American holidays. On certain holidays, such as Thanksgiving and Christmas, schools and community organizations arrange special dinners and celebrations for foreign students. You may also receive an invitation to spend a holiday at the home of an American friend. You should not hesitate to accept such invitations, for you will not only please your host by allowing him to spend time with you and introduce you to his family, but you will have the opportunity to join an American family and thus learn about American family and community life through actual experience.

During your visit to the United States you may be invited to speak on some aspect of your home country or perhaps to demonstrate examples of the culture of your country. If you can accept such invitations without taking time from your studies, you may be sure of interested audiences.

seeing the country

When traveling, it is advisable to look through a guidebook in advance. Free maps, listing local points of interest, are available at gasoline and railroad stations. In many cities the Chamber of Commerce publishes free booklets on local points of interest. Stationery stores and some newsstands sell maps of cities which have street guides including house numbers, postal zones, and subway, automobile, and bus routes.

To see the country, you may want to travel by private car, train, bus or bicycle. Students who own cars often advertise in college newspapers or on college bulletin boards for passengers who will share the expense of gasoline. Sharing someone's car can be an inexpensive means of transportation, although it may not take you to the exact place you wish to visit.

In most cities there are companies which rent cars. The fee for renting a car is approximately $9 per day plus 9 cents a mile, or $40 per week plus 9 cents a mile. Weekend rates are higher than weekday rates.

Secondhand cars may be purchased for under $1,000. If you plan to buy a used car, have it checked by a mechanic or by a friend who knows a good deal about automobiles. If you plan to drive a car, you will need a driver's license and, of course, a knowledge of American rules of the road. A car must be registered and have a license plate before you can drive it. Many states require automobile insurance. In any case, do not drive a car without insurance, for if your car is in an accident you may be sued for damages. If you are a member of the automobile club of your home country you are eligible for reciprocal services from the AAA (American Automobile Association). Any driver may join the AAA. Members of the AAA can, upon request, receive detailed road maps, lists of good hotels and automobile service free of charge.

If you plan to buy a car for use during the school year, first check the regulations of the institution you attend. Some colleges and universities do not allow their students to keep automobiles at school. (This is often because of lack of parking facilities.) Speed limits vary throughout the country. Signs along the road indicate the rate of speed allowed. Both state and federal highways are numbered. State highway numbers are enclosed in a circle or triangle on road signs and maps. Federal highway numbers are enclosed in a shield and are preceded by the letters "U.S."

Special bus tickets, providing 99 days of unlimited bus travel in the United States for $99, may be purchased prior to your departure to the United States. They *cannot be bought in the U.S.;* you *must* buy them abroad or not at all. The tickets are available from many travel agencies, including American Express and Thomas Cook & Son, and may be used on all major bus lines, including the Greyhound and Trailways companies.

During the summer, steamer service is available between various ports on the Atlantic coast, the Great Lakes, and the Hudson, Ohio, Mississippi and Columbia Rivers. Many of these steamers have auto-ferry facilities.

If you plan to do some traveling on a bicycle, obtain information on youth hostels. The American Youth Hostels headquarters is at 20 West 17th Street, New York, N.Y. 10011. This organization sponsors inexpensive outdoor trips including station-wagon tours and cycling and walking trips.

Hitchhiking is not recommended anywhere in the United States. Not only is it dangerous, it is also illegal in many states.

You can obtain travel information and assistance in planning trips from local travel agencies and organizations such as the International Student Service (291 Broadway, New York, N.Y. 10007) and the Council on International Educational Exchange (777 United Nations Plaza, New York, N.Y. 10017). The New York office of the International Student Service has a service called VISIT which organizes study tours for individuals or groups from abroad who wish to travel in the United States and sometimes stay at the homes of American families. The Council on International Educational Exchange provides information on organized travel programs. The Council conducts TRIP, a shipboard Travelers' Recreation-Information Program. Wherever you travel in the United States, do not hesitate to ask for advice or help if you need it. Your Foreign Student Adviser receives travel information that he will be delighted to pass on to you; talk with him about your travel plans.

government regulations

PASSPORT AND VISA

Everyone except Canadian citizens and landed immigrants in Canada from Commonwealth countries must secure a *passport* from his government in order to gain entry into the United States. Passport and immigration regulations vary from country to country. Under the U.S. immigration law, some passports must be valid for at least six months beyond the date on which the traveler expects to leave the United States. Certain foreign governments have entered into agreement with the U.S. to recognize their passports as valid for return for a period of six months beyond the expiration date specified in the passport. Application for an extension of your visit to this country is discussed on page 244. All information on immigration regulations may be requested from the American consulate nearest your home.

After you have obtained a passport, application must be made to the nearest American consulate for a visa. When applying for a visa, bring your passport together with documents showing evidence of sufficient financial support for your stay in America. The U.S. Consular office in your country determines the type of visa which will be granted to you. Students usually apply for a nonimmigrant F-1 student visa or for a nonimmigrant J-1 exchange visitor visa. The F visa provides for initial admittance to the U.S. for a period of up to one year. A student may receive extensions of stay for one year at a time as long as he maintains good status as a student and has a passport valid for six months beyond the requested stay. Applicants for a student F-1 visa must have a Certificate of Eligibility for Non-Immigrant Student Status, Form I-20, from the U.S. educational institution granting them admission. You must also prove adequate scholastic preparation and command of English for fulfilling an intended program of study.

Applicants for a J-1 visa must have a Certificate of Eligibility for Exchange Visitor Status, Form DSP-66, from a sponsor whose program has been authorized by the U.S. Department of State. The time an Exchange Visitor can remain in the United States is limited. Students may remain as long as they are actively pursuing recognized degrees, and they may be permitted up to eighteen months for practical training. Sponsors may be educational institutions or private or governmental organizations.

Keep your Form I-20 or DSP-66 with you during your entire stay in the United States.

Certain medical documents are also necessary for obtaining a visa. These include an X-ray photograph of your chest to show that you do not have tuberculosis, and certification that you are in good health and that you have been vaccinated against smallpox within the last three years. Your vaccination certificate must also be shown at the port of entry when you arrive in the United States.

If your spouse and/or children are accompanying you, they will receive a visa at a U.S. Consulate upon presentation of your Form I-20 (if you have an F-1 visa) or Form DSP-66 (if you have a J-1 visa). If your spouse and/or children will join you later in the U.S., you should obtain from the appropriate school official a current Form I-20 (if you are an F-1 student) or Form DSP-66 (if you are a J-1 student). The school official will endorse the form to show that you are still enrolled in a full course of study or are still an exchange-program participant, and to indicate the date of expiration of your authorized stay in the U.S. as shown on your Form I-94, Arrival-Departure Record (see below). The Form I-20 or Form DSP-66 should then be sent to your spouse and/or children for presentation to the American consular office in applying for their visas.

Procedures which you must follow while in the United States vary according to your visa. If you hold a J Exchange Visitor visa, a visa sponsor is responsible to the United States Immigration and Naturalization Service for your activities. If you hold an F-1 nonimmigrant visa, you must agree that while in the United States you will not enroll in any educational institution other than the one you have been authorized to attend, unless permission is obtained from the District Director of the Immigration and Naturalization Service in the area where your educational institution is located. Students who enter the United States on F-1 nonimmigrant visas will receive Form I-94 from the immigration officer at the port of entry. This form is called the Arrival-Departure Record. The law requires that you keep this form with you at all times, since it serves as evidence that you have been legally admitted to this country on a temporary basis. The Form I-94 must be surrendered to an authorized person when you depart from the U.S. If you wish to leave the United States temporarily, consult with your Foreign Student Adviser for procedures to follow.

Although it is expected that nearly all foreign students and scholars will apply for J or F-1 visas, it is possible that in certain unusual circumstances you may want to apply for one of several other types of visas. *Information and advice on visas should be obtained from the U.S. consulate nearest your home.*

REPORTING YOUR ADDRESS

After you have been admitted to the United States, you must report your address to the Immigration and Naturalization Service **every three months, un-**less you were admitted to the U.S. as a permanent resident. A *change of address* must be reported to the Immigration and Naturalization Service not later than ten days after it takes place. Make these reports on Form AR-11, which can be obtained at any post office.

In addition, all aliens and international organizations except foreign-government officials, must report their addresses to the Immigration and Naturalization Service *every January* on Form I-53, which is also available at post offices. Do not mail the completed form: submit it in person at a post office or immigration office.

If you plan to move, get a Post Office change-of-address card at any post office and fill it out, giving both your old address and the new one. Then return it to the post office to insure correct handling of your mail.

EMPLOYMENT

A nonimmigrant foreign student may not work without permission from the U.S. Immigration and Naturalization Service.

It is assumed that if you come to the United States to study, you will not undertake full-time employment during the regular academic year. But it may be possible for you to work *part time* (not more than 20 hours a week) under certain conditions. If you plan to apply for an F-1 (student) visa, and your school intends to offer you employment on campus, the school should indicate that fact on the Form I-20 it issues to you. Permission to work may then be given at the time of actual admission to the country.

To apply for permission to work after entering the country, fill out Form I-538 (Application by Nonimmigrant Student to Accept or Continue Employment) and submit it, with the appropriate countersignature of a school official, to the district office of the Immigration and Naturalization Service. No economic necessity need be shown for on-campus employment. For off-campus employment, for which Form I-538 should also be used, you must show genuine need based on changed financial circumstances. Permission to work is almost never granted, even for economic necessity, during the first year of study.

If you hold a J-1 (Exchange Visitor) visa, your program sponsor may authorize you to work part time if you need to because of changed financial circumstances. Approval by the Immigration and Naturalization Service is not required. It would be helpful if, before consulting your program sponsor, you discussed your plans with your Foreign Student Adviser.

A position held under the terms of a fellowship, scholarship, or assistant-ship is not regarded as employment. No permission is required for either F-1 or J-1 visa holders.

The U.S. Immigration and Naturalization Service decides every spring whether any F-1 students may be permitted to work during the coming summer. Authority to act on individual students' applications is delegated to the schools, usually to the Foreign Student Advisers. For J-1 students, program sponsors have *standing* authority to permit summer employment. Permission to work in other vacation periods is not granted, nor may students work after arriving in the U.S. before they begin their studies.

An F-1 or J-1 student may not work after completing his studies in the United States, except for practical training.

After completing his studies in the U.S., a nonimmigrant foreign student may be permitted to undertake paid practical training in his major field of study to supplement his academic work. An F-1 visa holder should apply for per-mission on Form I-538. The Immigration and Naturalization Service may grant him a six-month period for practical training, on recommendation of his school. Two additional periods may be granted if justified. (Practical training may be authorized *before* the completion of studies in special circumstances—for ex-ample, in agriculture when there are seasonal factors.) A J-1 student should apply for permission for practical training to his program sponsor.

The spouse and children of an F-1 student who are accompanying or joining the F-1 student in the U.S. are issued F-2 visas, which do not permit them to work for pay in the U.S.

The spouse and children of a J-1 student are issued J-2 visas. A person in the U.S. on a J-2 visa may be permitted to work in the U.S. if it is necessary for the support of the J-2 aliens—but not for the support of the J-1 alien. The J-2 person who wishes to work should apply in person or by letter (there is no form for the purpose) to the Immigration and Naturalization Service.

income taxes

You must file a federal income-tax return on Form 1040 NR (U.S. Non-resident Alien Income Tax Return) if you earn more than $600 during a calen-dar year. You can obtain the form by writing to or visiting any office of the Internal Revenue Service. Some tax forms are also available in banks for several months beginning around January 1. Fill it out and mail no later than June 15 to the Office of International Operations, Internal Revenue Service, Washington, D.C. 20225. Inquiries may also be directed to that office.

It might be useful to ask the Office of International Operations to send you Document No. 518, *Foreign Scholars and Educational and Cultural Exchange Visitors;* Document No. 519, *United States Tax Guide for Aliens;* and Document No. 513, *Tax Information for Visitors to the United States.*

Income from fellowships and scholarships is not recorded as compensation for services and is therefore not taxable. However, if you earn part of your expenses through a teaching assistantship or in a similar manner, you should consult the nearest office of the Internal Revenue Service with regard to any tax liability.

Whether a person is a resident alien or a nonresident alien, as defined for tax purposes, will affect his tax liability. Generally, the Internal Revenue Service

242

considers an alien whose stay in the U.S. is restricted by the immigration laws to a definite period to be a nonresident alien. Under certain circumstances, however, an alien with a limited visa may be considered a *resident* for tax purposes. An alien who has lived continuously in the U.S. for more than two years is considered to have been in the country for an "extended stay" and may be considered a resident alien. A nonimmigrant alien who thinks he may be a "resident" for tax purposes should consult the District Director of Internal Revenue. It may be appropriate for him to file a certificate of residence on Form 1078 with the treasurer's office at the institution or agency to which he is attached.

The U.S. income tax is levied against a resident alien's *entire* income, just as it is against a citizen's entire income. And a resident alien may claim personal exemptions and deductions to the same extent that a citizen may claim them. On the other hand, the income of a nonresident alien — that is, an alien who is a nonresident for tax purposes — is taxed only to the extent that it is from U.S. sources, with certain categories of such income exempt by law or treaty. But a nonresident alien may claim only *one* personal exemption (unless he is a resident of Canada or Mexico or, in certain situations, of Japan), and only *certain* kinds of deductions.

The Internal Revenue Code allows a deduction for "traveling expenses (including the entire amount expended for meals and lodging) while away from home in the pursuit of a trade or business." Thus, a visiting scholar receiving a salary from an American institution may, under certain conditions, deduct an allocated amount in computing taxable income.

If part of your wages were withheld for the income tax and you are entitled to a refund because your earnings were not more than $600, you must file an income-tax return in order to get the refund. For the correct procedure, see Document No. 519, referred to on page 242.

To avoid double taxation of nationals of one country who are nonimmigrant aliens in another, there are reciprocal tax treaties between the United States and various other countries (Australia, Austria, Belgium, Canada, Denmark, Finland, France, Germany, Greece, Ireland, Italy, Japan, Luxembourg, The Netherlands, New Zealand, Norway, Pakistan, South Africa, Sweden, Switzerland, Trinidad and Tobago, and the United Kingdom; the treaties with Belgium and the United Kingdom also apply to certain of their former territories that are now independent countries). Under them, professors and teachers from those countries are exempt, subject to certain qualifications, from U.S. taxes on income from sources in the United States for contracted teaching or lecture courses. The list of countries is, of course, subject to change.

Keep a copy of all tax forms that you have submitted to the U.S. government. You will need them later in obtaining clearance for any departure from the country. (Pre-departure procedure is discussed on page 245.)

You should consult the Foreign Student Adviser at your school about any income-tax obligations you may have under the laws of the state where you are located.

TRANSFER TO ANOTHER SCHOOL

If you hold an F-1 visa and wish to transfer to a different institution, discuss the situation with your academic advisers and your Foreign Student Adviser. You should apply by letter to the district office of the Immigration and Naturalization Service for permission 15 to 30 days before you wish to transfer. Your request should be accompanied by Form I-20 showing that you have been accepted by the school to which you wish to transfer and by your Arrival-Departure Record (Form I-94). When you actually withdraw from the school you are leaving, give your Foreign Student Adviser the date of withdrawal and reason for withdrawing and your new address.

If you have a J-1 visa and wish to transfer from one Exchange Visitor program to another, you must have the prior approval of both your current sponsor and the prospective new sponsor. The current sponsor must release you with a statement that the change is in the best interest of your plan of study or research, and the new sponsor must assume responsibility, in writing, for your continued stay in the country. The sponsors' statements should be made on Form DSP-66, which should be sent to the district office of the Immigration and Naturalization Service together with a letter of request and your Arrival-Departure Record, between 30 and 60 days before the desired transfer.

It is suggested that you use registered mail when sending documents.

EXTENSION OF STAY

If you are in the U.S. as an F-1 student and need an extension of permission to stay, send Form I-539, endorsed by an official of your school, and your Arrival-Departure Record to the district office of the Immigration and Naturalization Service 15 to 30 days before the period in which you are authorized to stay expires.

If you are in the U.S. on a J-1 visa and need permission to extend your stay, send a letter of request, a new Form DSP-66 filled out by your sponsor to show the time and terms of the extension and your Arrival-Departure Record to the district office of the Immigration and Naturalization Service between 30 and 60 days before your current authorized stay expires. You must indicate whether you intend to return home when the extension expires.

If necessary, your passport may be renewed at your country's embassy or one of its consulates in the U.S.

The U.S. immigration laws make provision for nonimmigrant aliens to acquire immigrant status while in the U.S. or soon after leaving. Exchange Visitors may not ordinarily be given such status until they have been outside the U.S. for two years after the end of their stay in the U.S.

MILITARY SERVICE

If you are in the U.S. on an F or J visa, you need not register for military service.

If you are in the U.S. as an immigrant and were born on or after September 15, 1925, the Military Selective Service Act of 1967 requires you to register for military service within six months of your entry into the country or five days after your 18th birthday, whichever occurs later. Your Foreign Student Adviser will be able to give you the address of the appropriate local board of the Selective Service System. As an immigrant, you may be required to serve in the armed forces just as a citizen may be.

According to current regulations under the Selective Service Act, nationals of about 40 countries associated with the U.S. in mutual-defense activities will, under certain conditions, be exempted from training and service *but not from registration.*

LEAVING TEMPORARILY AND RETURNING

Before leaving the U.S. for a temporary absence, give your Foreign Student Adviser or Exchange Visitor program sponsor the date of departure, port of exit, and means of transportation and your address during that period.

In order to return to the U.S. as an F or J visitor after a temporary absence, you should have a valid passport, a valid visa, your Arrival-Departure Record, and a new Form I-20 (from your school) or current Form DSP-66 (from your sponsor). If your previous visa is no longer valid (because it will have expired when you return or you have already used it for the allowable number of entries into the country), you will have to get a new one from a U.S. consul abroad. In certain circumstances, it may be possible to have it revalidated in Washington before you leave; apply to the Director of the Visa Office, U.S. Department of State, Washington, D.C., 20520.

It would be advisable to consult your Foreign Student Adviser or program sponsor before leaving the U.S. for *any* temporary absence.

DEPARTURE

All aliens (except those listed below) must obtain a certificate of compliance from the Internal Revenue Service before leaving the country, temporarily or permanently. The certificate, popularly known as a "sailing permit" or "exit permit," indicates that the person to whom it is granted does not owe any income taxes to the U.S. government. It may be obtained by filing Form 1040C (Departing Alien Income Tax Return) or Form 2063 (Department Alien Income Tax Statement) with the District Director of Internal Revenue. Employees in the office of the District Director will inform the alien which form is appropriate and, if necessary, assist in filling it out.

The following aliens are not required to obtain a "sailing permit" upon departure from the U.S.:

1. A diplomatic representative, members of his household and his servants;
2. A visitor for pleasure admitted solely on a B-2 visa;
3. An industrial trainee admitted solely on an H-3 visa who has received no income from U.S. sources other than expense allowances and the value of services or accommodations incident to his training;
4. A visitor for business admitted on a B-1, or on both a B-1 visa and a B-2 visa, who remains in the U.S. not more than ninety days;
5. An alien in transit through the United States;
6. A military trainee who departs from the U.S. on official military travel orders; and

245

7. A student admitted solely on an F visa who has received no income from U.S. sources other than expense allowances and the value of services or accommodations incident to his study.

You should apply for your "sailing permit" 30 days or less before leaving the country at the office of the District Director of Internal Revenue in the area where you have been living or, if there is no District Director there, in the city from which you are departing. Bring your passport and alien registration form with you, your transportation ticket or confirmation of it, and, if you have been employed in the U.S., an official record of earnings and tax withheld from earnings since the most recent January 1 and a copy of any U.S. income-tax return (with receipts for taxes paid) for any of the three previous years. To substantiate deductions claimed on income-tax returns, bring with you receipts, bank records, canceled checks, and any other pertinent papers. It is also advisable to have with you evidence of student teaching, or research status, such as letters of admission or appointment to a college or university and statements about scholarships, fellowships, or research grants that may have been awarded.

Any taxes on U.S.-derived income that may be due when the "sailing permit" is applied for must usually be paid at that time.

If you are entitled to a refund for income tax that has been paid, consult Document No. 519, referred to on Page 242, for the correct procedure to follow.

All aliens, whether they are still in the United States or not, may be required to file a final income-tax return at the end of the year. Filing Form 1040C does not necessarily relieve the alien of this responsibility.

Your Foreign Student Adviser can give you further information on government regulations. The staff of the Institute of International Education will also attempt to answer any questions. You may write to the Institute at 809 United Nations Plaza, New York, N.Y. 10017, or to any of its regional offices, listed on the inside back cover, either before your departure from home or after your arrival in the United States.

THE UNITED STATES OF AMERICA
Showing selected principal cities

MINNESOTA

WISCONSIN

eapolis

MICHIGAN

Milwaukee

Detroit

Buffalo

NEW YORK

VERMONT

MAINE

NEW HAMPSHIRE

Boston

MASSACHUSETTS

RHODE ISLAND

CONNECTICUT

IOWA

PENNSYLVANIA

New York

Chicago

INDIANA

Cleveland

Pittsburgh

Philadelphia

NEW JERSEY

ILLINOIS

OHIO

Cincinnati

Baltimore

DELAWARE

Washington

MARYLAND

SSOURI

Kansas City

St. Louis

WEST
VIRGINIA

VIRGINIA

KENTUCKY

NORTH CAROLINA

ARKANSAS

TENNESSEE

Memphis

SOUTH
CAROLINA

ALABAMA

Atlanta

Birmingham

LOUISIANA

GEORGIA

MISSISSIPPI

Jacksonville

ston

New Orleans

FLORIDA

Miami

Scale of Miles

0   100   200   300

DATE DUE

Demco, Inc. 38-293